Praise for *The Strategic Positioning of Acad*[illegible]

'This is the most challenging period for [illegible] career as a professional librarian. The peri[illegible] finances means nothing is sacrosanct, and this welcome book provides valuable advice and tools to help the library director show that their service is "business critical" in a period of furious competition for limited funds. It is well worth the time of any library director, as well as anyone aspiring to become one.'
Simon Bains, University Librarian, University of Aberdeen

'This timely book is an essential guide for navigating and positioning the academic library in the turbulent landscape of higher education. It illuminates the complex role of academic libraries and demonstrates why strategic positioning is critical for reputation, influence, and sustainability. With sharp insights into internal and external dynamics, it offers practical strategies and tools in response to global and local challenges. A must-read and go-to resource for academic library staff and higher education professionals seeking clarity and direction in an era of uncertainty and change, and for library students – equipping them with the insight and confidence to shape the future of academic libraries.'
Dr Jessica Bates, Programme Director for Library and Information Management, Ulster University

'A timely and really useful book that will help everyone concerned with academic libraries negotiate and navigate the unprecedented global, national and local challenges and changes facing us today. John Cox rightly identifies active positioning as a critical contributor to organisational success that has received limited attention from library strategists. Drawing on professional experience and scholarly research he provides an expert guide to the subject that is required reading for administrators, practitioners and students alike.'
Sheila Corrall, former professor of library and information science, University of Pittsburgh, USA

'John Cox has pioneered understanding of the strategic positioning of academic libraries in our complex and increasingly uncertain world. Readers will welcome this extended and updated analysis. Cox's reflections on the wider context within which libraries operate is fascinating. He also offers realistic insights into libraries' strengths and weaknesses. The toolkit included in the book offers practical ways to put strategic positioning into practice. The book will appeal both to practitioners wanting to reflect on how to position their own library, and scholars of librarianship and strategy.'
Andrew Cox, senior lecturer at the School of Information, Journalism and Communication, University of Sheffield

'John Cox has written an excellent guide to academic library strategic positioning, by which he means both identifying what the library should be doing and conveying the library's value to stakeholders. Cox brings his personal experience and a comprehensive review of the literature to the task. He is clearheaded about the challenges but is ultimately optimistic. His SWOT analysis and the resource tool kit are especially useful. Any librarian looking to find the way forward, especially those conducting a formal planning process, will find the book essential reading.'
David W. Lewis, Dean Emeritus of IU Indianapolis (formerly IUPUI) University Library, USA and author of *Reimagining the Academic Library*

'A fantastic, compelling and unflinching examination of academic libraries that is in equal parts terrifying and optimistic. It describes the most critical and complex challenge I face as a library director. A must-read for anyone shaping the future of academic libraries and for all library staff seeking to make sense of the forces changing their jobs.'
Ciara McCaffrey, University Librarian and Director of Library and Information Services, University of Limerick, Ireland

'This timely work provides essential strategic guidance for academic libraries navigating disruption. Understanding the complex global, political, economic, and technological context is vital for making informed positioning decisions. The book's comprehensive SWOT analysis and practical positioning strategies offer leaders the understanding and the tools to respond effectively to intensifying challenges – from artificial intelligence to identity blurring to declining institutional position. In an era of rapid change, this strategic framework is indispensable for academic libraries seeking to remain central to their institutions' missions.'
Dr Caroline Williams, University Librarian, The University of Sydney, Australia

The Strategic Positioning of Academic Libraries

The Strategic Positioning of Academic Libraries

Global Challenges, Local Politics and Strategy Development

John Cox

facet publishing

Published by Facet Publishing
www.facetpublishing.co.uk

Facet Publishing is wholly owned by CILIP:
the Library and Information Association.

British Library Cataloguing in Publication Data
A catalogue record for this book is available from the British Library.

ISBN 978-1-78330-690-9 (paperback)
ISBN 978-1-78330-691-6 (hardback)
ISBN 978-1-78330-692-3 (PDF)
ISBN 978-1-78330-693-0 (EPUB)

First published 2026

MIX
Paper | Supporting responsible forestry
FSC www.fsc.org
FSC® C013604

The manufacturer's authorised representative in the EU for product safety is Logos Europe, 9 rue Nicolas Poussin, 17000 La Rochelle, France (contact@logoseurope.eu, www.logoseurope.eu).

Typeset from author's files by Flagholme Publishing Services in
10/13 pt Palatino Linotype and Open Sans.
Printed and made in Great Britain by CPI Group (UK) Ltd, Croydon, CR0 4YY.

For Maureen, Dylan and Niamh,
the lights of my life

Contents

Figures, Tables, Reflective Journal Extracts and Case Studies

Figures

Tables

Reflective journal extracts

Case studies

About the Author

John Cox writes about and analyses issues impacting academic libraries and their strategic positioning, drawing on more than 30 years of leadership experience. He retired as University Librarian at the University of Galway in November 2023, having previously been Deputy Librarian there and held other library leadership roles at University College Cork and the Wellcome Trust. Projects led have included advocacy and strategy development for a new library building, digitisation of the Abbey and Gate Theatre archives and consortium negotiations with publishers to increase open access to Irish research publications. Among his committee memberships have been the Consortium of National and University Libraries (CONUL), the Irish Universities Association Librarians Group and the SCONUL Executive Board.

John's publications include a two-part SWOT analysis of academic libraries, a literature review on positioning the academic library in the institution, an overview of the higher education environment driving academic library strategy and a case study of the evolution and politics of a library building project. His maintenance of a weekly reflective journal since 2008 has complemented his writing with in-the-moment insights into events as they happened. He holds a Master's degree in Latin and has both enjoyed and endured half a century of following Everton Football Club. He continues to research with curiosity the fortunes of academic libraries.

Acknowledgements

A book of this nature can only come to fruition with the support, wisdom and inspiration of lots of wonderful people whose generosity has meant so much. The staff at Facet Publishing have been uniformly knowledgeable and helpful throughout. I am particularly grateful to Pete Baker and Andrew James. Pete was immediately enthusiastic about the idea for the book and encouraged me through the proposal process. The proposal itself was hugely improved by the perceptive insights of Jessica Bates, Sheila Corrall and Andrew Cox as expert writers about academic libraries. Pete and his successor Andrew offered valuable and vital advice at all points of the writing journey. It was a real pleasure to work with them both and with their staff, especially Michelle Lau, whose calm expertise saw the manuscript through to publication. I also benefited greatly from the meticulous copy-editing of the manuscript by Stephen York.

As I wrote the book, I frequently drew on my own experience, which has been shaped by collaborations and conversations with many colleagues and friends. My time at the University of Galway was especially influential and I learned so much from people across the whole campus. It was a great privilege to lead such a committed and capable library staff for 15 years and each of them taught me something. My predecessor and successor as University Librarian, Marie Reddan and Monica Crump respectively, both set the highest professional standards for me. Marie's passing just as I was completing the manuscript represents a huge loss. I owe a lot also to my colleagues at different times in the library leadership team when I was at its head, namely Evelyn Bohan, Catriona Cannon, Peter Corrigan, Cillian Joy, Ronán Kennedy, Niall McSweeney and the late Ann Mitchell. Their knowledge contributed to lots of enlightening discussions about many of the issues in the book.

I was able to access all the documents I needed for each chapter thanks to the wide-ranging collections at the University of Galway Library. My special thanks go to the Collections Team, and in particular Hugo Kelly and Niamh

Walsh for continually developing the collection, Rioghna Moggan for such prompt turnaround of book orders and Gabi Honan for rapid access to interlibrary loans. I also received invaluable technology support from Christian Warren.

Conversations with colleagues across the library world and beyond educated me at regular intervals and this stood me in good stead as I wrote. I was fortunate to share membership of CONUL and the Irish Universities Association Libraries Group with consistently excellent directors. Informal chats with library staff and others at conferences and elsewhere helped to develop my thinking. Others in leadership positions outside libraries often provided inspiration, among them John Gibney, Caroline Loughnane, Iain Mac Labhrainn, Nuala McGuinn and Dónall Ó Braonáin.

Writing has become a passion for me and I am eternally thankful to Terry Hanson, a great friend and thinker, who generously included me in his publications earlier in my career. The support with writing from Terry, Leo Appleton, Helen Fallon and my sister Olga Cox Cameron has helped me greatly. This is also true of the constant encouragement and interest from Jim Browne, Dan Carey, John Gaffney, Barry Houlihan, Liz McConnell, Donncha O'Connell and Ann Torres along the journey that has been writing this book. I hugely appreciate too the thought-provoking writings of many outstanding authors, including Sheila Corrall, Andrew Cox, Lorcan Dempsey, Roisin Gwyer, Richard Heseltine, John Howard, David Lewis, Lai Ma, Bryan Mathews, Tim Schlak, Caroline Williams and various researchers at Ithaka S+R and OCLC.

My biggest debt of gratitude is to my wife Maureen, who makes all good things possible and inspires me every day with her love, kindness and steadfast support. She is my pillar of strength. I am so proud also of our son Dylan and daughter Niamh for all that they represent and do. Lastly, huge thanks to our lovely dog Foof Foof, greatly missed since his recent passing but until then a faithful companion and writing supervisor every step of the way!

Abbreviations

ACRL	Association of College and Research Libraries
AI	Artificial intelligence
ALA	American Library Association
ARL	Association of Research Libraries
CAUL	Council of Australasian University Librarians
CILIP	Chartered Institute of Library and Information Professionals
CNI	Coalition for Networked Information
CoARA	Coalition for Advancing Research Assessment
CONUL	Consortium of National and University Libraries
DEI	Diversity, equity and inclusion
DORA	Declaration on Research Assessment
GDP	Gross domestic product
HyFlex	Hybrid-Flexible
IBM	International Business Machines
IT	Information technology
LIBER	Ligue des Bibliothèques Européennes de Recherche – Association of European Research Libraries
NCSU	North Carolina State University
NIH	National Institutes of Health
PEST	Political, economic, social and technological
PESTLE	Political, economic, social, technological, legal and environmental
RBV	Resource-based view
RPV	Resources, processes and values
SCONUL	Society of College, National and University Libraries
STEEP	Social, technological, economic, environmental and political
SUNY	State University of New York
SWOT	Strengths, weaknesses, opportunities and threats
UNESCO	United Nations Educational, Scientific and Cultural Organization

VLE	Virtual learning environment
VRIN	Valuable, rare, inimitable and non-substitutable
VRIO	Valuable, rare, inimitable and organisation-supported
VUCA	Volatility, uncertainty, complexity and ambiguity

Introduction: 'A luxury that we can't afford' – Are Academic Libraries Dispensable?

I was waiting to board a plane at West of Ireland Airport in December 2024 when a link to an article in the *Chronicle of Higher Education* dropped into my mailbox. Its title jumped out at me: '"A luxury that we can't afford": why one university axed its entire library faculty' (Lu, 2024). This was the story of Western Illinois University, where leaders had found themselves needing to make $22 million worth of cuts to a $100 million annual operating budget following a 40% drop in enrolments during the previous decade. They decided to target the library in their quest for savings. Nine professional library staff there enjoyed faculty status but, having laid off one of their number in the previous month, the leadership now decided to terminate the employment of the remaining eight with effect from May 2025 among a total of 89 staff redundancies.

The article noted that the library was the only department to lose all of its faculty members in this latest round of measures. It had endured cuts over a prolonged period of time, reducing its faculty librarians by half and its collections budget by a fifth. The elimination of its entire faculty librarian team represented a new level of devastation, however, leaving only a dean and five paraprofessional staff members to manage and operate the library. There was shock and outrage on and outside the campus, generating over 10,000 signatures to a petition to reverse the decision. Library staff came out fighting, extolling the value of their work through various media, including a website (https://savewiulibrarians.org), YouTube channel (Bowers Sharpe, 2024) and articles in the *Chronicle* and *Inside Higher Ed* (Lu, 2024; Palmer, 2024). Faculty members also lent their support through fulsome testimonials about the difference the faculty librarians had made for them and their students.

Frustratingly, all of the public advocacy only escalated after the decision to delete the faculty librarian team had been announced. The *Chronicle* noted that 'the provost's office viewed librarians through another lens' in coming to its decision. As Christopher Pynes, Interim Associate Provost, ominously put it: 'The faculty librarians are an important part of the university. The problem is that, where we are now, they are a luxury that we can't afford if we're going to provide instruction in certain disciplines. . . . [they] are not offering courses that students need to take to progress in their degree completion.' As he and the other decision-makers prepared to wield the axe, he somewhat incongruously added a familiar but now hollow refrain: 'I love libraries too!' (Lu, 2024).

What this book is about

Some of the major themes of this book intersect in the recounting of the unhappy library experience at Western Illinois University:

- changes in today's world have upended former orthodoxies and assumptions are risky;
- higher education is under major pressure and the competitive climate in which institutions act is mirrored within their campuses;
- the position of the academic library is multifaceted, complex and challenging, while its value is often underestimated;
- effective positioning is vital for academic libraries to combat decline, ensure accurate perceptions of what they contribute and support their advancement.

That a university could deem its professional librarian cohort an unnecessary luxury seemed heretical, although Bangor University had signalled something almost as drastic previously (Curtis, 2005). Nothing is sacred anymore. So how did we get here? What do major shifts in the external environment mean? Where are academic libraries situated in higher education institutions? How can we not only avoid such a nightmare scenario but instead position ourselves and our libraries for ongoing progression?

This book will address such questions in a spirit of empathy, balance and practicality. It sets out to enable a full appreciation of trends in the wider world and in higher education alongside a deep understanding of academic library strengths, weaknesses, opportunities and threats in order to provide an essential foundation for effective library strategy formulation and positioning. Its central thesis is that positioning is a high-stakes venture which can only succeed through an intimate understanding of both the inner and external worlds of academic libraries, specifically their history, current situation and wider operating environment. Unsuccessful positioning is bad news, with damaging immediate and long-term consequences.

The positioning challenge confronting academic libraries

Academic libraries face daunting challenges to their position and strategic positioning. They inhabit an unstable global environment, characterised by escalations in war and political polarisation, a return to trade wars, a climate crisis representing a threat to the future of the planet and the rapid advance of artificial intelligence (AI) as both an opportunity and a threat. Features of this world which are antithetical to library values include disinformation, fake news, distrust in experts, inequality and culture wars. Higher education, the key operating environment for academic libraries, has also experienced major disruption over a long period, notably in terms of funding, student recruitment, competition, government intervention and public criticism. A highly competitive positioning environment has developed on campus, with less collegiality and more aggressive striving for position and resources. Students, too, have become more demanding, consumerist and pressured.

It seems appropriate to ascribe the collective mix of Volatility, Uncertainty, Complexity and Ambiguity (VUCA), commonly cited in management and military circles, to this combination of disruptive factors as it operates at global, national and campus level. For academic libraries it all adds up to a very difficult, multi-layered climate of instability, coming on top of a series of challenges and a sense of decline in their position experienced across recent decades.

Academic libraries today typically account for less than 2% of their parent institutions' annual expenditure (Association of Research Libraries, 2013; SCONUL, 2023), half the level they enjoyed in the early 1980s. Of 88 UK library directors surveyed in 2017 only four reported to the head of the institution, while an even lower proportion, ten out of 662, emerged from a subsequent survey of US directors (Gwyer, 2018; Frederick and Wolff-Eisenberg, 2020b). Larger university management teams and the creation of new units as strategic priorities evolve have distanced the academic library from positions of institutional leadership and influence. Other departments such as IT, research, teaching and learning development and institutional research present strong competition for funding and jurisdiction. Competition from beyond the campus is even more severe, with Google but one of many well resourced entities providing services in the library domain. Reduced funding leaves academic libraries chasing rising prices, new demands and a broader cost base. This loss of competitiveness in a very intense operating environment is significantly disadvantageous.

Other factors are equally concerning. The shift to digital information fundamentally changed academic libraries. They lost their monopoly on access to information as users became more independent of them. The library value proposition became much more diffused, often co-delivered with others and harder to demonstrate or explain than in the era of print dominance. This has contributed to a less solid identity and some loss in clarity of purpose, in turn impacting how key stakeholders see the academic library. There has been a tendency to underestimate the library contribution, retain traditional perceptions of what it does and take it for granted. Indifference is evident in this comment from one institutional leader: 'The library is not a priority for my attention or the attention of the senior team' (Baker, D. and Allden, 2017, 15).

Benign neglect serves the academic library poorly, as does the sense that it belongs to everyone and to no one (Budd, 2018). It is also necessary to understand the profile of strengths and weaknesses internal to academic libraries alongside the forces influencing them from without. As noted below, their strengths represent an enduring asset but weaknesses such as over-cautiousness, tendency to focus too much attention inwards rather than on what is happening elsewhere and limited agility towards moments of opportunity have contributed to the difficult positioning environment in which academic libraries find themselves.

Positioning strategy is important and is the focus of the second chapter. Its key components include clarity of identity, distinctiveness from competitors and effective communications. It shapes stakeholder perceptions by projecting the identity of the academic library, what it stands for and how it contributes. Positioning impacts reputation, influence, recognition, resourcing and prospects. It is also a highly competitive and frequently political venture. Academic libraries are in a fight for position and support, the stakes are high and an effective response to their current situation is vital. Their strengths, weaknesses, opportunities and threats are key to the areas in which they excel or struggle. A detailed knowledge of them and of their external world can lead to well targeted positioning strategies and advancement instead of drift or decline.

There are major challenges in the operating environment but significant opportunities too, including institutional focus on the public good, the advance of open scholarship, data-driven research, the potential of AI and the opening up of deeper roles in community building. As they look to position themselves for success, academic libraries can call on substantial strengths, notably trusted status, broadly based engagement across their institutions, strong connectedness as places of community, effective partnerships and a solid base of goodwill pointed in their direction. These are all valuable assets at a juncture in their history when making the right positioning moves will be critical. The prize of greater influence, better resourcing, a more secure future and a library contribution which is fully recognised, valued and achieving its full potential offers a real incentive.

How the book will support academic library positioning

Readers of this book will develop their understanding of positioning strategy, global developments, directions in higher education, the political and other dimensions of the operating environment on campus and what happens when the strengths and weaknesses of academic libraries collide with these forces. By filling in gaps from the past, joining dots in the present and proposing strategies for the future the book aims to be a valuable guide and an important resource for navigating and responding to a complex environment. The main takeaway is that academic libraries, armed with a deep understanding of their macro-environment and effective strategies, can mitigate the weaknesses and threats they confront and will have much to build on through their established strengths and the opportunities available to them.

The operating environment for academic libraries is subject to a range of political, economic, social and technological drivers and can be difficult to read or to understand. This analysis helps to grasp its complexity, nuances and often unpredictable or even sometimes contradictory effects as different factors interact with each other. It also explains the current situation in which academic libraries find themselves and how they have got to this position, while putting forward appropriate positioning strategies. These are practical, achievable and situated in the real world in which library staff are active.

The overall approach is distinctive, starting from the outside world, viewing the environment of academic libraries through a wide-angled lens and distilling the bigger picture before exploring its impact and implications for library situation, strategy and positioning. The book takes on some challenging and often less covered topics, notably the complex political nature of the campus environment and how academic libraries have sometimes contributed to their own difficulties. An additional and unique feature is the embedding at regular intervals of some in-the-moment reflections drawn from a journal maintained across 15 years by the author as an academic library director (Cox, J., 2016b). These extracts offer insights into events linked to the book's coverage as they happened rather than with the benefit of hindsight, thereby adding some authentic case studies, observations and perspectives.

Who the book is for

Busy jobs may limit the attention library staff can give to making sense of the many external influences impacting their work, but this analysis will save them time. Academic library directors and leadership teams will find the book valuable for reflecting on their current situation, formulating future strategy and positioning or perhaps repositioning their library in its parent institution. Other academic library staff at all levels should find the analysis helpful in understanding the changes shaping their working lives and the potential for library advancement or decline. Students of library and information science will benefit from the helicopter view of where academic libraries fit in, how they are perceived and their possible future directions.

Although academic libraries are the focus here, many of the global trends and influences analysed have implications for public libraries, archives services and museums. The strategies proposed are relevant for those sectors too. There is also a potential audience among leaders, administrators and academic staff in higher education. As already noted, academic libraries are often poorly understood and commonly underestimated within institutional leadership teams. The book may help to redress this. It foregrounds an area of immediate interest to them, namely the world of higher education, how it is shaped by global events and how these in turn influence academic libraries and their role in and beyond the institution.

This analysis is intended to appeal to an international audience because the issues it addresses are global in nature and confront academic libraries everywhere in some form. It is recognised, however, that each library has its own characteristics and influences based on its particular geographic or other circumstances. This is taken into account throughout and there is therefore no question of trying to adopt a 'one size fits all' approach. The book takes a high-level view as it surveys academic libraries and their world. Readers will therefore not need an advanced level of professional expertise or a detailed knowledge of any area of library practice to understand the coverage of this volume and the messages it conveys. The aim has been to write in an accessible style, recognising that 'an overloading of the suitcase will make for a sluggish journey' (Barnett, 2022, 9).

The author's journey

I enjoyed a 40-year career in academic libraries, 30 of them in senior leadership positions and the last 15 at director level as University Librarian at the University of Galway in Ireland. When I retired in late 2023 I embraced the opportunity to write the kind of book I could profitably have read earlier in my working life. So much seemed to happen in a blur in those leadership roles and I often found myself time-poor but pressed to take consequential decisions without a full appreciation of everything around me. The significance of campus politics and effectively communicating the contribution of the library to the institution were not overtly stated but I soon learned that these were at the core of my different roles. Making the case for a major library building investment, eventually successfully, proved to be a highly instructive grounding in politics, persuasion and positioning (Cox, J., 2024). It involved projecting a new vision for the library, winning support across multiple constituencies and competing for tight funding, while fighting the library corner tenaciously and sometimes robustly.

Aside from my practical experiences of strategic positioning, I spent lots of time thinking about it. The reflective journal I commenced as part of a leadership programme in 2006 proved to be an invaluable tool, helping me to make more sense of what was happening each week and how I could make best use of upcoming opportunities (Cox, J., 2016b). My professional reading evolved, too, and I focused on publications that explained the bigger picture. This in turn prompted me to return to writing, an old passion, and I authored a number of review articles on positioning the academic library, the higher education environment driving library strategy and a two-part analysis of the position and prospects of academic libraries (Cox, J., 2018; 2021; 2023a; 2023b).

In each of those articles I was trying to make sense of a fragmented library literature and drawing increasingly on material from other disciplines. Writing this book seemed a natural progression, enabling me to expand, deepen and update the analysis, turning it into a collective whole while sharing some of what I had learned across my own career. My primary motivation, however, has been towards you as a reader. The recency of my own experience helps me to empathise with the challenges you face, the limited time at your disposal and the importance of taking an informed and practical approach which, while rooted in reality, explores big themes in the broader environment. Ideally, this volume will add to your perspective and help you to advance the position and positioning of your library. I am always happy to continue the strategic positioning conversation at john.cox@universityofgalway.ie.

Navigating the book

This book is arranged in three parts. Sense-making in relation to the wider operating environment for academic libraries is vital to their strategy and Part 1 emphasises this. It looks outwards, going well beyond the library literature to identify key developments, recent trends and shifts in perspective globally and in higher education, analysing what these mean for the position and strategic positioning of academic libraries. The opening chapter offers a historical perspective on the evolution of the position occupied by academic libraries and how they have positioned themselves. Chapter 2 examines positioning strategy as defined in the business and marketing literature, with some examples of it in practice, emphasising its importance for academic libraries and some challenges it presents. Next, working initially from the outside in, Chapter 3 surveys a highly complex mix of political volatility, economic uncertainty, societal change and technological advance in today's world. Changes in higher education generating new pressures for, and expectations of, its institutions and their libraries receive particular attention in the following chapter.

Shifting to an inside-out perspective, the focus turns to analysing the current situation of academic libraries and considering the evolving interpretations of their strengths and weaknesses relative to opportunities and threats in their environment. Part 2 comprises a Strengths, Weaknesses, Opportunities and Threats (SWOT) analysis across its four chapters. Each chapter explores four factors chosen for the long-term impact they have on the status and strategic positioning of academic libraries. Sixteen factors therefore feature in Part 2, ranging, for example, from centrality as a strength through stakeholder misperceptions as a weakness and AI as an opportunity to uncertainty as a threat. These factors are examined in terms of their evolution, impact, significance and implications for strategy, incorporating counterweights to each, overlaps between them and connections to the historical and external influences in Part 1. Summary tables conclude each chapter.

Part 3 opens with Chapter 9, which pulls together earlier coverage to summarise the contemporary position and profile of academic libraries based on many external and internal influences. This chapter offers a balance of positives and negatives, outlining some library own goals and identifying contradictions in the SWOT analysis, as well as some common experiences with other professional services in higher education, before looking towards the future by considering three intensifying trends. Chapter 10 puts forward ten strategies intended to improve the situation of academic libraries and advance their position in the institution. These include taking a highly active approach to positioning, prioritising contribution to institutional goals and maximising campus connectedness, while maintaining long-term perspective. The alignment of resources with positioning is also addressed and the chapter closes with an outline of what the well-positioned academic library looks like. A toolkit offering resources to guide practical library positioning comprises Chapter 11. It is followed by the concluding chapter which extracts the lessons from the book as a whole and ends on a note of optimism for the future.

Back to the future

Academic libraries have always been subject to global influences and interacted closely with the academic world. They have a long history and have experienced many ups and downs during their existence. Their position and positioning challenges did not begin just recently. Rather they have evolved over a long period and there is much to learn from their past, including their resilience, adaptability and distinctive values-driven mission. Chapter 1 charts concisely and thematically how they have fared across eight centuries and is a good starting point for framing the rest of this book.

PART 1
Positioning Context

Introduction to Part 1

Part 1 focuses on the library positioning environment and lays the foundations for Parts 2 and 3. Context is fundamental to understanding where academic libraries stand and what directions they might take.

History affords a valuable perspective on how academic libraries came to their present situation and their possible responses to future challenges. Chapter 1 consists of an overview of how their position and positioning have evolved, especially in the face of the transformation in user behaviour and in their own role wrought by the digital information revolution from the late 20th century onwards. It concludes with a brief assessment of whether the changed library value proposition has resulted in an advance or decline in position relative to previously. Chapter 2 explains positioning strategy and emphasises it as a vital focus and difference-maker for academic libraries. Its study of positioning is an essential precursor to the consideration of their contemporary operating environment and sets out five key components of particular significance for them as they navigate times of rapid change and ongoing uncertainty. This chapter urges academic libraries to pay close attention to their clarity of identity, distinctiveness from competitors, understanding of audiences, effectiveness of communications and alignment of resources.

The remaining chapters in Part 1 study the characteristics and influences of the environment in which academic libraries operate. Chapter 3 explores the political, economic, social and technological dimensions of the world at large as a source of both opportunities and threats. Developments highlighted include political polarisation, economic instability, intensifying climate change and the advance of artificial intelligence. These and other trends described are highly dynamic with many implications, highlighted throughout the chapter, for academic libraries and their parent institutions. The changing higher education environment is examined in Chapter 4. This is the primary sector in which academic libraries operate and it continues to experience a range of challenges and upheavals. They include tightened funding, increased government intervention, negative public perceptions and rapid technological shifts, often linked to the global developments outlined in the previous chapter. All of these factors impact the campus operating climate, in turn influencing the library position and informing its positioning strategies.

CHAPTER 1

The Historical Evolution of Academic Library Position and Positioning

Overview

The historical development of academic libraries is the focus of this opening chapter which:

- explains how historical perspective promotes an understanding of the identity, successes, failures and significance of academic libraries;
- provides a short overview of their history from the 13th century to the first decade of the 21st;
- examines how their position and experience has evolved in terms of collections, buildings, staffing, director/administration engagement, funding and technology;
- charts the positioning of the academic library by itself and others as well as its evolution;
- pays particular attention to the impact of late 20th-century developments in technology on position and positioning;
- concludes with a brief assessment of the current status of the academic library relative to its standing in the past.

The value of historical perspective

Why take time to understand the history of academic libraries when current needs and future directions are of such pressing concern? Budd (2022) notes a common view that the past is of limited, if any, relevance, as it is so different from the present. He is emphatically opposed to such a perspective, however, pointing out that change happens far more gradually than people often think and that this is particularly true of universities and their libraries. An understanding of what has gone before is vital to their success today and there is much to be learned not only from earlier successes but especially from previous mistakes. To emphasise this, Budd quotes the observation that

'Those who cannot remember the past are condemned to repeat it' (Santayana, 2017, 132).

McCallon and Tucker lament a relative paucity of scholarship on the history of academic libraries. They see this deficit as contributing significantly to 'professional myopia, a failure to grasp the large conceptual issues of our high calling and a failure to facilitate wide dialogue about the meaning and value of what we do' (McCallon and Tucker, 2022, 3). Consequences for library staff include short-term thinking and limited capacity to participate in campus discussion of institutional development, evolving trends in higher education and the definition of the role of the library in the university. Salisbury and Peseta (2018) have similarly identified the absence of the library from debate around the idea of the university.

A stronger sense of historical perspective and a deeper engagement with the campus community on wider academic issues, past and present, would help to address a common scenario in which there is 'both a minimal understanding of and a limited expectation about what librarians do, thus thwarting the library's potential to impact the educational enterprise' (McCallon and Tucker, 2022, 5). Understanding the history of academic libraries therefore offers opportunities to improve the strategic positioning of the academic library on campus. It also opens the way to a deeper appreciation of its identity, deeds, characteristics and significance. Extending back to the 13th century, academic libraries have a longer history than many institutions on and beyond the campus.

The next section traces that history in brief, outlining the major developments ahead of later discussions of how the position and positioning of the academic library have evolved, primarily in the past century and up to the first decade of the current one. While acknowledging variations per country, coverage emphasises developments in Western Europe and the USA on the grounds that the models adopted there have in general exerted a strong influence on the development of higher education (Altbach and de Wit, 2023) and academic libraries across the world (Shiflett, 1994). A further point to mention is that the history of academic libraries is intimately connected with that of higher education and the section which follows reflects this.

A short historical overview of academic libraries

The University of Bologna, founded in 1088, is the oldest in continuous operation in the world and was followed by universities at Oxford, Salamanca and Paris. There were 56 universities in Western Europe by 1400 (Budd, 2018) and progress across the different regions of Europe is well charted by Hoare (2015). Universities did not immediately have libraries and students bought or rented books from local booksellers. The University of Paris was the first to have a library, in the middle of the 13th century (Rubin and Rubin, 2020), and the catalogue of the Sorbonne listed 1,722 volumes by 1338 (Budd, 2018). Early academic libraries were small, with usually fewer volumes than the Sorbonne. University students were partaking of church-controlled professional education aimed at ministers, civil servants and the law. The range of subjects taught was limited, focusing on theology, philosophy, law and the sciences. The mode of instruction involved recitation of what was imparted in lectures, with no encouragement of wider reading which would have necessitated larger library collections. Later, a similar model took hold in colonial America (Weiner, 2005), with the first university founded at Harvard in 1636.

Four major developments came together to transform the educational model and to stimulate the growth of academic libraries in Europe. The advent of printing in the middle of the 15th century hugely increased the number of books available, rising from a maximum of 15 million in 1500 to 180 million by 1600 (Rubin and Rubin, 2020). This promoted greater literacy and interest in a wider range of subjects and library collections grew accordingly, rising from a few hundred volumes in 1450 to many thousands commonly by 1550 (Feather, 2013). The Enlightenment of the 17th and 18th centuries advanced a new intellectual curiosity which questioned received wisdom and encouraged a broadening of the mind well beyond the narrowly constricted classical training at the universities which had preceded it. Concomitantly, the role of libraries in enabling wider reading became more important.

The Industrial Revolution in the latter half of the 18th century provided another motivation towards a more diverse curriculum. A growing industrial economy called for a variety of technical skills. One further development proved critically important towards far larger and richer academic library collections. Germany was at the heart of this change. It had 24 universities by 1800 (Ratcliffe, 2006), but the foundation of the University of Berlin in 1810 had the greatest influence. This was the first university to make objective research its focus, a model which then became characteristic of German scholarship and spread to other countries later in the century (Shiflett, 1994). For libraries, the focus on research meant a need for far more extensive collections, extra space and greater staffing support. The trajectory followed at the University of Cambridge was typical of research libraries, with growth from 1,000 volumes in 1650 to under a million in 1900 and over three million by 1980 (Thompson, J., 1980).

Academic libraries in the USA had been small until the 1800s and Atkins (1991) cites an estimate of just over 26,600 volumes across all libraries in 1783.

Similar factors to those in Europe brought change in the 19th century. The American Enlightenment and Industrial Revolution happened later than their counterparts in Europe but had the same effects. There was a strong desire to move away from the constraints of the classical model of education towards a more liberal and diverse offering, alongside an impetus to develop the skills needed in a new country and a strong attraction towards the German research university model. The Morrill Land Grant Act of 1862 provided an additional stimulus, with states taking an active stance towards higher education by distributing 30,000 acres of public land to establish public universities which majored in applied sciences and technology (Rubin and Rubin, 2020). A key moment was the foundation of Johns Hopkins University in 1876 as an institution with research at its centre, including a seminar model of teaching which required consultation of a wide range of sources.

Others soon adopted that model, with profound implications for academic libraries. Rapid expansion of collections was the most obvious manifestation and Shiflett (1994) notes growth in the USA by a factor of five to ten, even 20, between 1875 and 1925. Libraries established reference departments to support the use of their growing collections (Weiner, 2005). In the UK universities and libraries expanded in the second half of the 19th century and early in the 20th century, notably the civic universities in major cities (Ratcliffe, 2006). The establishment in 1919 of the University Grants Committee, which took a strong interest in libraries across the UK, was a significant development. Globally, the two World Wars and the Great Depression from 1929 to 1939 slowed growth but a pattern of building the most comprehensive collection possible to support local teaching and research had become established as the primary focus for academic libraries.

Libraries benefited from further government investment in higher education in the period after World War 2, both in research and in initiatives to widen participation. The former enhanced collection development, while the latter generated increased student numbers, and both combined to necessitate new or extended library buildings. Atkins (1991) characterises the period from 1945 to the mid-1960s as one of unprecedented growth for both higher education and academic libraries in the USA. For the UK, Smethurst (1980) noted a period of evolution rather than revolution until the 1960s, with steady growth as more students went to university, their number increasing by 46% between 1953 and 1963 (Mowat, 2006). The number of universities in Australia grew from six in 1930 to 19 by 1980 (Harvey, 2015).

The 1960s represented an exceptional period of growth in both the USA and the UK. Holley (1972) cited some remarkable US figures for the decade, including increases in academic library staffing from 21,100 to 48,000 and in operating expenses from \$183.7 million to \$600 million, while Atkins (1991) noted the construction of 500 new campuses. Service developments included separate graduate and undergraduate libraries, subject departments and area studies units specialising in specific regions (Rubin and Rubin, 2020). Writing about the UK, Roberts observed 'splendid new library buildings, imaginative extensions, larger and larger bookfunds and staffing ratios that had some regard, at least, for ideas of library service' (Roberts, 1980, 114). An average growth rate of 33% obtained for senior library staff between 1966 and 1971 (Smethurst, 1980), while the Parry Report in 1967 recommended that 6% of institutional income should be allocated for annual expenditure on libraries (University Grants Committee, 1967).

Unfortunately, the 1960s proved to be the high-water mark for academic library expansion in the 20th century. Retrenchment was a more common theme throughout its remaining decades. The seeds of trouble were sown in the USA in the late 1960s as public distrust of universities grew. Anti-war protesters expressed opposition to research conducted with government funding for military and defence purposes, while civil rights movements reacted with deep concern to racial tensions on campus. The upshot was widespread public disenchantment with higher education and an increased focus on the practical relevance of university degrees, translating into a much stronger government emphasis on accountability (Atkins, 1991). Governments in other countries also started to take a more interventionist line, shifting from previous support for expanding higher education to questioning funding awards, seeking return on investment and turning the conversation in the direction of impact, outcomes and value. The journey towards today's marketisation, competition and consumerism in higher education, described in Chapter 4, was well under way.

Economic circumstances were highly challenging in the 1970s and 1980s, characterised by periods of high inflation. As new disciplines emerged and the volume of published output increased alongside continuing high student participation, academic libraries were very hard pressed to meet growing demand for collections and related services. Budgets did not always keep pace with the rate of inflation, which in turn was regularly surpassed by publisher prices. An improvement in the economic situation in the second half of the 1990s was very welcome but by then the costs of electronic information and a range of new technologies were making additional calls on the library budget. If funding was the main constraint as academic libraries entered the 21st century, technology, most notably via the advance of the World Wide Web, had emerged as the most important factor in shaping their situation and strategy in the face of new challenges, opportunities and competitors. The rest of this chapter examines how the position and positioning of academic libraries has evolved across the past century.

How the position of academic libraries has evolved

This section examines a number of factors strongly influencing the position and experience of academic libraries during their history: collections, buildings, staffing, director/administration engagement, funding and technology.

Collections: first and foremost

Collections have already featured prominently in this chapter and their significance is encapsulated in the observation that 'Throughout their history libraries have existed primarily as collections of information' (Mowat, 2006, 391). Academic libraries enjoyed a monopoly on access to information in the printed era and local collections underpinned the teaching, learning and research activities of the campus community. The overarching priority for the library staff was to build, make available and preserve the most comprehensive collection it could afford 'for prospecting by students and researchers' (Dempsey and Malpas, 2018, 69). Where funding allowed, the approach was geared towards comprehensiveness rather than selectivity, just in case rather than just in time, on the basis that publications might not be needed immediately but could prove valuable at some future point when they might no longer be obtainable.

The building of large collections was replicated across libraries, with the goal of maximum self-sufficiency at each location. James Thompson (1980) cites impressive rates of growth for individual libraries alongside aggregated figures for US research libraries showing increases from 138 million volumes in 1935 to 280 million in 1955 and 791 million in 1973, noting a similar trend in Germany, Denmark, Sweden, Canada, Australia and New Zealand. The prevailing view was that size mattered. Ratcliffe (1980, 6) noted 'the undoubted dignity and "presence" conferred by great collections on universities'. Commenting on the synonymity between great and large with regard to US collections, he was quick to add that 'no one would suggest that such large American libraries are anything but good'. Collections remained the primary professional preoccupation throughout the 20th century. For example, the majority of a 1980 book titled *The Library in the University: Observations on a Service* was taken up by chapters on selection, acquisition, cataloguing, lending, interlibrary loan and storage (Higham, 1980).

Large and rapidly growing collections created storage challenges. A study of US libraries by Fremont Rider (Rider, 1944) found that college and university libraries on average doubled in size every 16 years, ringing alarm bells in terms of projected collection sizes and the ongoing need for additional storage space. Funding for new construction became tighter in the latter decades of the 20th century and the advent of online publications was welcome in terms of alleviating storage pressures; it did, however, turn the previous approach to local collection building on its head as part of a new value proposition for academic libraries, discussed in the section about the evolution of positioning later in this chapter.

Buildings: from grandeur to flexibility

Collections dominated academic library buildings as well as their other activities. Even in the 1970s it was observed that 'A library is, in the most basic sense, a store-house: a room or series of rooms of which the primary function is the preservation of a collection of written records' (Gormley, 1974, 4). Many libraries consisted at the outset of just one or two rooms, sometimes within other buildings (Weiner, 2005), but as their institutions and collections grew in size from the middle of the 19th century they distributed their space between book storage and study areas. Their standard pattern between the 1890s and 1930s combined spaces for catalogues, open and closed bookstacks and a central reading room (Feather, 2013). A tendency towards monumental, imposing buildings, reflective perhaps of how libraries had radiated wealth and power in ancient times, continued into the 20th century but gave way to a more pragmatic, functional approach as the century progressed (Conner, 2014).

The move towards more flexible and modular buildings with more open space was generally welcomed by library staff as they needed to adapt space to changing circumstances. Over time, changes included opening up access to a greater proportion of the collection, replacing card catalogues with online equivalents and introducing network cabling as well as more pervasive electrical power supply to support access to electronic information and a wider range of equipment, including devices owned by users. The postwar expansion of higher education saw the foundation of many new universities and with them new library buildings at central campus locations, frequently offering more welcoming and spacious entrances (Latimer, 2011). Funding challenges stalled growth from the 1970s onwards but new demands were emerging at the turn of the century, notably a desire for spaces to support collaborative learning. This led to a reconceptualisation of academic library buildings as the balance of collections and user space shifted strongly in favour of users, facilitated by access to information in less space-intensive formats.

A single main library building has been the most common model on university campuses. This has not been the case universally, however. A tradition of separate departmental libraries controlled by faculties or specialist institutes established itself from early on in some European countries, including Germany, Italy, Spain and Portugal. Hoare (2015) describes this trend as well as later efforts to reverse it, including in the Netherlands at Utrecht, where the number of departmental libraries was reduced from as many as 144 to eight between 1974 and 1991. Multiple libraries, including separate buildings for undergraduates, were established on US campuses too (Shiflett, 1994). Decentralisation has generated challenges in terms of standardisation, service development and optimal use of scarce resources.

Staffing: professionalisation, status and organisation

Untrained personnel staffed academic libraries for a long period of time. A common model was to put an academic with an interest in libraries in charge, but this practice was far from universal in the USA at least and 'If it were convenient to place a student or someone else such as the janitor in charge of the library, that was done' (Lynch, 1997, 50). By 1900, however, it was necessary to have a library school degree certificate to take charge of a US university library (Weiner, 2005). Progress in Europe was slower and the scholar-librarian model endured for some time, with trained librarians becoming the norm only in the early 1930s in the UK (Hoare, 2006) but somewhat later than that in Spain and Portugal (Hoare, 2015). The establishment of the American Library Association (ALA) in 1876 was followed in 1887 by the first library school, the School of Library Economy at Columbia University, founded by Melvil Dewey. By 1923, 15 US institutions were providing professional training programmes for library service, albeit with a very practical focus to the exclusion of any theoretical foundation to support scholarly enquiry (Lynch, 1997). This led to criticism of low intellectual quality which took over half a century to reverse (Atkins, 1991). University College London established the first postgraduate school of librarianship in the UK in 1919, but it took until 1963 for the next one to be formed at Sheffield, with others following soon after (Orne, 1980).

Concerns about the low status and pay of library staff surfaced even in the period of higher postwar funding (Lynch, 1997; Smethurst, 1980). A nationally negotiated structure for academic-related library staff in the UK was agreed in the 1970s but was not always applied consistently across institutions (Mowat, 2006). The case for faculty status for professional librarians began to be made in the USA, resulting in a statement published in 1972 setting out a justification based primarily on the importance of library work to the academic mission, including teaching responsibilities and the contribution to institutional governance made by professional librarians (www.ala.org/acrl/standards/jointstatementfaculty). Barriers to faculty status identified included the absence of a PhD as the standard qualification for professional librarians (McCallon and Tucker, 2022; Shiflett, 1994) and insufficient academic rigour in the scholarship about academic libraries (Atkins, 1991). Whatever the arguments, the track record of US institutions in granting faculty status to professional librarians was and remains highly variable (Walters, W. H., 2016).

A preference for bureaucratic models of organising staff may have held academic libraries back from a more advanced position in the institution. Characteristics included departmental silos, rigid hierarchies, cumbersome decision-making processes, inflexibility and limited agility (Conner, 2014; Simons, 2017; Smethurst, 1980), all especially inhibiting as the operating environment called for rapid and fundamental change from the 1980s onwards. Academic libraries were slow to adopt participative management, 40 years behind the business world in one estimate (Kaplan, 1988), with only gradual progress in and after the 1960s. Changes in staff structures happened very gradually and were considered to comprise reshuffling and recombining rather than anything truly radical (Simons, 2017), despite exceptions such as the University of Arizona Libraries (Stoffle and Cuillier, 2010), outlined in Case study 1.1. Some new roles, notably subject librarians and IT specialists, emerged later on to challenge the traditional dominance of cataloguers (Mowat, 2006).

Rigid structures begat risk aversion, exacerbated by 'the fact that the profession attracted and, worse yet, retained people who crave security and status quo' (Stueart, 1984, 1726). The delayed response to calls for major change in response to new paradigms and greater competition in the networked environment raised questions of complacency (Ross, L. and Sennyey, 2008). Tennant (2002) observed an inclination to treat change as a temporary phenomenon, deferring the actions it required. For Atkins (1991), while their service ethic was admirable, a reactive approach and failure by library staff to take the initiative in seeking out faculty contributed towards difficulties in the political arena encountered by academic library directors, as described in the section on the challenges directors faced.

Case study 1.1 Staffing reorganisation at the University of Arizona Libraries, 1993–2008

While conservatism more typically attended changes in staffing organisation, the University of Arizona Libraries adopted a radical approach in the last decade of the 20th century (Stoffle and Cuillier, 2010; Stoffle, Renaud and Veldof, 1996). Its leadership recognised the winds of change blowing through higher education and their implications for academic libraries, notably intensifying financial pressures, increased accountability, technological change and a more demanding student body. There was a realisation that sustaining traditional collecting and processing activities was no longer affordable and that bureaucratic, siloed staffing structures could not be sustained at a time of rapid change calling for greater agility. The new staffing structure adopted in 1993 represented a shift of emphasis away from separate departments processing and managing collections towards a team-based organisation focusing on customers and providing value-added service.

The principles driving organisational change included:

- giving autonomy to cross-functional teams
- maximising the deployment of staff without a professional library qualification
- deploying professionally qualified staff specifically to roles requiring a qualification
- focusing on customers rather than things
- adopting technology wherever possible and making it easily accessible
- doing more with fewer staff as regular cuts ensued
- anticipating future needs, sometimes at the expense of functional day-to-day work
- adapting the structure as needed, including four more reorganisations between 1993 and 2008.

A flatter, less hierarchical structure, coupled with a willingness to question all existing operations and let go of some traditional activities, enabled fundamental change and greater responsiveness to evolving user needs and technological opportunities as information became increasingly digital. A sense of urgency in the face of major change was evident in the view that 'The choice is clear. Change now and choose our futures. Change later, or not at all, and have no future' (Stoffle, Renaud and Veldof, 1996, 224).

The library director: political and other challenges

Gwyer provides an excellent review of the status and experience of the academic library director, charting an overall decline from an earlier position of strength in which 'The library was a stand-alone unit and the library director had a high status within a small senior management team' (Gwyer, 2018, 437). The centrality of printed collections to teaching and research contributed to this, but changes were under way by the early 1970s, even before digital information became commonplace. A key issue for McAnally and Downs (1973) was the expansion of university management teams in the USA at that time, experienced elsewhere later, with additional vice-presidents interposing a layer of officers between the library director and the president. Previously the director had often reported directly to the president but growth in institutional size and complexity generated new leadership roles and distanced the library. This made it difficult to present the library case such that 'the director could not even get to the point of a showdown, much less win one' (McAnally and Downs, 1973, 109).

Relations between directors, presidents and vice-presidents appear to have been fraught in the early 1970s, with Atkins (1991) noting a number of feuds which resulted in departures. Seven of the directors at the Big Ten universities left their post in the academic year 1971/72, all but one before the normal retirement age (McAnally and Downs, 1973). Atkins indicates that much rested on the director as almost the sole interface between the library and the institutional leadership, rendering poor relations and instability highly problematic. Accounts of the director's experience suggest high levels of disillusionment. McAnally and Downs describe an unfavourable combination of factors, including user dissatisfaction, pressures from different quarters, declining status, the lack of a power base from which to operate and absence from decision-making bodies. Writing in 1991, Atkins confirmed the difficulties confronting the director, including a feeling of being left out of the political arena and seen as an outsider, with the library virtually isolated from policy councils. Interviews with institutional leaders at five universities in the late 1990s painted the same concerning picture (Grimes, 1998), representing an unpromising position from which to secure library funding.

Funding: an eternal struggle

The most typical funding model for academic libraries has been an annual allocation from the institutional budget. This has not been the case in every country, however, with funding provided directly from the state in some instances, notably in parts of Europe (Hoare, 2015). One common experience has been a sense of insufficient financial resources. Roberts (1980) captured this when writing that, with a very brief exception in the 1960s, there has been an eternal resourcing struggle, with libraries settling for a lower funding baseline than should have been the case and suffering accordingly. Another shared experience over the decades has been a mix of ups and downs, outlined earlier in this chapter, as a postwar boom gave way to retrenchment from the 1970s. That decade featured double-digit inflation regularly, increasing competition for funds from the campus computer centre and the beginning of a stronger focus on accountability which set the tone for the rest of the century.

A study of movements in library expenditure as a percentage of total institutional outlay is instructive. For the USA this figure stood at 3.3% in 1949/50 in aggregated figures for higher education included by Atkins (1991), rising to 4.0% in 1975/76 and then declining to 3.4% by 1985/86. The Association of Research Libraries (ARL) (2013) charts a steep fall from 3.7% to 1.8% across 40 member institutions between 1982 and 2011, illustrated in Figure 1.1. This represents on average a halving of the proportion of institutional expenditure accounted for by the library in that period. Data for the UK show a figure of 2.2% in 1913/14, rising to 4.5% by 1976/77 but translating to 'A barely perceptible annual increase' (Roberts, 1980, 120). Unfortunately, the pattern has been one of steady decrease since then to 1.7% in 2021/22 (SCONUL, 2023).

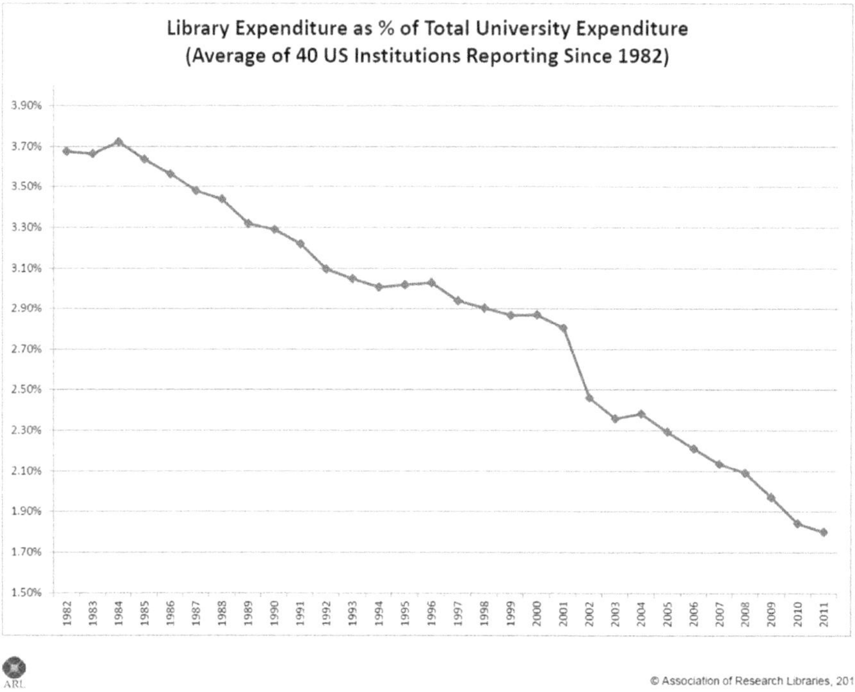

Figure 1.1 *Library expenditure as % of total university expenditure (average of 40 US institutions reporting since 1982), CC-BY 4.0* Association of Research Libraries, 2013, www.libqual.org/documents/admin/EG_2.pdf

One clear implication of this pattern has been a consistent decline in the proportion of books to journals purchased for academic library collections. Roberts (1980) showed a narrowing margin of 51% to 49% in favour of books in 1976/77 but the need to maintain journal subscriptions at costs usually higher than inflation has shifted the balance emphatically in the other direction since then. Recurrent subscriptions accounted for 73.8% of US library materials budgets in 2020 (American Library Association, 2020).

Overall, an ongoing pattern of struggle to keep up with user demands and operating costs has been evident over a long period.

Technology: initial applications

Technology costs made increasing demands on the academic library budget in the latter decades of the 20th century. Library deployment of technology in the 1970s and 1980s was primarily geared towards internal collections management operations, including circulation and shared copy cataloguing via national or regional co-operatives. Implementation and maintenance costs were significant and, while productivity improved, university administrators expected more savings than actually materialised (Atkins, 1991). Libraries were in the vanguard of early technology adoption on campus, however, and were well positioned to influence the development of campus IT infrastructures (Lynch, 1997).

Users began to see the benefits of new technologies from the mid-1980s. Online library catalogues became commonplace, as did access to a range of databases and reference services via compact discs. The really significant change was the emergence from 1993 of the World Wide Web as a medium for publishing and remotely accessing essential information resources, as well as new online services at any time or location. More than any other development earlier in the century, this impacted the positioning of the academic library, the focus of the remainder of this chapter.

The evolution of academic library positioning

This next section considers how the academic library has positioned itself, or been positioned by others, primarily over the past century and especially since the shift from printed to digital information. It addresses many of the positioning components detailed in Chapter 2, notably identity, perceptions, distinctiveness, value and competition.

Identity and perceptions

Academic libraries seem to have maintained a distinctive identity on campus for much of their history. Atkins (1991, 162) asserted that 'The academic library has always had an identity separate from that of the rest of the university', linking this to resistance to change and noting that it had happened despite warnings from within the profession of the risks of remaining isolated from the academic mission of the institution. Connected to this may be a lack of participation by the library in the campus debate concerning the idea of the university, noted earlier. A tendency to engage with the rest of the university from a practice-based perspective has been observed, such that 'investigations are confined to the life-world of librarians' (Salisbury and Peseta, 2018, 252). A shift was evident later in the 20th century, linked to the sense of major upcoming change occasioned by the digital information era. Sapp and Gilmour (2002) identified a sentiment towards increased visibility at university level from various writers, including that 'librarians must become active partners in the scholarly process' (Woodsworth et al., 1989, 138). It was acknowledged that 'Library directors can be too myopic in their view of the library in relation to campus-wide problems' and should take a stronger interest (Hardesty, 1991, 227).

The inclination towards limited participation in campus life seems surprising today, given the focus of academic libraries more recently on engagement and alignment with the mission of the institution at large. The most likely explanation lies in the importance associated with collections not just by library staff but also by the campus community at large. Academic staff and students relied on the locally created and curated collection to get their work done. Collections were also a major asset in attracting scholars and universities often linked collection size to institutional prestige, attractiveness, quality and effectiveness, with large libraries a source of pride for administrators and faculty (Atkins, 1991). A strong association with scholarship was also helpful. Ratcliffe (1980, 7) captured this in stating that 'The relationship between scholarship and libraries has been from the earliest times a most intimate one: the two are utterly interdependent.' The centrality of collections to the academic mission was probably seen as a sufficient basis for academic library positioning on campus such that a degree of separation from other activities in the institution was not a concern.

Metaphors can be deployed effectively in positioning and those associated with academic libraries were favourable towards them. The library as 'heart of the university' was one of the most common and promoted centrality and importance. Salisbury and Peseta (2018, 250) cite a list of more than 20 metaphors, historical and contemporary, ranging from 'academic temple' and 'storehouse/warehouse of books' to 'laboratory' and 'commons', adding a sense of the significance and distinctiveness of the academic library. Further weight towards positive identity and positioning was added by influential external bodies, notably the University Grants Committee in the UK, which variously referred to the academic library as 'the power-house of the university', its 'central organ' and 'core' (Higham, 1980, 11; Hoare, 2006, 319; Ratcliffe, 2006, 367).

These complimentary words and associations, as well as the importance accorded to collections, did not necessarily translate, in the absence of active positioning effort, to attention and support. A separate identity contributed to invisibility in the literature of higher education (Weiner, 2005), the director's absence from key decision-making fora already described and a lack of understanding by administrators. One institutional leader viewed academic libraries as the object of little administrator attention, 'unlikely to be the cause of either a crisis or a coup' (Munn, 1968, 52). Atkins (1991) characterised the general attitude as one of benign neglect and believed that library leaders had made insufficient effort to educate university leadership about the library. Academic staff had a stronger appreciation of the value of the library and its collections, albeit with a limited understanding of its operations. Professional library staff felt a closer affinity to academic staff and fought for faculty status in the USA. A positioning challenge for academic libraries earlier and now was their occupation of a space in between academic and administrative staff, being neither entirely of one or the other and running the risk of being overlooked by either or both (Higham, 1980). There existed the potential for their work to be identified as scholarly or administrative and perceptions veered more commonly towards the latter (McCallon and Tucker, 2022).

Service offering

Its service offering has always been an important part of academic library positioning. Collections were the main focus of library staff energy to begin with, although Melvil Dewey had introduced some innovations as head librarian at Columbia University in the 1880s, including the first reference department to support users, something which became a feature of most US academic libraries before World War 1 (Weiner, 2005). McKenna (1980) describes limited user needs in the UK until the 1950s, when lectures began to be supplemented by seminar tuition. This required students to make greater use of libraries, which in turn needed to provide additional support for an increasing number of first-generation students as government initiatives to widen participation in higher education took effect. Evolving user needs and postwar expansion resulted in the development of a greater range of library services, described as a 'shift almost everywhere from concentration on book-processing to concentration on reader service, from seeing the library primarily as a repository to seeing it as a centre of information' (McKenna, 1980, 93).

Users of academic libraries were able to partake of a range of new or expanding services. These included access to more collections, longer opening hours and expanding programmes of education in how to use libraries and find information, supplemented by increased emphasis on reference and enquiry services. Access to these services was open to all users, while others were targeted at academic staff and research students, including online literature searching, current awareness services and an expansion in interlibrary loans. Subject librarians played a vital role both in service delivery and in identifying new or upcoming library needs from different departments, establishing a base from which stronger engagement by academic libraries with the wider campus could grow. Developments in compact disc technology in the 1980s and 1990s enabled users to do their own literature searching, an early foreshadowing of how the digital revolution would change the role and positioning of academic libraries as users enjoyed more choice and independence.

Digital horizons

Higher education, including academic library staff, experienced a sense of foreboding as the 1970s progressed amid funding challenges and increased questioning from government and public sources. The term 'information society' was coming into use, but libraries were unsure of their likely place in it. Into this atmosphere of uncertainty and introspection dropped in 1978 an impressively prescient book titled *Toward Paperless Information Systems* by F. W. Lancaster, professor in library science at the University of Illinois. Lancaster (1978a) foresaw much of what was to come, outlining a future in which information would be available online via networks, discoverable and accessible directly by users at any time or place. For libraries such a future offered potential space savings, faster and more comprehensive access and more powerful retrieval capabilities. More attention was paid, however, to the threats it posed if users could bypass the library and if the printed collections at the heart of the library's identity no longer needed to be assembled and preserved. Lancaster himself (1978b, 356), in a provocatively titled article, 'Whither Libraries? or, Wither Libraries?' asked the key question: 'Can libraries survive in a largely electronic world?' whose components he expected would be well established by the year 2000.

Sapp and Gilmour (2002; 2003) have digested the academic library reaction to the challenges set forth by Lancaster to its position and positioning. While some level of apprehension and indeed denial would have been in the air, a robust debate ensued and many understood the major implications involved, foreseeing new roles and practices. These included providing users with the skills to navigate this new information landscape, taking on stronger teaching roles, acting as guides and filters and developing partnerships. Veaner (1985) saw the importance for academic libraries of positioning themselves as the primary information providers on campus even if their monopoly on access to information was coming to an end. He called for stronger visibility and breaking down of barriers within the library and across the campus, along with marketing the library as a service rather than a place. Another highly influential publication in the early 1990s was Michael Buckland's *Redesigning Library Services: A Manifesto*, providing a measured, realistic and cogent view of how print and electronic collections could co-exist (Buckland, 1992). Buckland offered guidance on actions libraries needed to take, including integrating electronic materials into workflows and budgets, combining access with ownership and enabling greater self-service by users, while acknowledging some blurring of boundaries with computer centres, museums, publishers and other information providers.

The second part of Sapp and Gilmour's review (2003) shows a realisation that collection size was no longer to be the main barometer of academic library effectiveness and that the ability to match services to user needs was more important. The traditional and human skills of library staff would continue to be vital. Local collections could take a more selective approach, augmented by access to online resources provided from elsewhere. As the 1990s progressed and the World Wide Web revealed itself there was greater optimism that academic libraries could position themselves successfully in this new world with relevant and valued skills and services. Reinvention was under way, with information literacy, end-user support and digitisation all becoming established early in the 21st century. Uncertainty remained, however, and Sapp and Gilmour (2003) identified big questions around the function of the library in a networked university, the future of interpersonal engagement and how to compete effectively with other providers.

Competition via technology

The advance of technology generated some new competition for academic libraries. On campus the rise of the computer centre was observed with some wariness, both as a competitor for resourcing and also as an important player in information access and management (Atkins, 1991). A close and collaborative relationship was advocated (Sapp and Gilmour, 2002) but libraries saw scope for tension in terms of values (Stoffle et al., 2003). There was also a significant trend towards convergence of the two departments into a single information services unit (Hanson, T., 2005; Mowat, 2006), often led by the library director, although some such arrangements were also reversed over time. Another model involved the establishment, separate from either department, of a vice-presidential role of Chief Information Officer. The need to cultivate not only support from this source but also an understanding of library technology and culture was a cause of concern in some quarters (Atkins, 1991; Stoffle et al., 2003).

Academic libraries had not faced real competition from external agencies prior to the advent of the web. By early in the 21st century it had become apparent that students could draw upon web sources for their assignments and no longer depended exclusively on the library. Search engines proved easy to use and more appealing than library catalogues. Companies also saw opportunities through services such as Google Answers, Questia Media and YouTube, the latter two packaging information resources targeted at students for a fee (Stoffle et al., 2003). The web lowered the cost of entry into such markets and challenged libraries to offer unique value when other avenues to information were conveniently available.

Positioning shifts

The beginnings of a shift in academic library positioning were becoming apparent at the start of the new millennium. Soundbites had come into vogue at that time in political and other domains and can be used to highlight some of the changes of direction:

- from collections to services
- from user education to information literacy
- from provision to facilitation
- from collections to connections
- from ownership to access
- from collection to selection
- from local to global
- from passive to active
- from storehouse to commons
- from gatekeeper to gate opener.

These headlines were not necessarily all in use at that time, nor did a statement that encapsulated what was happening come from then: 'The old library was passive . . . The new library is active, an aggressive, educating force in the community'. Surprisingly, that sentiment belonged to a speech by Melvil Dewey in 1888 (Conner, 2014), evidence perhaps that a paradigm shift had long been on the academic library agenda. The direction of travel was at any rate becoming clear by 2000. The overarching change, later summarised by Dempsey and Malpas (2018), was from the collections-based library to the services-based library. Two other thought leaders embraced the shift and put forward new agendas which acknowledged the value of traditional offerings and practices but clearly signalled the importance of moving on from what they both called 'legacy print collections' to the new opportunities on offer in an increasingly digital environment (Brindley, 2006; Lewis, 2007).

For an institution which had experienced such clarity of purpose and general consistency in its operations for so long, the changes occasioned by the digital era were destabilising and disruptive. An unprecedented level of repositioning was called for, but the essential purpose of the academic library was unaltered. As Gorman (1992) emphasised, the means had changed but not the mission.

Conclusion

Academic libraries have been in existence on university campuses for eight centuries and are a well-established entity in higher education. Their beginnings were modest, but growth accelerated after the introduction of printing in the 15th century and especially from the second half of the 19th century onwards. For much of that time the academic library was recognised and measured according to the scale and coverage of its collections which underpinned academic endeavour and conferred prestige on it and its director. The association with collections provided clarity and solidity in terms of identity and value proposition but perhaps too much so as, apart from the size of its main building, the library otherwise seemed to lack visibility and political influence in the institution. As universities expanded, new layers of administration and other competitors emerged, moving the academic library further away from the centre of gravity. The shift of emphasis from printed to digital information has also loosened the foundations on which the library stood, disrupting its operations, revising its value proposition and demanding an ongoing repositioning effort.

Have academic libraries advanced or declined in recent decades? This chapter has provided evidence of a decline in funding, at least as a share of the institutional budget, some slippage down the organisational hierarchy, a struggle to keep up with increasing demands, a strengthening of competition on and beyond the campus, a loss of monopoly position in access to information and greater user self-sufficiency. On the other hand, trust in the academic library remains high, its traditional values are appreciated even more as a counterweight to excessive marketisation and competition in higher education, engagement and alignment with the institutional agenda have strengthened, the social and community role played by the library building and its staff have been heightened and its value proposition is more diverse and broadly based than in the print era. An entrenched professional tendency towards pessimism and soul-searching, evident also in earlier writings (Atkins, 1991; McAnally and Downs, 1973; Roberts, 1980), may promote a more negative assessment of the status of the academic library in any era than is actually warranted.

Celebration of achievements, including library reinvention and the creation of new value in the digital era, deserves more emphasis, as does the long-term perspective generated by an appreciation of the historical development of academic libraries. History has shaped the strengths, weaknesses, opportunities and threats of the academic library over time. They in turn inform strategy development, which itself must be situated in the context of trends in global politics, economics, society and technology (Chapter 3) and of contemporary developments in higher education (Chapter 4). A knowledge of the concept of positioning also underpins academic library strategy and is the subject of the next chapter.

CHAPTER 2

Positioning Strategy

Overview

This chapter introduces the concept of positioning and:

- identifies its objectives and recurrent features via definitions gleaned primarily from the marketing literature;
- explores the importance of positioning, the range of significant issues it influences, the pitfalls of getting it wrong and the benefits of its successful execution;
- analyses the key components of positioning strategy;
- illustrates these components by successful and occasionally unsuccessful examples from the business world, including specific considerations for academic libraries;
- outlines the complex positioning environment academic libraries confront in the world at large, in higher education and on campus;
- considers how academic libraries might best navigate the tightrope between positioning themselves according to traditional and newer value propositions.

Positioning and its importance

The concept of positioning is difficult to pin down and a literature review of over 150 publications is unable to locate a coherent definition on which scholars and practitioners agree (Saqib, 2021). Definitions typically have a marketing context and a focus on products, services or organisations as the objects of the positioning action. The classic work in the field is the book *Positioning: The Battle for Your Mind – How to be Seen and Heard in the Overcrowded Marketplace* by Al Ries and Jack Trout, originally published in 1981 (Ries and Trout, 2001). Their definition emphasises the mind of the potential customer or user: 'positioning is not what you do to a product. Positioning is what you do to the mind of the prospect. That is, you position the product in the mind of the prospect' (Ries and Trout, 2001, 2). The idea of a battle for the mind of the customer is reinforced in another definition of positioning as 'the act of designing the company's offering and image so that they occupy a meaningful and distinct competitive position in the target customers' minds' (Kotler, 1997, 295). Achieving a desired perception by the target audience towards whatever is being positioned emerges as a key objective.

The elements of competition, distinctiveness and communication feature strongly too. One textbook sees the essence of positioning as 'understanding how customers compare alternative offerings on the market and building strategies that describe to the customer how the company's offering differs in important ways from those of existing or potential competitors' (Hooley et al., 2020, 175). Dunford (2019) goes a step further in urging a position of best among, rather than merely distinctive from, the competition. Writing about public libraries, Walters, S. and Jackson (2013, 69) point out that positioning not only identifies the uniqueness of the offering but also 'directs your message specifically to those who need and want to know about your services', thereby incorporating a vital communication function.

Beyond the marketing domain, the *Oxford English Dictionary* provides helpfully neutral definitions of both *positioning* and *position*. The general entry for *positioning* reads: 'The action of putting a person or thing in a certain position, esp. an effective or advantageous position; (also) the fact of being in a certain position or location' (Oxford University Press, 2022). The latter part is reinforced in the definition of position as 'The place in which a person, thing, etc., is located or has been put; situation, site, station'. This is valuable in highlighting that, if a specific position is not claimed for a product or organisation, one will be assigned anyway as perceptions build around that entity. In the absence of clear positioning people 'will invent a position for you, one that potentially hides your key strengths and misrepresents your value' (Dunford, 2019, 11). This points up the risk of being passive or indefinite and the need for organisations, including academic libraries, to take a highly active approach to positioning, discussed later in this chapter. It is also worth emphasising that, although the marketing literature is the most common source for definitions of positioning, its political dimension is highly developed. Countries aim to position themselves politically for influence in the world, while departments seek to position themselves for political advantage on campus.

Why positioning is important

Positioning is important and its effect on the perceptions of target audiences carries significant influence. In one view it can underpin an entire business strategy, potentially making the difference between success and failure (Dunford, 2019). In another it can help a company to become an authority in its field, achieve better brand recognition and create new markets (Writer, 2021). Getting it wrong can be costly and Writer takes the view that incorrect positioning can kill a brand, targeting it at the wrong market or making it unattractive to the right audience. Kotler (1997) identifies four major errors whose consequences he summarises as follows:

1. *Underpositioning*: customers have only vague perceptions of a company and its products, seeing nothing special about them.
2. *Overpositioning*: customer understanding is too narrow, perhaps limiting engagement to just a few of the company's offerings.
3. *Confused positioning*: there is a lack of clarity among customers about a company's position due to frequent changes and contradictory messaging.
4. *Doubtful positioning*: customers do not believe the claims made by the company for its products and services.

In many cases, including that of academic libraries, the target audience for positioning will include the stakeholders responsible for their funding. This is an issue recognised by Penniman (1997), who identifies the need to influence positively the choosers as well as the users. Cox (Cox, J., 2018) outlines possible negative consequences if an academic library is poorly positioned with its stakeholders, including less influence with the leadership of the parent institution, a lower position in the organisational hierarchy, grouping with professional instead of academic services and a tendency for the library contribution to be overlooked. In summary, he sees strong positioning in the institution as critical to the recognition, resourcing and prospects of any academic library.

Walters, S. and Jackson (2013) recognise the importance for public libraries of positioning. They see it as the most crucial decision the library will make, because it expresses its core values and identifies for whom they will make most difference. The current book also puts forward values as a significant strength for academic libraries and a key force in their positioning. The emphasis placed by Walters and Jackson on the benefits and opportunities of successful positioning is appropriate. These include achieving competitive advantage, influencing customer behaviour in ways that deliver stronger interaction with services and potentially moving libraries to the next level.

They see value in the journey as much as in the destination, noting that libraries which spend time on positioning 'develop a better understanding of who they are, of their strengths and their purpose. They become stronger, more focused, and united and have a clarity of purpose to move forward to meet the challenges of the future' (Walters, S. and Jackson, 2013, 104).

Having established the importance of positioning, it is opportune to examine its key components, including some practicalities and examples of successful practices but also of mistakes, in the next section.

Key components of positioning strategy

The definitions at the beginning of this chapter provided some pointers towards the key components of positioning strategy. An attempt to summarise them in one sentence might run as follows: pitching a clearly identified offering which is differentiated from closely monitored competitors and of significant value for a deeply understood user base to whom it is communicated effectively, while fully aligned with the resources and strengths of the positioning entity. On that basis, the key components are clarity of identity and distinctiveness from the competition, as well as an understanding of the needs of target audiences, all underpinned by impactful communications and strong resources. Each is interlinked and aimed at influencing perceptions in the minds of identified user groups.

Clarity of identity

Identity may be defined as who you are, what you do and who benefits from your products or services (Walters, S. and Jackson, 2013). A clear identity makes it as easy as possible for users to understand the offering and its value. This can be further facilitated by belonging to a definite market category (Dunford, 2019), easily recognisable in the way that Apple is associated with technology, for example. Assigning academic libraries to a single market category is challenging, however, and Corrall (2000) has noted debate over a long period about the core business of libraries, including their potential to be described as belonging to any of the information, knowledge or learning businesses.

More encouragingly, 'In any positioning program if you start with a strongly held perception, you'll be that much ahead in your efforts to establish your own position' (Ries and Trout, 2001, 141). This is advantageous for libraries, given the strength of their brand, built over many centuries. Academic libraries have been an identifiable part of universities since the 13th century and have often been described as the heart of the institution

(Salisbury and Peseta, 2023). They enjoy the benefit of having been first in their area of influence and therefore getting into the mind of their user community first, something which Ries and Trout (2001, 47) see as the 'essential ingredient in securing the leadership position'. They highlight the example of IBM, which did not invent the computer but 'was the first company to build a computer position in the mind of the prospect' (Ries and Trout, 2001, 24).

Distinctiveness from the competition

A clear identity supports the distinctiveness of any institutional offering. The level of differentiation achievable is also linked to the strength of the competition faced. Paying strong attention to competitors is recommended as there are opportunities to learn from them (Walters, S. and Jackson, 2013). Asking what customers would do if your solution did not exist is a starting point in understanding alternative options available and getting focused on differentiation (Dunford, 2019). A valuable tool in understanding the competitive environment for any entity is Porter's Five Forces framework (Porter, 1979). This enables an analysis of customers, suppliers, potential entrants, substitute products and competitive rivalry within a sector, helping to identify areas of actual or potential differentiation in order to create a distinctive position.

Having analysed competitive alternatives, Dunford (2019) advises isolating the capabilities that make an organisation and its products or services stand out from competitors. This generates thinking around the value proposition as perceived by the target audience (Levitt, 1980). Academic libraries have competitors, as discussed later in this and other chapters, and need to consider their points of distinction, which include place, service and knowledge of local needs. Hooley et al. (2020) identify six dimensions of differentiation: price, technical quality, service, innovation, benefit differentiation or customisation. Southwest Airlines in the USA offers a good example of differentiation on price (Porter, 1996). Its entire business model is based on containing operational costs and offering lower fares than other airlines to target price-sensitive customers. The Irish airline Ryanair operates a similar model of distinctive positioning in Europe.

Understanding of target audiences and their needs

Distinctiveness is linked with value offered, which in turn depends on having a deep understanding of the needs of the audiences targeted. These, as noted earlier, may include funders as well as users. Hooley et al. (2020) identify this connection when observing that companies need to know the value they create and how customer perceptions of value may change. In essence, effective positioning requires that you know both your value and your customers. This holds true in all sectors, including libraries, where there is recognition of the need for 'very detailed knowledge of users and their hopes, fears, needs, wants, attitudes, behaviours and values' (Kendrick, T., 2021, 8). More specifically, Dempsey (2012) sees the importance for academic audiences in relation to positioning of understanding the structure of disciplines, the norms of scholarship and changes in publishing.

Acquiring that intelligence about target audiences involves multiple approaches. These include developing market-sensing skills in staff, maximising the generation and analysis of customer demographic and transactional data available from IT systems and regularly monitoring levels of user satisfaction through surveys and other interactions (Hooley et al., 2020). Most service providers today have opportunities to make extensive use of data about customers but the value of in-person engagement with service users remains strong and Dunford (2019) recommends identifying and knowing those core users who really value the offering and will tell others about it. Academic libraries recognise the merits of regular human interaction with users through their deployment of liaison, engagement and relationship management roles (Eldridge et al., 2016).

Effective communications

A reminder of the earlier definition that 'Positioning is what you do to the mind of the prospect' (Ries and Trout, 2001, 2) serves to highlight the importance of communicating effectively with target audiences. The same authors offer their advice on how this might be approached. First, they recommend staying inside the head of the user and concentrating on how the intended message may be received. This involves looking from outside in rather than from inside out and recognising that the solution to effective communications lies in the mind of the prospect rather than in that of the provider. They also urge conciseness of messaging, observing that less is more and that the best approach in an over-communicated society is the over-simplified message. Examples include Nike's 'Just do it', promoting action and aspiration, and Apple's 'Think different', capturing the distinctiveness of its products.

Generating a very simple message which advances strong positioning is easier said than done for libraries and information services. Corrall (2000, 72) warns against alliterative taglines such as 'education, enlightenment and entertainment' or 'information, imagination and innovation', which look neat but may have little originality or meaning for users. The use of language needs due attention too and the library tendency towards terms like service and support may not resonate as intended. Interviews with a group of provosts in the USA found perceptions of service terminology as indirect and reactive rather than proactive (Connaway et al., 2017). More optimistically for libraries, the value of a strong name in capturing space in the audience mind has been emphasised, noting that 'A strong, generic-like, descriptive name will block your me-too competitors from muscling their way into your territory' (Ries and Trout, 2001, 72). The word 'library' has resonance by virtue of its longevity and carries valuable strength when it comes to communications.

Alignment of resources with strengths

Effort in the areas of identity, distinctiveness, audience research and communications will be undermined if positioning does not line up with the strengths of the organisation. Aligning resources with strengths is therefore vital to positioning and this means looking inwards to a far greater extent than for the other components described. A body of research into the resource-based view (RBV) of the organisation is helpful towards this end. An early leader in this field, Jay Barney, identified a need to balance the focus on external threats and opportunities with the development of tools to analyse internal strengths and weaknesses (Barney, 1995). He deliberately referred to capabilities as well as resources, recognising that less tangible assets could represent important strengths. These might include brand reputation, relationships with customers and a long-established competitive position in the marketplace (Hooley et al., 2020), as well as specialist internal knowledge and processes. Coca-Cola has calculated that most of its value resides in its intangible assets, primarily its brand (Knox, 2004).

Resources generating a particular competitive advantage are identified as Valuable, Rare, Inimitable and Non-substitutable (VRIN) according to the framework developed by Barney (1991). Their resistance to duplication by competitors is a key characteristic, defending the competitive position of an organisation and its offerings. Porter (1996) documents an example from the 1990s, when Continental Airlines tried to compete via its Continental Lite service with the low-cost model offered by Southwest Airlines, described earlier. It failed because it was unable to commit fully to replicating all the business processes of its rival as Continental continued to operate its full-service model and fell between the two stools, driving the Lite service out of business within two years. In 1995 Barney updated the VRIN framework to Valuable, Rare, Inimitable and Organisation-supported (VRIO). In doing so, he emphasised the need for a company to be organised through all its processes and systems to exploit its resources and capabilities (Barney, 1995). As an example, he described a negative instance at Xerox, whose reporting structure, management control systems and compensation policies prevented the company from taking full advantage of innovations developed at its Xerox PARC research laboratory in Palo Alto, California, during the 1960s and 1970s.

The key message emerging for academic libraries is the need to recognise and capitalise on their strengths, aligning their tangible and intangible resources accordingly for optimal positioning. The frameworks of Barney and Porter also highlight the importance of an intimate knowledge of strengths, weaknesses, opportunities and threats for successful positioning and strategy development. The second part of this book encompasses a SWOT analysis of academic libraries to support the identification of positioning strategies in the final part.

The positioning environment for academic libraries

Positioning an academic library today happens in a noisy world with multiple channels of communication, filtered and unfiltered. Ries and Trout (2001) emphasised the difficulties of getting attention in what they saw as an over-communicated society even in 1981, prior to the advent of social media and with 24-hour news broadcasting in its infancy. Everything is more fluid now, with many moving parts. As described in this section, the operating environment for academic libraries is more volatile and uncertain than before globally, in the higher education sector and on campus, so positioning is complex. Academic libraries are aiming at a series of moving targets against a background of disruption, instability and complexity.

Global uncertainty

Trends in the global environment are the subject of Chapter 3, but a few developments are worth noting here, each contributing to an uncertain platform for positioning. The political environment has become characterised by an upsurge in polarisation, identity politics and culture wars between Left and Right, with a move in a number of countries towards the Right (Fukuyama, 2020). This can lead to big shifts in direction when administrations change, along with high levels of government intervention in all sectors, including higher education, regardless of who is in charge. An area of common ground, unfortunately, appears to be a lack of urgency in acting to mitigate the current and future effects of climate change which is gathering momentum and represents a major existential threat in many parts of the world.

The global economic picture is similarly insecure. Many governments, institutions and individuals are heavily burdened by debt following unprecedented levels of borrowing, creating the potential for a major economic crash (Roubini, 2023). The globalisation of the economy means that the effects of a financial meltdown in one country can be quickly felt elsewhere. Free trade is under major threat in the face of increased protectionism. Positioning needs resources but an uncertain economic climate brings further challenges. Although the economic effects of the COVID-19 pandemic have not proved to be as disastrous as feared, profound social changes have followed. These include new, commonly hybrid, patterns of work (Williams, C., 2021) and changes in human behaviour, notably an increased tendency to interact with services digitally rather than in person. New expectations among users have implications for academic libraries, as does the need to position their services to a changed mix of on-campus and remote audiences.

Digital disruption

Academic libraries have to work harder at positioning than in the print-only era, when their offering centred on collections, generating a clear and solid value proposition. The move to an increasingly digital environment, accelerated by the advent of the World Wide Web, meant that users became largely self-sufficient in performing a number of tasks for which they had formerly depended on library mediation. Academic libraries shifted to a much more diversified value proposition, characterised as a move from collections to services and centred on new contributions to teaching and research, working in partnership and reconfiguring library space for creative experiences.

Obligations towards printed collections nevertheless remain and academic libraries continue to be 'encumbered by their legacy infrastructure, practices, and culture' (Lewis, 2016, 10). This limits their agility towards repositioning compared to new competitors who have not needed to make trade-offs with their existing activities (Porter, 1996). Perceptions, as already noted, play a big part in positioning and some of these competitors, notably Google and Amazon, may be seen by users and administrators as a benchmark for academic libraries in terms of cost and performance. The age and condition of the library's building also represent a key positioning factor, with newer spaces offering far greater flexibility, convenience and digital capacity to meet evolving expectations than structures built for a different purpose prior to the web (Cox, A. M., 2023).

A further technological disruption in the shape of AI is playing out in society at large, with significant implications for higher education and academic libraries. Artificial intelligence is not new but the recent advance from extractive to generative AI, capable of creating text, images and sounds almost instantly (Pelletier et al., 2023b), has attracted much attention and features prominently in Chapters 3 and 4. Generative AI raises many questions about academic library roles and positioning. It represents a further level of self-sufficiency felt by users relative to previous library mediation. Expectations will be subject to change and it is likely that the role of academic libraries in supporting users to understand and use AI appropriately will need to evolve.

Higher education in flux

Chapter 4 covers changes in higher education in greater depth. The sands have certainly shifted under this sector, which comprises the key operating environment for academic libraries, in recent decades. Its whole identity has been questioned, its purpose challenged, its actions scrutinised and its future rendered uncertain amid an ongoing state of crisis, creating an unstable climate for library positioning. Cox (Cox, J., 2018; 2021) identifies multiple drivers for radical change, including greater accountability, more intense competition for students and research funding, rising student expectations, internationalisation and difficult economic conditions. Funding has been a particular issue, with varied models operating in different jurisdictions but a tightened resource base in common relative to a much-increased student population.

Institutional strategies have been prone to frequent shifts, with new items added to the agenda via not only the global and technological changes already outlined, but also in many countries by a high level of government intervention which emphasises institutional accountability and contribution to national economic goals (Clancy, 2021). Among the evolving priorities for institutions have been student success, internationally recognised research, local community engagement, global reputation and reach and demonstration of societal impact (Cox, J., 2018). The COVID-19 pandemic has, furthermore, changed how teaching and learning happen as well as who is on campus when.

The ongoing degree of change and uncertainty presents positioning challenges for academic libraries. Lewis (2016) sees some positivity in this, as it offers them an opportunity to be assertive in making necessary changes and to take a leadership position on campus, especially in harnessing digital technologies effectively. As argued at the end of this chapter, there is definite merit in an assertive approach to positioning. It is also important, however, to acknowledge the difficulty that a continuously changing campus environment presents for library efforts at alignment with institutional priorities.

Campus challenges

Academic libraries have a broad user base and interact with many parties. These include academic staff, students, professional services staff, institutional leadership, members of the local community, funders, donors and professional bodies. Pitching to such a diversity of audiences presents a positioning challenge. Students comprise the largest stakeholder community. Their number has grown hugely in recent times, as has their diversity in terms of age, ethnic origin and socioeconomic background, with more studying part-time than before. This diversity brings a range of outlooks, expectations and needs to which academic libraries strive to relate and bring meaningful value.

Institutional leaders are key stakeholders and, as noted earlier, positive positioning towards them is vital to the resourcing and success of an academic library. A problem in this regard is that studies have shown a lack of awareness among this group of what their libraries do and the contributions they make to the institutional mission (Cox, J., 2023b; Gwyer, 2018). Some hold very traditional views of the library and others exhibit indifference towards it, seeing it as of limited strategic concern and therefore not requiring attention. This is not a promising situation and addressing it through effective positioning is not straightforward, especially where the library has moved further away from the top table as leadership teams have grown additional layers in increasingly complex organisations.

A final campus challenge to note is that other departments have increasingly been overlapping with libraries in terms of expertise. Newer areas of engagement such as research data management and digital scholarship involve multiple contributions. They represent shared activities and are not the exclusive preserve of academic libraries (Dempsey, 2016). Partnership on campus has generally proved healthy for libraries, but there is an awareness that it 'could have elements of both a smooth, fruitful collaboration or a competitive struggle for resources' (Cox, A. M., Pinfield and Rutter, 2019b, 324). Collaborators can also become competitors, while relatively newer units may intersect with or seek to absorb library functions. Bibliometric analysis of research outputs is an example in the case of institutional research units. Library positioning therefore needs to incorporate an appropriate balance of collaboration and competition.

The positioning environment for academic libraries is complex and all of the themes identified briefly in this section are the subject of more detailed coverage in later chapters. Case study 2.1 recounts a range of challenges and opportunities experienced in repositioning the University of Leicester Library.

Case study 2.1 Repositioning the Library at the University of Leicester

The experience of the University of Leicester Library provides insights into the challenges and opportunities of repositioning an established academic library on campus (Wynne et al., 2016). Changes in research such as digital scholarship, the increasing importance of research data management and expectations of open access to research outputs, alongside an emphasis on independent learning, provided opportunities for the Library. These included partnership roles in knowledge creation, a publishing function and the development of more broadly defined information literacy programmes. The Library leadership also recognised the ongoing importance of traditional roles relating to information access and knowledge sharing.

A staff restructuring in 2012 resulted in the creation of new research services and learning and teaching services teams with remits to extend the role of the Library into the emerging areas of research mentioned above, to develop its role in learner development and to strengthen relationships with academic departments. Despite some initial successes there was an early acknowledgement of the importance of effective communication of the new role and positioning of the Library. The establishment of a cross-service Marketing and Communications Group, supported by the addition of a communications remit to an existing post and the engagement of a marketing consultant, proved key in developing a more systematic approach to marketing. This helped to avoid difficulties commonly experienced by academic libraries, including a tendency to confuse promotion with marketing in addition to challenges with resourcing and sustaining effective marketing. Instead, data analysis, focus groups and lots of listening delivered new insights to inform communications to segmented audiences and campaigns to coincide with new services.

Positive outcomes included improved relationship building, new partnerships, a broader range of involvements and sometimes leading roles in teaching, learning and research alongside wider committee representation. All of these contributed to a repositioning of the library and its role on campus and changed perceptions by stakeholders. The strategic approach to positioning adopted by the Library proved vital and was further sustained by the creation of a full-time marketing role and a rolling communications plan, with marketing integral to the Library strategy rather than separate from it. Many of the key elements of positioning outlined in the current chapter are prominent in this case study, notably influencing of user mindsets, understanding of target audiences, effective communication and the alignment of resources with the intended position while appreciating the importance of traditional strengths.

The academic library positioning tightrope

How to leverage optimally their strong traditional brand alongside a changed value proposition in the digital world is an overarching positioning issue for academic libraries. This can feel like walking a tightrope, necessitating careful handling to maximise the benefits of the older and newer models.

Maximising traditional value

Academic libraries have enjoyed longevity and an established presence on campus, supported by resonant values and a solid value proposition. Their values promote ensuring free and equal access to information, protecting intellectual freedom, advancing the public good, delivering exemplary service and being socially responsible (American Library Association, 2024; Association of College and Research Libraries, 2018). These generate loyalty, support and trust and chime well with a list identified by Walters, S. and Jackson (2013) of characteristics to which people are attracted, including authenticity, clarity, approachability, passion and reliability. The values academic libraries espouse are an asset for themselves as well as being well supported by their users.

Lewis identifies three functions that libraries have always performed, along with their purpose:

> 1. They have kept documents for the long haul.
> 2. They have provided the knowledge and information that the communities and institutions that fund them need.
> 3. They have assisted individuals in finding and using information.
>
> They have done so to assure that communities and individuals are productive and so that civilizations are long-lasting.
>
> (Lewis, 2016, xi)

These functions remain relevant, essential and appreciated. The shift towards digital libraries has radically changed how they are fulfilled, generating a new value proposition, but one which sits alongside the traditional perception of the library as printed collections continue to be important for users and need to be appropriately resourced.

Promoting a changed value proposition

The relatively solid value proposition promoted by the monopoly position of academic libraries as repositories of access to information in the print-only era has given way to a much more diffuse and less concrete or concise offering. Academic libraries now frame their value in a multiplicity of ways: as partners, publishers, stewards of research data, places of community and well-being, spaces for social learning and creativity, proponents of digital literacy and enablers of student success and employability to name but a few. Their buildings often host a range of services in partnership with other campus providers, including academic writing and mathematics support hubs, assistive technology units and digital scholarship centres.

New paradigms have been proposed to move away from the limitations of old mantras and to communicate the changed value proposition. These include the library as platform, the computational library, the library as infrastructure and the boundaryless library (Pinfield, Cox and Rutter, 2017). Presenting such a diversified value proposition to its target audiences in a neat and concise way is not easy. The Association of College and Research Libraries (2016) and SCONUL (2012) have published statements of academic library value, building on an earlier review and report by Oakleaf (2010), and it is noticeable that their lists are lengthy, multidimensional and require close reading. They do, however, helpfully combine examples of traditional and new value, a commendable approach rather than trying too hard to project only the latest offerings.

The diffusiveness of the value proposition also raises an issue of potential loss or compromising of the traditionally strong library identity amid such a diversity of services, spaces and partnerships. Distinctiveness, identified earlier as a key component of positioning, is important and Lewis (2016) advocates a focus on what libraries can do either uniquely or better than any other unit on campus. Earlier, Corrall (2000, 72) sensed the 'real danger of formulating a mission statement which could equally apply to a bookstore or an IT unit, or a cybercafe' and recommended the demonstration and differentiation of value provided as a vital task for information service managers.

Reflective journal extract 2.1
Changed value – and language

From the author's journal: 24 October 2014

Excellent discussion at Irish Universities Association Librarians Group today about 21st century libraries. Important point about avoiding terminology such as 'the library service' which puts us in the admin/services camp rather than the academic area where we must align – expertise and advanced skills are our unique selling point for the future, not services and transactions.

A brand crisis?

Writing of US public libraries over a decade ago, Suzanne Walters and Kent Jackson (2013, 10–11) identified a 'brand crisis'. In doing so, they drew upon the results of an OCLC report (De Rosa and Johnson, 2008) which revealed a strongly positive public perception towards those libraries but found that this sentiment was rooted in a very traditional view of what they offered. They concluded that: 'In effect the public does not identify with the library as a venue for transformation and value-added programs and services – there is disconnect between how libraries see themselves and how they want the marketplace to see them.'

Whether or not one chooses to term this a brand crisis, there is evidence in a number of studies of a similar disjunction applying to academic libraries (Baker, D. and Allden, 2017; Pinfield, Cox and Rutter, 2017; Gwyer, 2018; Murray and Ireland, 2018; Blankstein, 2022). A survey of 261 academic library staff in the UK indicates awareness of this issue from within the library (Pinfield, Cox and Rutter, 2017). More than 70% of participants agreed that senior institutional decision-makers needed to be educated that the library was not all about books, while of those expressing a definite opinion a majority believed that students did not know what services the library provided. The authors of the report containing the survey took this finding as a very definite signal that academic libraries needed to communicate their current and future role better, creating a compelling vision and engaging multiple stakeholders with the specific value they provide (Pinfield, Cox and Rutter, 2017).

Assertive positioning

'Position' as something that can be assigned if it is not claimed emerged early in this chapter, specifically in the *Oxford English Dictionary* (Oxford University Press, 2022) definition of it as the place where something has been located or is put. Walters, S. and Jackson (2013, 69) confirm this by asserting that 'if you don't consciously create a positioning strategy for the library, the community and your stakeholders will do it for you', while another author states unambiguously that 'When you don't own your position, you are putting your company at a competitive disadvantage' (Dunford, 2019, 11). The need for an active and assertive approach to positioning emerges clearly for academic libraries, not only to combat misperceptions of their value proposition but also to advance their status, improve their prospects and take greater control of their destiny. A few specific considerations follow.

Assertive positioning involves taking the upper hand, including projecting the academic library as a leader to the maximum extent possible. It has been observed that alignment with the institutional agenda should not just be reactive (Pinfield, Cox and Rutter, 2017), while risks were noted earlier in this chapter that terminology such as 'service' and 'support' may lack proactivity and create a passive impression (Connaway et al., 2017). Academic libraries have exerted leadership in areas such as learning space design, digital literacy and open access publishing. Their positioning messages can capitalise on these roles.

Dilution is a risk in academic library positioning. There can be a pressure to be all things to all people, something labelled 'the everybody trap' by Ries and Trout (2001, 60). They emphasise the need to avoid this and to practise audience segmentation in order to focus on delivering and communicating specific value to identified groupings. Walters, S. and Jackson (2013) support this view and exhort libraries to prevent dilution by intentionally prioritising certain audiences. This should be based on an intimate knowledge of their target market, one of the key components of positioning described earlier. Although published some time ago, the statements of academic library value by the ACRL (Association of College and Research Libraries, 2016) and SCONUL (2012) provide resources to support positioning towards segmented audiences, as does the report by Oakleaf (2010).

It can be tempting to focus positioning messages on the newest parts of the value proposition but maintaining a balance with promoting traditional strengths and contributions of value is important. Academic library values, as argued in Chapter 5 especially, are an asset, providing a helpful anchor in times of change. Personal service, trusted advice and commitment to objective pursuit of the truth add authority to the library's position and positioning. Ries and Trout (2001) counsel against changing a basic positioning strategy, advising that it should simply be improved rather than replaced. Their firm view is that 'Owning a position in the mind is like owning a valuable piece of real estate. Once you give it up, you might find it's impossible to get it back again' (Ries and Trout, 2001, 193).

Finally, while a strong commitment towards service characterises those who work in libraries, there can also be a scepticism towards marketing, 'seeing the two as somehow in conflict with each other' (Walters, S. and Jackson, 2013, xvi). Such a mindset needs to be overcome if the academic library is to position itself successfully. It is important to heed the warning that 'In our noisy times the fight for attention is severe and brutal. Being the best kept secret is dangerous positioning' (Kendrick, T., 2021, 2).

Reflective journal extract 2.2
Asserting the Library's role in online teaching and learning
From the author's journal: 25 April 2020
The Library's role in helping to move the University to an all online teaching and learning environment is a big issue just now [early in the COVID-19 pandemic] . . . Our role and contributions are not fully understood – in a way we were almost too proactive in building a great digital library so there's been no panic with the move online in the short term. This is a long-term proposition now and we need to gear up for it and communicate our role . . . it's about what the University needs to do to deliver online teaching/learning at scale; within that we in the Library need to be clear about our contribution and how we organise it. We are doing a lot but it's being taken for granted, so we need to articulate what we do, what resources it takes, how we offer it, what our structure is, who is involved and, especially, what difference it makes.

Conclusion

Positioning matters and perceptions matter, especially in a competitive environment. Delivering and communicating distinctive value to intimately understood target audiences is fundamental and resources need to be aligned towards that end. An unwanted position may be assigned in the absence of active positioning, so an assertive approach is required. The rewards for successful positioning are substantial. For academic libraries these can translate into a well understood offering, preferred over competitors, valued by stakeholders and recognised by institutional leadership in terms of support and resourcing. Positioning failures can have the opposite effect and academic libraries face a highly challenging environment, characterised by instability and uncertainty at global and campus level. Disruptions in higher education and the digital world are major ongoing features of their environment. These mean shifting priorities for their parent institutions and a significantly changed, potentially diluted, library value proposition respectively.

Getting attention for positioning messages is difficult in this dynamic and somewhat chaotic arena. Academic libraries find themselves battling strong competition, misunderstandings of their contribution and a tension in balancing their traditional and newer value propositions. They can, however, draw upon distinctive strengths. Foremost among these are their longevity, established presence on campus, strong brand and enduring values. Academic libraries are naturally keen to put their new value front and centre in the face of a persistent association with books or quiet, especially when people speak of their loss of relevance or fail to understand the range of new contributions they make to the institution. It is important to remember, however, that positive perceptions towards the traditional form of the library as a central part of the campus remain in many quarters. Furthermore, the desire for places of contemplation is heightened in today's noisy world. Academic library values are constant and offer a good bridge between the traditional and contemporary value propositions. Positioning may gain from starting with traditional value as an easily understood and solid backdrop to the diverse range of recent contributions, while keeping the message tight for specific audiences through segmentation.

This chapter has provided a context for academic libraries within the concept of positioning, having in the opening chapter examined their history and evolution. An understanding of the past and of today's positioning components and challenges offers a good foundation for the analysis of academic library strengths, weaknesses, opportunities and threats in the chapters comprising the second part of this book. This in turn is helpfully informed by a more detailed account in the next two chapters of developments in the contemporary global and higher education environments.

CHAPTER 3

The Global Context: Politics, Economics, Society and Technology

Overview

Global developments impact academic libraries and this chapter:

- introduces recent developments, as well as their potential future direction and convergence;
- uses summary tables in each section to link academic libraries to the global political, economic, social and technological factors discussed;
- outlines the key elements of today's political climate, notably polarisation and increasing global tensions;
- examines the economic setting, identifying globalisation as a key influence;
- describes the social environment, including demographic shifts, working life and climate change;
- surveys the technological landscape, highlighting the power of AI but also concerns raised by it;
- reviews an unstable and challenging global situation overall and considers its headline impacts for academic library operations and strategy.

The world we live in

Higher education and academic libraries operate in the wider world. They are part of a broader canvas, interacting with and shaped by political, economic, social and technological developments worldwide and those specific to their own country or region. Global events and trends are a key context for them. That context was positive until relatively recently. Politically, democracy had been on the rise, reflected in a trebling of the number of electoral democracies between the early 1970s and the first decade of the 21st century; during that time economic progress had seen a quadrupling of the world's output of goods and services (Fukuyama, 2018). Life expectancy had increased and quality of life improved, aided by medical advances and technological innovations.

The global recession of 2008 may be seen as a turning point in economic terms, with long-term effects in many countries, including a build-up of debt to new levels and a transfer of manufacturing activity from West to East. The political climate also became more fraught in the new century, characterised by geopolitical competition, instability and division (Thompson, H., 2022). Gorman's (2015) list of influential trends and changes for libraries extended in number to 20 from the 16 identified in 2000, incorporating 12 new entries which included climate change, financial collapse, cybercrime and social media. Events since 2020 have generated a sense of concern, even doom. These have included the COVID-19 pandemic, new outbreaks of war, tensions between global superpowers, a period of rising inflation and interest rates, famine, energy insecurity and extreme weather events linked to climate change.

Speculation about the future generates little optimism. Roubini (2023) foresees severe consequences as megathreats converge, including unsustainable debt, protectionist trade policies, deepening inequality, demographic collapse and technology-induced job losses. A rise in polycrises as multiple crises interact to intensify their individual impacts already features in the *2025 EDUCAUSE Horizon Report, Teaching and Learning Edition* (Robert et al., 2025). Peston and Koria (2023) calculate a 41% chance of one of the following five events happening within five years: nuclear strike; economic war; AI attempting to destroy the human race; severe climate events killing millions of people; another viral pandemic. The predictions of Guillén (2021) are less dystopian but very clear that major changes are on the way by 2030, among them an ageing population, a shift in economic power towards Asia, intensification of climate change and technological disruption. He and others emphasise linkages between trends, adding to their momentum. It is not difficult to see a line of connection, for example, from economic inequality to political polarisation, from protectionist policies to immigration curbs or from climate change to demographic shifts.

The Political, Economic, Social and Technological (PEST) analysis technique offers a helpful framework for this chapter (Makos, 2024). It focuses on the external environment and enables the grouping of a multiplicity of developments according to each of the four dimensions involved, while acknowledging that many are closely related, even interdependent. There is therefore some overlap between the sections of this chapter. A further point to note is that higher education, a key context for academic libraries, is covered separately in Chapter 4.

The political environment

Politics plays a major role in everyone's lives. Susskind (2021) urges a broad interpretation of this term, looking beyond a narrow, but common, focus on the people and institutions comprising the key actors in the political process to a wider view encompassing all the forces that shape our existence. The domain of politics extends across how we are governed, where governments stand on a continuum from democracy to authoritarianism, the ways in which different views are represented, the degree of government intervention or regulation experienced by sectors and individuals, levels of taxation or state support and relations between countries. In summary, politics strongly influences our freedom to act and our ability to get things done.

The rise of identity politics

A stable political climate is important for the current operations of, and future planning by, any organisation, including an academic library, but instability has been more characteristic of late, with the increasing prevalence of identity politics a key factor in many parts of the world. The traditional Left–Right political divide centred on economics but has shifted in the current century towards questions of identity (Fukuyama, 2020). The Left is less preoccupied with achieving greater economic equality than with advancing the rights and interests of a range of marginalised groups, while the Right is focused on protecting what it sees as a traditional national identity and set of values under threat from forces such as modernity, liberalism and multiculturalism (Fukuyama, 2018; Sotirakopoulos, 2021).

The causes of this shift in emphasis are complex to define. They include rising economic and social inequality, a sense of loss at being left behind as globalisation has moved manufacturing jobs eastwards and a feeling of invisibility and being ignored by governments and elites. Social justice is a particular motivation for the Left, with a desire to secure recognition, inclusion and equal opportunities for groups disenfranchised in the past according to multiple criteria, including gender, ethnicity, class, disability, age, sexual orientation and religion. On the Right, there is a wish to stop globalisation, minimise immigration, put national interests first and restore past identity and prosperity. On all sides the feeling of resentment towards elites whose wealth and influence escalated during the era of free trade and financial deregulation has intensified since the 2008 economic crash. That shock exposed flaws in neoliberalism and brought long-lasting pain to people at all levels.

Polarisation and populism

The default to group identity feeds tribalism and polarisation, manifested in various theatres of struggle, often termed culture wars. Free speech is one of these, with incidents of protest, intimidation and cancellation of speakers, on university campuses in many instances (Sotirakopoulos, 2021), and over 1,000 cases of infringement in the USA archived by the Foundation for Individual Rights and Expression (2025). Another feature is a dismissal of 'experts' and a disregard for the facts, preferring instead to believe simple untruths, deceits or items of fake news favourable towards the worldview of the group rather than engaging with the complexities behind many issues (De Paor and Heravi, 2020; Campbell, 2023). Reasoned debate is a casualty of this approach, stirring up hate, often via social media, and sharpening the culture war divisions even further. The tribalist mentality also promotes what Sotirakopoulos (2021) sees as a dangerous loss of belief in individual agency. This creates a sense of victimhood and vulnerability in the face of forces on the other side, driving people into the perceived safety of increasingly fragmented groups.

This atmosphere of polarisation and vulnerability provides an opportunity for populism to thrive. Populist movements claim to represent the people at large, or at least a majority, in protest against the established order, sometimes emerging as political parties (Worsley, 2001). They tend to be more common on the Right, clearer about what they oppose than what they support or will do, capable of convincing people that their problems are the fault of others and keen to undermine institutions that act as a restraint on power (Campbell, 2023). A nationalist perspective is common, characterised by opposition to globalisation and immigration and their linkage to a range of problems such as crime, job shortages and lack of housing. Populist parties have gained ground in a number of countries worldwide, sometimes taking power or at least increasing their share of the popular vote significantly (Fukuyama, 2020; Campbell, 2023; DeRosa, 2023). At a minimum this trend creates electoral uncertainty about the political complexion of future administrations.

Democracy under threat

The democratic system of government has been under threat and Fukuyama (2018, 91) observes that 'democracy has retreated in virtually all regions of the world', giving way to authoritarian regimes in a number of countries.

Campbell (2023) cites a decline in the previous 15 years, with 20% of the global population living in totally free countries compared to an earlier figure closer to 40%. The rise of populism is not the only threat to democracy. Voter apathy and disengagement, along with a decline in political participation among young people, have been noted, reflective of lower confidence in the democratic system (Campbell, 2023). A loss of trust in the authority of traditional institutions such as political parties, churches, trade unions and the media has accelerated over time as part of a growing social fragmentation (Fukuyama, 2020). Refusal to accept election results has become more common, jeopardising loser's consent, an essential component of democracy (Thompson, H., 2022). The increasing power of AI to support undemocratic practices such as invasive surveillance and biased decision making, discussed later in this chapter, has also attracted concern (Crawford, 2021).

Polarisation and culture wars can compromise effective government too, leading to distracted and dysfunctional administrations in which routine government becomes an exercise in brinkmanship (Fukuyama, 2018). A focus on identity politics may fragment leadership attention, resulting in insufficient practical focus on large-scale issues. Climate change is an example, calling for big decisions around major challenges which demand strong focus and determination by governments. To date, however, and despite rising urgency, government actions relating to climate change have been characterised by markedly slow progress.

Global tensions

Rising tensions among global superpowers and the increased incidence of war in recent years have created an unstable political background, with ripple effects across the world. Rising war casualties reflect this. Campbell (2023) cites an average of 32,000 people killed annually in conflict between 2016 and 2020, a doubling of the figure for the previous five-year period. That increase has been far surpassed in the years since as a result of the outbreak of major wars in 2022 and 2023 between Russia and Ukraine and Israel and Palestine respectively. Those new wars have also engendered fears of an extension of conflict into other countries.

Politically, a notable tension exists between China and the USA. China has executed a very rapid rise as a major economic power since 1990, facilitated by a strong technological base which is the foundation for its aspiration to become the global leader in AI. This, allied to increasing political friction in recent years, has created a rivalry with the USA, for long the leading economy in the world but at risk of being overtaken by China at some point. Protectionist trade policies, economic disruption and prevention of flows of data have the potential to generate severe impacts well beyond the two countries involved. These and other sources of political uncertainty are a cause for concern and further hamper the level of global collaboration needed to address challenges such as climate change effectively.

Table 3.1 connects academic libraries with the global political factors identified in this section.

Table 3.1 *Impact of the global political environment on academic libraries*

Political factor	Academic library perspectives and implications
Identity politics	• Diversity a core value for academic libraries • Discomfort with culture wars • Threats to campus diversity, equity and inclusion (DEI) initiatives
Polarisation and populism	• Opposition to fake news, dismissal of expertise and undermining of authoritative sources • Destabilisation via diametric shifts in ideology when governments change
Democracy under threat	• Intellectual freedom challenged • Concern at loss of trust in traditional institutions and undemocratic applications of AI
Global tensions	• Unstable and uncertain operating environment • More expensive imports, disruption of supply chains and data flows • Support towards refugees from, and libraries in, war zones

The economic environment

Economics exerts a strong influence on the position and prospects of the world at large. Key factors shaping and shaped by the economic environment include trade, labour markets, employment rates, wages, income distribution, costs and inflation. The global economy also impacts energy supply, currency exchange rates and cycles of growth or recession. For academic libraries the state of the economy affects their purchasing power and ability to maintain current services as well as to keep pace with emerging needs.

Globalisation and labour

The importance of globalisation for politics emerged in the previous section but it has been a vital economic factor too. One definition summarises globalisation as 'the widening, intensifying, speeding up, and growing impact of worldwide interconnectedness' (Held and McGrew, 2001, 324), facilitating the cross-border exchange of goods, services, finance, labour, technology and information. Globalisation is not new but has intensified in recent decades, facilitated by near real-time communication which has created a more integrated, fluid and competitive marketplace. This, along with a shift from manufacturing to services, has profoundly affected labour markets. Manufacturing accounted for a quarter of all US workers in 1970 but that figure is now less than a tenth, with the service sector employing more than eight in ten workers (Susskind, 2021). Labour supply and demand operate worldwide in a globalised economy and manufacturing has moved gradually away from the USA and Europe towards countries in Asia and elsewhere offering lower labour costs. Services, for example call centres and computer programming, have also proved transferable and remotely deliverable.

The economic impact of global free trade has been uneven. It has brought cheaper goods to everyone and new manufacturing jobs to Eastern countries. There has been a lot of focus on job losses in the West or intensification of competition for employment through increased labour migration. However, the working-age employment rate reached an all-time high in over half of rich countries in 2019 (Williams, C., 2021). Technology has been identified as a stronger influence on the job market than globalisation, while immigration has proved essential and brought many benefits (Guillén, 2021; Roubini, 2023). Nevertheless, the negativity towards immigration in Western countries described earlier persists, fuelling support for populism and protectionist policies in place of free trade, including the imposition of tariffs on imports. Roubini (2023) terms this approach deglobalisation and warns against consequences such as higher prices and reduced global output as well as disruption to supply chains and movement of labour, data and technology. Tensions between those favouring and opposing globalisation look set to continue.

Debt and instability

The 2008 global recession has cast a long shadow in many countries. One of its legacies is high levels of public and private debt. Governments borrowed at low interest rates then and even more extensively when the COVID-19 pandemic struck in 2020. Private debt owned by corporations and individuals is also high, notably through housing and higher education costs in the case of households. A combined global public and private debt figure of 350% of Gross Domestic Product (GDP) at the end of 2021, up from 220% in 1999 and likely to head towards 400% by 2030 is cited by Roubini (2023). He sees this as a highly vulnerable situation, with governments, companies, banks and households owing more than they can realistically pay.

Previous crises show what can happen, notably the long-term damage done in 2008 via unemployment, increased inequality, the costs of bailing out banks and a destabilised Eurozone. More recently, inflation in 2022 reached levels unseen since the 1980s, with severe impacts for households as the cost of living rose and for public debtors in the face of interest rate rises. The first half of 2025 saw new tariffs on imported goods, affecting many countries negatively. Roubini (2023) has identified a range of possible causes for a fresh economic crash with potentially dire implications for heavily indebted organisations and individuals. Among the triggers he mentions are inflation pushing up interest rates, another pandemic, escalation of wars, intensification of climate change and economic mismanagement by populist governments. Consequences could include debt default, ongoing inflation and severe reductions in government services through public spending cuts.

High levels of uncertainty prevailing today threaten to add to the difficulties presented by another severe economic crash. Neoliberal approaches minimising the role of the state were discredited in 2008 and cannot be relied upon anymore. New job creation is likely to become harder to achieve as technology, especially AI, begins to replace existing jobs to a greater extent than previously without stimulating new ones in return. That trend will be discussed later, as will the uncertainties surrounding climate change.

Inequality

The economic environment may be subject to ongoing change, but one constant is inequality, which Susskind (2021) describes as being as old as civilisation itself. In one definition inequality relates to the privileges and valuables of prestige, respect, power or wealth and their uneven distribution according to race, gender, religion or culture (Pennock, 2001). That definition also notes that the politics of the world are beset by tensions arising from inequality either within or between countries, reflecting the social and political as well as economic consequences attaching to it. These tensions have been exacerbated in recent times by an intensification of inequality, with the proportion of total income accounted for by the wealthiest 1% having increased significantly since 1981, doubling in the USA and UK in that period (Susskind, 2021). The same author notes that the richest 0.1% of people in the USA have as much wealth as the poorest 90%. He also highlights a pattern whereby the proportion of wealth going to workers has decreased, as productivity went up by 30% but pay by only 16% in 24 countries across two decades since 1995.

Susskind sees technology as playing a vital role in this deepening inequality, with the owners of the latest machines and systems increasing their capital at the expense of workers whose main capital, labour, reduces in value as technology replaces more jobs. Support for this point of view comes from Acemoglu and Johnson (2023), who draw upon 1,000 years of history as evidence that new advances have enriched elites and been no guarantee of widespread prosperity. Sharing of economic benefits, they believe, has only happened due to pressure from electoral competition, trade unions and legislation to protect workers' rights, all of them weaker forces now than in the past. Looking to the future, it is estimated that the lowest earning 40% of workers in the USA will be 14 times more likely to be forced to change occupation by 2030 than the highest paid as AI advances (Ellingrud et al., 2023). Finally, economic inequality according to gender remains stubbornly problematic. Only 10.4% of the Fortune 500 companies had women as Chief Executive Officers in 2023 (Hinchcliffe, 2023), while women were paid less than men by an average of over 30% worldwide in the same year (World Economic Forum, 2023). All the signs point to economic inequality remaining a significant issue well into the future, one which will continue to exercise governments, motivate social justice campaigners and cause social unrest.

Table 3.2 summarises linkages between academic libraries and the global economic factors identified in this section.

Table 3.2 *Impact of the global economic environment on academic libraries*

Economic factor	Academic library perspectives and implications
Globalisation and labour	• Access to wider pool of labour, products and services • Global suppliers and competitors • Disruption, trade wars via increasing protectionism
Debt and uncertainty	• Uncertain funding situation • Increased possibility of rising inflation, job cuts and economic crashes • Higher education affordability issues a threat to student numbers
Inequality	• Equality a core value for academic libraries • Political and social instability

The social environment

A knowledge of social trends helps to understand the wider environment in which institutions operate. Social factors include demographic changes such as population size and life expectancy as well as education levels, attitudes, behaviours, lifestyles and expectations. Values are also significant, notably towards social justice and sustainable development. Academic libraries are people-centred organisations and social changes shape their ongoing work and strategic positioning.

Shifts in population and perspective

Demographics are a core factor in the social environment. The world has experienced sustained population growth, rising from about half a billion people in the late 17th century to over six billion by 2000, a twelve-fold increase (Zelinsky, 2009). Growth has continued in the current century, reaching just over eight billion people at the end of 2023 (Nguyen, 2023). This is a highly mobile population, characterised by high levels of migration, with a change in flow evident in recent times such that there are far fewer European migrants than previously and many more Asians, Latin Americans, West Indians, Middle Easterners and Africans on the move (Zelinsky, 2009). Roubini (2023) foresees a further acceleration in migration from poorer to richer countries due to a range of factors beyond economic globalisation and including climate change, failed states and poverty. Another trend has been towards increased urbanisation, reflected in a growth rate of 1.5 million city dwellers per week as cities account for 55% of the world's population and 80% of energy consumption and carbon emissions (Guillén, 2021).

Changes in the composition of the population are also evident. It continues to become more ethnically diverse, especially among young people in Europe and the USA. Guillén (2021) expects that the minorities of today will be in the majority within a decade, positing that in 2030 less than half of those in the 15–34 age group in the USA will be non-Hispanic Whites compared with 78% in 1980. He also observes an ongoing decline in the US middle class, with their number of households falling below that of rich and poor families combined in 2015, a big change from 1971 when middle class households were comfortably in the majority. Becoming middle-class is seen as harder now due to changes in the labour market and Guillén shares a concern that this trend may contribute to an increase in the polarisation of society in the USA and Europe by 2030, with a higher proportion of children born to rich or poor families. McRae (2023), however, foresees a significant growth in the middle class in other continents by 2050.

The world's population shows an ageing demographic. The birth rate is in decline, while advances in medicine mean older people are living longer and those aged over 60 represent the fastest-growing group (Guillén, 2021). This situation brings challenges for governments in terms of the funding of healthcare and pensions, creating the potential for social unrest as experienced in France in 2023, when measures to raise the pension age were introduced. Tensions between generations may also be fuelled by the economic inequalities described earlier, to which younger people are far more exposed and may become the first generation in a long time to be worse off than their parents. Generation Z, those born between 1995 and 2010 and accounting for the majority of students in higher education, face many challenges. There is optimism that they are well placed to make a major contribution to society as well travelled, knowledgeable, caring and open-minded people with an orientation towards problem-solving, backed by strong awareness of the world's problems and a concern for social justice (Seemiller and Grace, 2016).

Changes in working life

The shock of the COVID-19 pandemic landed in 2020 and stimulated a number of social changes and debates. Among these have been a shift towards more online and less in-person engagement across a range of activities, greater incidence and awareness of mental health issues and wider discussion of work–life balance. Changes in work patterns necessitated by the pandemic have become established, most visibly hybrid working. Instead of being based entirely at their work location, people in many jobs now spend at least some of their working hours operating from home or some other location remote from their employer's main base. This has been a major development relative to previous generations and is seen to have been accelerated by the pandemic, delivering increased flexibility, job satisfaction and other benefits (Williams, C., 2021).

As with many other recent changes described in this chapter, however, there has also been a strong element of inequality. During the pandemic, lower-paid workers doing essential jobs in sectors such as food, transport and healthcare had to attend work at a time of major health risk. The option of hybrid working was unavailable to them then or since. Job losses tended to hit their positions harder and automation has since been especially targeted at manual work (Susskind, 2021).

In his book *A World Without Work: Technology, Automation and How We Should Respond*, Daniel Susskind (2021) identifies the pandemic as the forerunner of further changes in work everywhere. Artificial intelligence, discussed in the technology environment section of this chapter, is expected to result over the coming decades in less work for humans. This will have major social consequences, causing people to revise their purpose in life in the absence of work and raising questions about government policy. A particular issue highlighted by Susskind, again drawing on the precedent of pandemic welfare payments, will be the role of what he calls the Big State in ensuring economic support, possibly through a universal basic income. Funding a society with a significantly smaller proportion of the population at work will be a real challenge with potential to threaten social cohesion if those in work are asked to bear a much higher tax burden. Difficult times may lie ahead.

Climate change or climate crisis?

Concerns about climate change are rarely out of the headlines. It has become a major global threat as industrialisation and population growth have intensified, resulting in rapid increases in energy consumption and the emission of greenhouse gases which have warmed the temperature of the Earth. Problems escalated in the 20th century as the average global temperature rose by 1 degree centigrade, including a 0.4 degree increase in its last two decades alone (Palmowski, 2008). Global warming has a number of effects. One of these is an expansion in the volume of oceans, exacerbated by melting polar icecaps. Rising sea levels cause flooding, soil erosion and collapse of land, thereby putting coastal dwellers and their properties at risk of death and destruction. Alarmingly, 90% of the world's urban areas lie along a coast, comprising 75% of the global population and leaving Asia particularly vulnerable (Guillén, 2021). Other effects, already in evidence, include droughts, fires and extreme weather events such as storms, hurricanes and typhoons. Among their consequences are loss of life, desertification, famine, collapse of water supply and crop failure, forcing sudden mass migration (Roubini, 2023).

The effects and consequences of climate change are clear to see but taking the necessary actions to mitigate them has proved much harder. Goals have been published, including zero emissions by 2050 and a maximum temperature rise of 1.5 degrees relative to pre-industrial levels at the end of this century. By 2024 the latter target had already been breached for a full 12 months (Henriques, 2024). Challenges abound, including finance and entrenched practices. Daunting costs of between US$3 trillion and US$5 trillion annually to take the necessary actions have been estimated (Roubini, 2023). The use of fossil fuels is deeply embedded in industry and daily life. Helen Thompson (2022) highlights not only a dependence on oil in transport and in the food chain, but also the role of petrochemicals in the manufacture of solar panels, batteries and electric vehicles, all of which are key to sustainable development. Among other challenges she points out are difficulties in containing the cost of both renewable and traditional energy sources, a reliance on (or hope for) technological solutions and ongoing increases since 1995 in the consumption of fossil fuels despite the availability of newer alternatives.

Achieving changes to established individual behaviours will also be very difficult, calling on governments to take unpopular measures in the face of public resistance. Examples include carbon taxes on fuels, the phasing out of non-electric vehicles and mandated changes in agricultural practices to reduce carbon emissions. Despite the promise of emerging technologies and the commitment by many institutions, including universities, to advancing the

United Nations Sustainable Development Goals (United Nations, 2015) it is hard to argue with the contention that 'It is more likely that there will be a long energy transition than a rapid one' (Thompson, H., 2022, 278).

Table 3.3 outlines the impact on academic libraries of the global social factors identified in this section.

Table 3.3 *Impact of the global social environment on academic libraries*

Social factor	Academic library perspectives and implications
Shifts in population and perspective	• Evolving user population, more mobile and diverse in its composition and expectations • Ageing population, requiring increased government funding in competition with higher education investment • Fewer students via lower birth rates
Changes in working life	• Increased online interaction with users since the COVID-19 pandemic • Hybrid working commonplace, but not for all staff grades
Climate change or climate crisis?	• Existential threat, especially in coastal regions • Maximally sustainable library buildings and operations emphasised and expected • Cost challenges

The technological environment

Technology has embedded itself into our daily lives, vital for staying connected with the world and for a host of regular tasks. At the institutional level it underpins progress, productivity, competitiveness, operational change and costs. There is a need to monitor developments such as AI, data use, cybersecurity, user expectations and levels of access to devices, networks and information amid an often-overlooked digital divide. Developments in technology have shaped academic libraries in recent decades, as outlined in Chapter 1, and continue to influence them in terms of service development and discontinuation, staff skills required, balance of digital and printed or in-person provision and anticipation of user needs.

The power of AI

Artificial intelligence has been in development and operation for a number of decades but has attracted a lot more attention in recent times. Its deployment has focused on the automation of tasks through robots and on analysis and prediction based on its ability to process vast quantities of data. The range of applications of AI is impressive. Susskind (2021) offers a lengthy list across agriculture, construction, manufacturing, education, law and medicine. He mentions the use of 3-D printing to construct entire homes, adaptive learning systems and medical diagnosis systems. Performance has exceeded or equalled that of humans in these applications and Susskind explains the increasing power of machines to learn how to perform tasks independently of human input and also to derive entirely new rules and patterns.

The capability of AI was already impressive before 30 November 2022, when ChatGPT was launched. This marked the beginning of public access to generative AI tools, with ChatGPT reaching 100 million users in two months, the fastest-growing digital service for consumers ever (Peston and Koria, 2023). Generative AI moves beyond prediction, opening up a whole new dimension by enabling the creation of texts, sounds and images resembling those created by humans. Trained on large datasets, it can, for example, generate articles, compose music, write poetry, communicate in typical human language and turn natural language instructions into computer code (Acemoglu and Johnson, 2023). The ongoing advance of AI promises to increase productivity, save time and enhance creativity by eliminating work to which it is well suited but which humans find tedious. There are, however, less positive and optimistic perspectives on the power of AI, as discussed next.

Concerns about AI and data use

The collection of data and their use, often to support decision making via AI, have been a source of much concern. The earlier advent of technologies such as personal computers, tablets and smartphones, coupled with internet access, empowered users. However, the massive datasets deployed by AI and machine learning require the kind of resources at the disposal of companies or governments rather than individuals for their effective use, shifting power towards those corporate entities (Fukuyama, 2020). Instead of facilitating increased democracy, AI and other technologies are seen as putting 'potent tools in the hands of both governments and companies interested in surveillance and manipulation', thereby promoting 'digital dictatorship' (Acemoglu and Johnson, 2023, 341). Crawford (2021) concurs, paying particular attention to the ways in which data have been collected, or extracted as she sees it. She emphasises the lack of consent sought by, or provided to, companies in building datasets from text, images and other materials published online by individuals, spoken into household devices or harvested via consumption of digital publications, music or other services. The absence of consent puts issues of privacy, ethics and equity at stake, as datasets feed into facial recognition systems, predictive policing tools and other machine training sources used for decision making.

Datasets reflect in-built societal bias, encoding existing power, and Crawford (2021) provides a full analysis of the risks involved, focusing on three datasets in the public domain. She is concerned at how classification schemes in AI tend to be over-simplified, thereby flattening complex social, cultural, political and historical relations into quantifiable entities, with negative impact for race and gender especially. An algorithmic failure to recognise nuance and complexity is damaging, even more so as AI may be deployed to adjudicate on matters vital to people's lives. Crawford cites a number of examples, including the erroneous identification of over 40,000 Michigan residents on suspicion of benefit fraud and accusations of gender bias in Apple's creditworthiness system. In another instance, students in the Netherlands with foreign-sounding surnames or living in areas with high levels of migration were disproportionately targeted for grant fraud (Dixon, 2024).

Beyond these issues, other concerns related to AI include its misuse to spread new types of fake news, covered later in this chapter, and to compromise academic integrity, as discussed in Chapter 4. Lastly, there is an even greater alarm that AI might become so powerful that it would become uncontrollable by humans, resulting in possibly catastrophic actions, a moment described as the singularity (Roubini, 2023). The development of AI will clearly need careful attention to ensure outcomes helpful rather than destructive to society.

Technology and jobs

There has long been a fear that new technology will make people redundant and AI has heightened this concern. Some recent writings are not encouraging. Artificial intelligence is seen as encroaching on more jobs than previous revolutions, with knowledge workers and those in creative roles at equal risk with people in manual jobs (Roubini, 2023). Research cited by Peston and Koria (2023) estimates that up to a fifth of all work globally could be automated by AI. Another study they mention indicates that AI could compromise the usual advantages of age and experience, allowing new employees to perform at the same level as those in the job for longer and exerting downward pressure on pay rates. A report from the McKinsey Global Institute suggests that 12 million US workers could need to change their occupation by 2030, foreseeing the biggest declines in office support, customer service and food service employment (Ellingrud et al., 2023).

There are, however, some more positive views about job prospects. Acemoglu and Johnson (2023) observe only a limited AI impact on employment for now, while Williams (Williams, C., 2021) finds slower growth in robot deployment than anticipated and low unemployment in countries with strong robot adoption. It is also noted that pessimistic predictions about job losses in the face of technological advances have proved wrong in the past as higher productivity has stimulated more demand and with it extra jobs (Susskind, 2021; Williams, C., 2021). The tendency up to now has been for automation to have a complementary role, leading to the substitution rather than elimination of work.

On a more cautionary note, nevertheless, Susskind (2021) notes that the average number of hours worked each year has continuously fallen over the past 50 years, albeit slowly. He also foresees a permanent turning point at which available work will actually decline as AI and other technologies enable a greater number of jobs to be done more effectively by machines than humans. This structural technological employment will mean fewer jobs to go around and will be a gradual feature rather than a sudden force, occurring over some decades. Its progress, according to Susskind, will be uneven and many roles will remain beyond automation, but machines will do more and humans less, with ongoing education and training needed across people's working lives.

Societal participation and communication

Technology has been both a force for good and ill when it comes to societal participation and communication. On the positive side, it has helped people to stay connected with each other socially while also facilitating easier communication online by organisations with their customers and service users. Beyond this, new cultures of participation have developed as additional channels of publication, sharing and collaboration have enabled interaction between producers and consumers of information. This has reshaped relations, for example, between writers and readers and between experts and laypersons (Corrall, 2022c). Sharing writings, ideas and other creations as they are being developed rather than only at the end has made it possible to incorporate feedback and to involve a wider range of contributors and co-creators. Technology has also promoted citizen science, participatory journalism and civic engagement, empowering individuals to participate in new ways.

Less positive has been the misuse of social media to spread extreme views and falsehoods, helping to foment the political polarisation discussed earlier in the chapter. Social media help to create echo chambers in which people are exposed mainly to others with the same opinions, opening themselves to targeted messaging (De Paor and Heravi, 2020). One study on the dissemination of true and false information online found that false news spread faster and further on Facebook (now Meta), assisted by algorithms (Vosoughi, Roy and Aral, 2018). Artificial intelligence has added to the fake news phenomenon through systems that can generate images or recordings, known as deep fakes, of people, usually public figures, saying or doing things that have never actually happened. The ownership of social media platforms by private interests makes regulation difficult and adds to concerns that a small number of technology companies wields an unhealthy amount of political power and influence.

Table 3.4 links academic libraries to the global technological factors identified in this section.

Table 3.4 *Impact of the global technological environment on academic libraries*

Technological factor	Academic library perspectives and implications
The power of AI	• Time-saving automation of routine work and decision making • New service possibilities and changed information behaviours via generative AI
Concerns about AI and data use	• Issues of privacy, bias, equity and democracy at stake, in conflict with core library values • Potential for generative AI to compromise academic integrity • Library opportunities in promoting data literacy
Technology and jobs	• AI-led library job losses at all levels expected, possibly with reducing pay rates • Support for evolving curricula, expectations and staff skills as jobs market shifts
Societal participation and communication	• Increasingly participatory knowledge-generation, information-sharing and publication practices • Library role in identifying and combating fake news

Conclusion

Each of the political, economic, social and technological dimensions of the global environment brings major challenges, existential in the case of climate change, unprecedented in terms of economic debt and unpredictable in regard to AI. Instability is a common thread, with changes of government liable to bring sudden shifts in ideology and policy, globalised economies exposed to events happening far from their shores, potential climate disasters unmitigated and employment prospects uncertain in many fields.

All of the factors described in the current chapter affect academic libraries. Their values are in tune with efforts towards achieving greater social justice but diametrically opposed to inequality, fake news and the concept of a post-truth society. Culture wars generate discomfort for libraries. Economic uncertainty, including the possibility of sustained high inflation, is a concern when budgets struggle to keep pace with user demand and increasing costs as the technology infrastructure of libraries expands. The memories of the 2008 global economic crash and its aftermath still hang heavy. Demographic changes continue to diversify the profile of user groups, while there is an imperative to respond to evolving societal behaviours and preferences, notably the increased appetite for digital information and online interaction since the COVID-19 pandemic. Fears for another pandemic endure alongside major concerns about the impact of climate change, creating an especially worrying scenario for academic libraries located in coastal regions and mandating maximum implementation of sustainable development practices everywhere. Artificial intelligence offers both opportunities and threats, from the automation of routine tasks and new roles in data literacy to compromised information integrity and the potential for job losses at all levels of library staffing. The power of major technology companies looms large, often as competitors.

Instability is a far from ideal backdrop to ongoing service delivery and future strategy. Shifting sands provide an infirm base for positioning. Academic libraries have, however, coped with major change and uncertain operating environments in the past, taking the opportunity to reinvent their value proposition and contribution to the mission of their parent institutions while maintaining an established position on campus. Uncertainty can beget opportunity and academic libraries may also take strength from the knowledge that they are not alone. As the next chapter describes, higher education is also navigating with difficulty a highly challenging and volatile environment.

CHAPTER 4

The Changing Higher Education Environment

Overview

This chapter provides an overview of higher education, recognising it as a critical context for academic libraries. Its coverage encompasses:

- an introduction to common challenges facing higher education;
- a survey of the higher education landscape in terms of key developments worldwide;
- discussion of issues such as mass student participation, internationalisation, funding, intensified competition, diversity and equality challenges and public perceptions;
- impacts on academic libraries;
- consideration of the campus environment which shapes how universities operate;
- the perspectives of academic staff and students amid major changes to their experience;
- a summary of how higher education reflects, interacts with and is influenced by a range of global trends identified in the previous chapter;
- a conclusion which seeks to balance the uncertainty surrounding higher education with an acknowledgement of its overall strength.

Challenges and variations, but common purpose

Higher education is the key operating context for academic libraries and a knowledge of its main developments and issues is essential to understanding their position and strategic positioning. A common set of challenges has confronted higher education institutions in the current century. These include accommodating rising student numbers, meeting tighter accountability requirements, funding teaching and research adequately, ensuring equity of access and contributing effectively to society. It is important to note that, while there is much common ground globally, there is no single system for organising and funding higher education across all countries. Each national government takes its own approach and this influences the experience in every country. Clancy (2021) provides a helpful overview of the main models and their operation in Europe, while Guri-Rosenblit (2021) examines systems internationally.

National variations need to be kept in mind throughout this chapter. The same is true of global shifts in size and influence. China has led a major expansion of higher education in Asia, recording an impressive growth rate of 500% since 2000 with a student population of over 40 million (Alexander, 2020). Research capacity, formerly dominated by the USA and Western Europe, has increased elsewhere through national investment. Despite these changes and the range of national systems, higher education has a common purpose, summarised by one writer as 'to prepare citizens to contribute to society through knowledge, understanding, critical thinking, and innovative ideas — developing and advancing society as a community' (Makoe, 2023, 303). Teaching, research and service to society had emerged as the three main pillars of activity for universities by the end of the 19th century and this tradition has endured across the world (Altbach and de Wit, 2023). Some other traditions established in the same period, notably public funding and university independence, have been less stable in recent times, as will be evident from the description in this chapter of higher education developments, perspectives and global influences.

The higher education landscape

This section selects and considers some trends and issues strongly impacting the world of higher education today.

Massification: rising student numbers

Participation in higher education, formerly experienced by a small minority, has increased hugely in the past half-century, a trend commonly labelled massification. The figures speak for themselves. Global participation more than trebled from 10% in 1970 to 36% in 2015 (Connell, 2019) and it is estimated that by 2030 or soon after half of all young people everywhere will enter tertiary education (Marginson, Callender and Locke, 2020). Rates of participation have varied across the world, ranging from over 80% in the USA and Europe to below 10% in Sub-Saharan Africa (UNESCO Institute for Statistics, 2022). In 2022 more than 230 million students were in post-secondary education worldwide (UNESCO Institute for Statistics, 2022), a significant rise from 150 million in 2009 (Altbach and de Wit, 2023). Some countries have, however, reached peak demand for the relevant age group and numbers have been declining in the USA over the past 15 years.

Why are so many people flocking to higher education? Government policies aimed at widening participation have played a part, but the main factor is probably that a degree or other higher education qualification offers opportunities for more rewarding work, better salaries and greater mobility in the employment market, as well as conferring social prestige. On a less positive note, concerns have been expressed about reduced quality in the overall system as it struggles to achieve the capacity required in the face of sustained increases in student numbers (van der Zwaan, 2017; Altbach and de Wit, 2023). Academic libraries are but one area on campus having difficulty in accommodating and supporting a student population which is not only much larger than previously but also more diverse in its composition and expectations.

Internationalisation: mobility across borders

Part of that diversity in the student population comes from a major increase in enrolments by students from other countries as the force of globalisation promotes international student mobility. Studying abroad provides opportunities for intercultural learning and personal growth as well as a far wider choice of access to academic programmes. Prior to the COVID-19 pandemic the number of international students had reached almost five million, doubling across the previous decade (de Wit and Altbach, 2021). A strong post-COVID recovery in student mobility, coupled with an increase in online programme delivery, has pushed that number upwards (Institute of International Education, 2025). Universities have also established branch campuses outside their own country, totalling over 380 across more than 80 countries (www.cbert.org/intl-campus). Internationalisation is vital to higher education and most institutions see it as essential to their strategy and indeed funding as students from abroad pay significantly higher fees. This has generated concern that, through their sharp focus on competition for revenue and reputation, institutions have lost sight of qualitative factors such as global citizenship development, employability and the quality of education and research (de Wit and Altbach, 2021).

Internationalisation has advanced a global approach to research as well as teaching. Global challenges such as climate change, health and poverty have promoted international research collaboration. Marginson (2020b) identifies some key trends, including an expansion in the number of research-active countries and an increase in the number of papers with authors from more than one country. The latter constituted less than 2% of papers in 1970 but reached 23% for science and engineering by 2020 (National Science Foundation. National Science Board, 2021). Open scholarship is likely to be an important future enabler. Beyond the USA and Europe other countries, notably Japan, China, Korea and Singapore, have increased their investment in research with a corresponding rise in publications and capacity for international collaboration. Factors casting a shadow over further growth in globalised research and wider student mobility are increased economic protectionism and immigration restrictions, which have limited cross border movement and made it harder for students and researchers to obtain visas for themselves and their families in some countries, including the USA and UK.

Funding and economic challenges

The state has traditionally been the main funder of higher education institutions, but this is no longer the case in all countries. Teixeira (2021) surveys a range of funding models in Africa, Asia, Europe, Latin America and the USA. These vary from systems in which students pay no tuition fees, for example Germany, France and Italy, to models where fees are payable and, in some instances, notably the USA, England and Australia, at rates that mean students need to take out loans for repayment after graduation. Governments absorb all of the fee costs in the first model but share or entirely transfer this expense to students in the second system. The latter approach is becoming more common, according to Teixeira, as part of a growing shift from public to private funding, likely to be further extended as governments come under greater pressure to allocate more funds to health and housing. This raises fears that many potential students will miss out on higher education, being either unable to pay fees annually or deterred by escalating student debt, which in 2025 had exceeded US$1.8 trillion in the USA (Hanson, M., 2025b).

The economic situation for higher education institutions has been challenging for some time. Many had not fully recovered from the effects of the economic crash of 2008 before the COVID-19 pandemic struck in 2020, bringing uncertainty through a mix of budget cuts initially followed by temporary increases for a period afterwards. Falling enrolments have exacerbated the situation in the USA and have begun to feature elsewhere. Some institutions have become increasingly dependent on revenue from international students but struggled to maintain numbers as competition in that market has intensified. Another factor has been the rising cost of technology infrastructures to support online delivery of teaching programmes and a range of administrative and research applications. Static or falling income levels at some institutions have resulted in staff savings as well as deletion of academic programmes or student services (Pelletier et al., 2023b). Institutional closure represents an even less appealing option but also a serious threat (Mintz, 2023).

The role of the state: increased accountability

Just as governments have different approaches to funding higher education in their country, they also vary in the extent to which they direct the system as a whole and its constituent institutions. Clancy (2021) outlines three models, with examples of European countries in which they prevail: state authority, academic self-governance and market-oriented. The level of institutional independence from the state varies in each case.

Although different models of state intervention are in operation, there has for some time been an increasing government focus on greater accountability in higher education. A growing pattern has been discerned towards 'a regulatory mode centered on the performance and the outputs of each institution and of the system as a whole' (Teixeira, 2021, 249). This has meant less detailed administrative intervention by governments and greater institutional autonomy, but within a framework of tighter accountability (Clancy, 2021). Value for money and contribution to national social and economic goals are expected and measured. The emphasis on accountability has made performance indicators, league tables, target setting and benchmarking commonplace. Performance-based funding has become more established, with state funding awards dependent on delivery against a range of metrics from student retention and graduation rates to diversity indicators across the staff and student population.

Another trend has been towards greater oversight by entities outside the institution. Examples are the engagement of external agencies to provide bibliometric data and analysis for research assessment (Stromquist, 2021) and an increase in external member representation on governing authorities (Clancy, 2021). The strengthening of accountability mechanisms has created negative sentiment. Over-reliance on quantitative metrics in the evaluation of research is one concern (Stromquist, 2021). Another relates to the administrative effort required to demonstrate compliance with requirements, including an estimate that 8% of the national university teaching budget in the UK was absorbed by quality assurance measures (Connell, 2019).

Marketisation and competition

Some countries, most notably the USA, Australia and England, have committed strongly over a lengthy period to the market-oriented model, also termed marketisation, privatisation or neoliberalism. One of its pillars is to stimulate greater competition between institutions in a self-regulating free market with the intention of improving quality, delivering better value for money and offering more choice for students than the state funding model provides (Cox, J., 2021). Other characteristics include liberalised market entry, commercialisation of research and greater privateness in the system, reflected especially in funding models which are rebalanced away from state contributions towards private sources and tuition fees paid by individual students, commonly via loans (Clancy, 2021; Teixeira, 2021). The emphasis is perceived to be on higher education as a private rather than a public good.

Responsiveness to the labour market, industry and the economy is a focus for institutions under this model. Employability following graduation is of keen interest to governments and to students paying high fees. This influences curricula and, in one interpretation, 'shifts focus from knowledge that academics want to produce onto the knowledge that business and governments want to consume' (Pearson, 2018, 72). There are fears that the heightened emphasis on market-oriented credentials threatens the traditional public service mission of the university (Fitzpatrick, 2019).

Marketisation intensifies competition between institutions not only for funding, donors, faculty and students but also for attention and position in the international league tables which rank universities. A variety of ranking systems has emerged, generating 'competition, hierarchy and frenetic striving for continuous performance improvement' (de Wit and Altbach, 2021, 309). These systems attract plenty of criticism, including perceptions that they fail to account for differences in type, distinctiveness or local context of institutions, are highly selective in coverage and prioritise research over teaching (van der Zwaan, 2017; Connell, 2019). Despite these concerns, universities accord high importance to their position in global ranking tables as well as investing much effort to improving it across the different systems, recognising the potential to influence student choice, staff recruitment or research funding.

Diversity, equity and inclusion

The strong societal focus on social justice evident in Chapter 3 is also reflected in higher education where diversity, equity and inclusion (DEI) has become a core value for many institutions. In common with other sectors, higher education has deficits in relation to DEI, including gender inequality at senior levels. Recognition of knowledge systems and equitable access to institutions stand out as problematic. Belluigi (2023, 137) observes that 'Central to the authority and functions of the university are the politics of knowledge recognition, legitimation, production, and reproduction'. However, knowledge generated by 'white bourgeois men from western Europe and North America' (Connell, 2019, 35) has long been foregrounded in writings, curricula, library collections and campus artwork. Barnett (2022) identifies academic coloniality as a related theme, resulting in the dominance of the institutions in the Global North at the expense of those in the Global South when it comes to knowledge recognition, acceptance for publication, research funding and global rankings alongside the primacy given to the English language.

Access to higher education is also unequal. Systems are highly stratified in many countries, ranging from highly selective research universities to mass-access institutions and vocational post-secondary institutions (Altbach and de Wit, 2023). Geiger (2019) highlights inequality in both access and outcomes in the USA, with level of wealth determining the type of institution students attend and the likelihood of academic programme completion. This situation is by no means exclusive to the USA. Unequal access according to race also persists (Alexander, 2020). It has been noted that the very stratification of the higher education system and the varying levels of prestige attached to institutions result in a further stratification of the academic profession, the student body, graduate degrees and the value placed on research (Eggins, Smolentseva and de Wit, 2021a).

Higher education institutions are striving to redress the range of DEI issues they confront. Efforts include recruitment of more diverse faculty and students, adaptation of admission systems, revision of curricula and reading lists to include a wider range of knowledge traditions, participation in open scholarship, making campuses more accessible physically and implementing a range of DEI policies. By no means everybody is supportive of the DEI agenda, however. Issues of free speech have surfaced on campuses, with protests and activism fomented by both Left and Right. There have also been claims that DEI policies and other initiatives compromise academic freedom (Altbach and Finkelstein, 2023; Sun, 2023), generating at institutions some of the polarisation evident in national politics. Challenges to DEI, initially at state level but more recently by the federal government, have become an increasingly common experience for US higher education institutions.

Higher education as a public good

In the face of perceptions of DEI deficits and an over-emphasis on marketisation and competition there have been calls from within and beyond academia for a renewed focus on higher education as a public good. Two eminent academics make the case for universities to reinforce their focus on service to society. Fitzpatrick (2019) argues for generous thinking and a renewed effort to build community with the public. Connell (2019) exhorts the good university to be democratic, engaged, truthful, creative and sustainable, rebuilding trust as a shared resource and a collective asset. Higher education institutions have paid heed to such sentiment and sought to emphasise their contributions to the public good and to society at large in their strategic plans.

Such contributions are multifaceted. Marginson (2020a) divides these into collective national local and global goods. The former include ongoing development of the professions, support for economic development and academic inputs to government policy and regulation. Among the collective global goods are creating and disseminating new knowledge, addressing global challenges via collaborative research and leading public opinion. Universities as places for reasoned, respectful debate and constructive argument in a polarised society are highlighted by Barnett (2022), who notes that academic freedom is important for the collective good. The guiding role of the university in society is also promoted by van der Zwaan (2017), who sees an opportunity, as the influence of other guiding institutions like the church declines, to ensure a flow of accurate and authoritative knowledge to society, supported by open scholarship. The cultivation and formation of students to contribute to the world in whatever ways their talent points them is a common thread. In one reading, 'This can be characterized as a "public good" in the sense that we all benefit from people being healthy, educated, and productive' (Rouse, 2016, 33).

Public perceptions

While higher education has shown that it plays vital roles in the economy and society and in educating increasing numbers of people, it often attracts negative headlines. This is more true in Western countries than in Asia (Andersson, 2018), especially in those places where the system has been marketised and students are paying high fees with low levels of government support. Nevertheless, some criticisms are applied more generally. Noorda (2018) notes sentiment that universities are elitist, arrogant, driven by money, too close to business and prone to fraudulent practices in research, resulting in a loss of trust. There is also concern at the promotion of specific political standpoints on campus and the protection of students from exposure to potentially offensive views (Cox, J., 2021).

A Gallup poll in 2023 revealed that only 36% of Americans had strong confidence in higher education, down significantly from 57% in 2015 (Smith, 2023). The *Chronicle of Higher Education* conducted a national survey in the same year which, while finding qualified public support for the value of a degree, also revealed that many participants felt that trade school provided a viable alternative to university (Kelderman, Elias and O'Leary, 2023). The same survey reported that less than a third of respondents believed that 'colleges are doing an excellent or very good job of leveling the playing field for success in society' (Smith, 2023), adding to a perception of private rather than public good. Negative sentiment about value for money in higher education has become increasingly commonplace in fee-paying systems, including political party attacks on a lack of preparation for the workplace via some degree programmes in the UK (Morgan, 2023) and a public sense of shame surrounding student loan debt in the USA (Alexander, 2020). Van der Zwaan (2017) emphasises the need for universities to do a better job of defending themselves against unfavourable public opinion.

Technology as a shaper of higher education

Finally in this survey of the higher education landscape, a brief consideration of the influence of technology is opportune. Technology, including virtual learning environments (VLEs) and access to online course materials and digital information resources, has underpinned teaching and learning over a long period. This proved even more true during and after the COVID-19 pandemic, when online delivery of academic programmes became strongly established. Students now expect flexibility in modes of access to higher education, including Hybrid-Flexible (HyFlex) delivery which enables them to move between onsite and online instruction within the same course (Pelletier et al., 2023b). Research, too, has been transformed by network-enabled international collaboration, data analysis, digital scholarship and faster dissemination of findings. Access to large datasets and their combination across different fields promotes new discoveries and interdisciplinary research (van der Zwaan, 2017).

Technology generates dilemmas for higher education too. It promises to help institutions with what has been termed the 'iron triangle', namely the challenge of simultaneously reducing costs, improving quality and increasing access and equity (Perna, Ruiz and Brickfield, 2023). However, costs have risen as digital infrastructure has expanded, the quality of online education has been questioned and digital equity is a persistent issue in terms of uneven online access and device ownership.

Artificial intelligence, described as a major technological force globally in Chapter 3, looms large in higher education too. Some applications, including handling student enquiries, delivering feedback and tracking progress via learning analytics, were already commonplace before generative AI became mainstreamed via the launch of ChatGPT in late 2022. Generative AI has been the subject of much debate, including concerns that it will produce biased outputs, diminish the role of academics, promote cheating by students and bring an end to creative expression and individual thought (Pelletier et al., 2023b). An alternative view is that the changes to student assessment necessitated by generative AI will enable a welcome emphasis on practising higher-order skills of analysis and creativity, academics will be freed from routine tasks and personalised learning will enhance the student experience (Pelletier et al., 2023a). As in society at large, AI has the potential to shape higher education for both good and ill and its overall impact remains difficult to predict.

Table 4.1 opposite summarises the impact of the factors in the higher education landscape discussed so far in this chapter, along with their implications for academic libraries.

The campus environment

How universities work

Although each higher education institution has its own identity, Barnett (2022) in chapter 13 of his book on *The Philosophy of Higher Education* writes cogently about the essence of the university, its structures, spaces, rhythms and characteristics. He finds it 'a strangely ephemeral entity' (Barnett, 2022, 156), noting that the very idea of the university is commonly in dispute, a view shared by Salisbury and Peseta (2018). Despite its longevity, the university's sense of itself is not settled. Barnett observes that it is a loosely coupled institution, with highly varied worldviews across its constituent parts. Rouse (2016) expands upon this in his characterisation of universities as complex adaptive systems. He explains that authority and responsibility are decentralised throughout the organisation, with the tradition of academic freedom meaning that faculty and indeed administrators often operate as independent agents who may work in competition with each other and feel comfortable in opposing institutional initiatives. The president or vice-chancellor and governing authority are only nominally in charge in this view and cannot control the daily activities of multiple independent agents, meaning that incentives to support a shared vision work better than mandates.

The *modus operandi* described by Rouse often renders it difficult to make things happen and decision making is often slow and cumbersome. There is a tension, too, with government expectations of efficiency, agile responsiveness to market forces and high levels of accountability. Bureaucratic structures and approaches are nevertheless commonplace and institutions strive hard to conform and comply with the regulations of government and other external

Table 4.1 *Key factors in the higher education landscape and their influence*

Factor	Impact on higher education	Implications for academic libraries
Massification	• Huge worldwide increase in student participation • More diverse student population requiring extra supports	• Challenges of supporting higher numbers • Wider range of student needs, including support with transition to higher education
Internationalisation	• Global student mobility • Higher fees paid by international students • Cross-border approach to research and teaching	• Multicultural user population • Heightened expectations of library service • Added impetus for global open access publishing function
Funding and economic challenges	• Diversity of funding models • Tighter budgets, cutbacks, closures on the increase • Spiralling student debt	• Funding typically static at best • Cost control imperative • More consumerist student body as fees burden rises
Role of the state	• Reduced funding role • Stronger accountability focus • Emphasis on performance metrics	• Unpredictable budgets • Greater bureaucracy • Demand for bibliometric and impact measurement support
Marketisation and competition	• Intense competition between institutions • Fees, private funding sources vital • Curricula driven by student employability emphasis	• On-campus environment more competitive • Emphasis on library as institutional competitive asset • Employability influential in creative spaces, new literacies
Diversity, equity and inclusion	• Historic and contemporary inequalities in focus • Government intervention for and against DEI	• Deficits in diversity of staffing and collections highlighted • Support for social justice initiatives
Higher education as a public good	• Emphasis on contribution to society and economy • Leadership of public debate • Community engagement, citizen science programmes	• Library values in tune with public good focus • Open access momentum • Stronger connectivity with wider public
Public perceptions	• Increased public criticism, rejection • Loss of public trust • Government hostility in some countries	• Defence of higher education through values, service, user experience • Library retention of trust often greater than that of institution
Technology	• Teaching, learning and research dependent on IT • Increased costs • Generative AI a source of opportunities and challenges	• Digital libraries essential to academic mission • Budgetary and cybersecurity challenges • Optimal AI deployment in focus

bodies while establishing a myriad of policies and procedures for observance by their internal communities. The scale of the effort directed at conformity generates cost and delay (Rouse, 2016). Crow, Anderson and Whitman (2018,

124) observe a 'self-imposed institutional conserver mandate' by which a fixation with compliance means emphasising the maintenance of external relationships and the conservation of existing resources rather than their development and expansion. Risk aversiveness slows the response to changes in the external environment and causes a loss of vitality at individual and institutional level (Crow, Anderson and Whitman, 2018; Barnett, 2022).

Regulatory compliance has been one factor driving a notable increase in the number of administrative staff on campus since the 1980s alongside the expansion of technology infrastructure and of student support services. This represents for Alexander (2020) a transformation in campus labour. Among new or expanded university functions requiring additional staffing support are audit, marketing, fundraising, diversity, mental health, disability and para-curricular centres improving proficiency in areas such as academic writing and mathematics. Stromquist (2021) notes that the focus on institutional reputation building and advancement in global ranking systems has spawned new administrative roles. She links this and the increased emphasis on administration and monitoring to a reduction in influence by academic staff in institutional decision making, seeing their role as limited to strictly academic affairs rather than involvement in decisions affecting the institution at large.

Clancy (2021) supports this view, observing that the heightened focus on externally imposed accountability has promoted managerialism as a pervasive ideology, shifting the power structure and strengthening the position of presidents and institutional leadership teams at the expense of faculty. Rising tensions between academic and administrative staff are a concern and van der Zwaan (2017) points to a problem of trust. The lived experience of the neoliberalist influence on campus life is captured in a number of individual stories by academic and other staff (DeRosa, 2023).

Academic staff perspectives

Academic staff have experienced major changes to their working life in the current century. A research project by the University of York Library aimed at understanding better the key motivations, frustrations and aspirations of academic staff in that institution provides valuable insights (Blake and Gallimore, 2018). Although many points of fulfilment emerged, the section on frustrations seemed to receive most emphasis, highlighting pressures from a range of sources, including student expectations, increasing volumes of administrative work and intensifying research assessment. Beyond the findings at York, marketisation, accountability, demanding targets and growing managerialism in higher education have caused disgruntlement among academics. This is epitomised in the sentiment that 'We now have strategic plans, goals and indicators. We benchmark with competitors. We consult our stakeholders, we pursue excellence, we are committed to our values, we drive change. The language is both vague and complacent; it is designed to conceal more than it reveals' (Connell, 2019, 125). A clash of cultures between traditional academic values of individual autonomy and the leadership or administrative pressure towards institutional imperatives is evident.

As already mentioned, there is a view that the emphasis on accountability has increased control from the administrative centre, compromising academic influence and independence. The academic reward system is heavily geared towards publication in high-impact journals, which in turn forms the basis of evaluation of research performance, funding allocations and career promotion decisions. Academic staff voice concerns about the lack of recognition for other contributions (Fitzpatrick, 2019) and the reduction of assessment to a narrow range of metrics generated by external companies at the expense of academic peer review (Stromquist, 2021). This system can lead to a loss of collegiality on campus as staff focus primarily on their own publication or promotion priorities, opting out of service to the wider institution, a tendency labelled competitive individualism by Fitzpatrick (2019).

The conditions of employment of academic staff have deteriorated over time, with many now engaged on temporary, often part-time, contracts for teaching and research. Geiger (2019) and Alexander (2020) note a trend across the current century towards insecure employment as the most common hiring pattern. The American Association of University Professors found that 68% of faculty at US institutions held posts, mostly part-time, which were off the tenure track in 2021, up from 47% in 1987 (Colby, 2023). The situation is similar in other parts of the world, including the UK, Australia and Germany (Locke, 2020; Guri-Rosenblit, 2021). Temporary staff may have fewer opportunities for professional development and may also feel less protected in terms of academic freedom.

A related trend in academic staff employment has been towards what Macfarlane (2011) calls 'unbundling'. This mainly relates to the appointment of staff to teaching-only or research-only roles. In addition, Macfarlane highlights the displacement of all-round academic staff by specialist para-academics such as learning technologists, research managers and advisers supporting student skills, including academic writing. He views this as an issue of identity, representing 'a "hollowing out" of what it means to be an academic' (Macfarlane, 2011, 69). Conversely, others may welcome the sharing of an expanding academic workload.

Recognition of teaching work is perceived by Macfarlane among others to have diminished. He sees more career opportunities in research or management, 'with teaching remaining as a Cinderella activity, rewarded through tokenistic prizes and "fellowships" rather than attracting mainstream kudos' (Macfarlane, 2011, 71). In the same vein, a university rector commented that the much higher valuation placed on research over teaching meant that 'a deeply-felt pecking order has emerged across the globe, one that is causing much discontent' (van der Zwaan, 2017, 51). Overall, there is a sense of academic staff under siege, with anger expressed in a variety of ways, including an increase in strikes, boycotts and bans in recent years (Connell, 2019).

Student diversity, expectations and challenges

The profile of the student body varies by institution type but is increasingly diverse in various respects. These include age, ethnic origin and socioeconomic class (Malpas et al., 2018). The number of first-generation students is increasing, there are more students with disability and more are studying part-time around their jobs or caring roles, with many also holding down jobs even when enrolled as full-time students in order to pay their bills.

Such students, formerly described as non-traditional, are now commonly termed new-traditional due to their much-increased share of the population on campuses. Their diversity of background and experience generates challenges, notably a need for institutions to support their transition to higher education and their progression through academic programmes. Today's students have different approaches to learning too. Sustained reading is less common and internet access via mobile devices offers both support for learning and also distraction from it. One study observes that 'What Generation Z students might refer to as multitasking is likely an inability to focus' (Seemiller and Grace, 2016, 181). It cites research indicating that the average attention span had decreased by half in the first decade of the current century. Geiger (2019) also notes a trend towards significantly fewer hours of study, down from between 38 and 40 hours a week in studies for the period to 1961 to a range of 24 to 28 hours weekly since 2000.

Affordability is a common issue for students in the face of rising tuition costs or, in systems with no or low tuition fees, higher accommodation bills. Even by 2010 the majority of undergraduate students in the USA were borrowers, with student debt rising from US$250 billion in 2003 to US$1.25 trillion in 2016 (Geiger, 2019), followed by a further increase to US$1.8 trillion in 2025 (Hanson, M., 2025b). Tuition fees have increased faster than inflation in the USA and debt has weighed most heavily on poor households (Alexander, 2020).

High costs have engendered a more consumerist view of higher education among students. Post-qualification employment prospects influence choice of programme or institution alongside expectations of internships, experiential learning and real-life problem-solving opportunities (Seemiller and Grace, 2016). As already noted, students want maximum flexibility in course delivery from providers. They also expect to be involved in shaping their experience at college and there has been an increased emphasis on staff-student partnerships (Salisbury, Dollinger and Vanderlelie, 2020; Weaver, 2020). Questions of affordability and return on investment impact decisions on whether to enrol in higher education at all, as prospective students match job opportunities against costs of participation (Pelletier et al., 2023b). Two notable trends have been a lengthy period of stagnation in wages for recent graduates and a greater willingness by companies to hire people without degrees (Alexander, 2020).

Student mental health has become a pressing issue in higher education. Record levels of stress, depression, anxiety and suicide ideation have been reported among the student body (Pelletier et al., 2023a). A range of factors already mentioned has contributed to this. These include transition to college from new-traditional backgrounds, loan debt, stress from examinations and coursework and a competitive job market (Johnson and Crenna-Jennings, 2018). These are in addition to rapid changes in body, mind and social relationships experienced by people in the years between 17 and 25 (Usher and Curran, 2017) and the negative social impact of the COVID-19 pandemic on young people in particular. University counselling centres have experienced levels of demand beyond their capacities and many institutions have striven harder to promote wellness and to distribute responsibility for mental health support across the organisation.

Global trends and higher education: current and future implications

The final section of this chapter provides a bridge to many of the global trends identified in Chapter 3. It summarises how higher education reflects, interacts with and is influenced by them.

Politics

The political influence on higher education is strong and is manifested in various ways which threaten academic freedom. Interference with the work of universities has been especially evident in the USA, where identity politics has led a number of conservative state legislatures to target campus diversity initiatives, also impacting public university libraries (Pokornowski and Schonfeld, 2024). The DEI legislation tracker maintained by the *Chronicle of*

Higher Education (2025a) has logged this activity, listing more than 135 bills since 2023 with a variety of aims, including preventing colleges from having DEI offices or staff, banning mandatory diversity training and forbidding the use of diversity statements in hiring. Further interventions in some states have included proposals to guide the content of research and teaching and to remove tenure from faculty (Pelletier et al., 2023a; 2024). US federal government actions impacting higher education, highlighted in the concluding chapter, have escalated from early 2025.

Political extremism has had damaging effects in other countries too. An anonymous academic writes of loss of freedom in Afghanistan, chronicling censorship and the imposition of religious observance on scholarly life (Anonymous, 2023). Hungary has experienced authoritarian state intervention in higher education, including the forced relocation of the Central European University from Budapest in 2018 (Clancy, 2021). Populism with a strong nationalist element has extended its influence geographically (DeRosa, 2023). Anti-intellectualism is part of its worldview, including a disregard for experts from universities and elsewhere (Andersson, 2018). Limits on immigration have been a common goal for nationalist administrations and these run counter to the expansive internationalisation strategies of most higher education institutions. The increased prevalence of war has led to the destruction of universities and major disruption of higher education in countries such as Cameroon, Afghanistan, Syria and Ukraine. Impacts may be felt beyond the immediate territory of conflict. The war between Israel and Palestine has generated protests on US campuses, leading to the removal of faculty and even presidents, as well as calls for institutional disinvestment from donors (Basken, 2023a; 2023b).

Economics

The economic rise of Asia is also reflected in higher education. For the first time two Chinese universities featured in the top 15 institutions in the *Times Higher Education* World University Rankings for 2024, with one Japanese university in the top 30 (Bothwell, 2023). A longitudinal analysis of six years of data for the same ranking system showed an improvement of more than 100 places in the average position of Chinese universities and declines for both the USA and UK in the same period. The trend in terms of future funding appears positive for Asia. Western countries by contrast may struggle to maintain or increase investment in higher education as they face pressures to direct more funding towards the health needs of ageing populations (van der Zwaan, 2017). A further significant factor identified by the same author is that, as Asian universities develop further, students from those countries will be more likely to stay at home rather than to travel elsewhere to obtain tertiary qualifications. This will negatively impact the balance sheets of many higher education institutions in the West.

Chapter 3 noted a trend towards fewer jobs over time as AI and other technologies take over work previously requiring human input. An over-supply of graduates has already been identified, with increasing risk of further saturation of the labour market in countries with unlimited access to higher education (van der Zwaan, 2017). An intensification of this trend will be of concern to universities and may make enrolment in academic programmes less attractive. Also worrying is an increased tendency for companies, including IBM and Google, to recruit to a greater proportion of jobs without any requirement for a degree (Smith, 2023).

Society

No person or sector, including higher education, can hide from climate change. EDUCAUSE has recognised this major global force through separate future scenarios, one based on a series of disasters rendering coastal regions uninhabitable (Pelletier et al., 2023a) and the other forcing thousands of families to relocate because of unsafe and unaffordable housing conditions (Pelletier et al., 2023b). The implications of climate change for higher education are profound, including its viability, enrolments, retention rates, modes of delivery and student mobility. Important roles are evident for universities in educating students about sustainability and in informing the public accurately about climate change in the face of misinformation from multiple quarters.

Demographics are also impacting higher education. The USA has seen a decline in enrolments of 8.4% since 2010 (Hanson, M., 2025a). A reduction in the main age population for university attendance has been the primary cause, with further decline expected from the mid-2020s due to a fall in the birth rate occasioned by the economic recession which commenced in 2008 (Alexander, 2020). Other countries with high participation rates have little margin for further growth and some may have reached peak levels of demand. A fall of 1.5% in acceptances occurred in the UK in 2023, albeit reversed in 2024 (Bolton, 2025), alongside two years of lower enrolments in New Zealand (Ross, J., 2024).

As people live longer their working lives will also extend, necessitating lifelong learning of new skills for the workplace. Higher education will be a vital enabler but institutions will need to maximise the flexibility of their offerings, including an intensification of the existing trend towards microcredentials. These are short programmes which can fit around work or other commitments and be combined over time as an alternative to linear, multi-year participation (Pelletier et al., 2023b). Competition in this area is already being provided by companies outside the sector, including Google and Amazon (Smith, 2023).

Technology

Artificial intelligence has emerged as a powerful driver of the need for lifelong learning. It has featured prominently in this chapter and the previous one as the single most important development in technology for higher education and the world at large, generating optimism and pessimism in equal measure. Mariët Westermann, then vice-chancellor of New York University Abu Dhabi, advised that 'In the decade ahead, no university will survive without a generative AI strategy' (Westermann, 2023). It is evident that an amount of policy development will be required to harvest the benefits of AI and to minimise its potential for harm. Ethical issues will arise regarding privacy, security, data use and potential bias, calling for institutional frameworks to govern the use of AI (Pechenkina, 2023). Without programmes to develop data literacy there is the potential for poor decision making (Pelletier et al., 2023a). Such programmes will also benefit students in terms of workplace preparation.

Institutions will be challenged to update their curricula dynamically to keep pace with developments in AI, as well as to blend technology disciplines with the humanities to maximise creativity and critical thinking and to ensure appropriate coverage of the ethical dimensions arising for society (Penprase, 2018). The impact of AI on jobs in teaching, research and administration is uncertain but there is potential for radical change. Finally, taking technology at large, cyberattacks are growing in their sophistication and ability to cause major disruption. They have been successfully targeted at higher education institutions in recent times and will continue to be a threat, calling for ongoing vigilance (Alexander, 2020).

Conclusion

A cumulative range of political, economic, social and technological factors is driving uncertainty about the future of higher education. The preceding pages have not painted a positive picture. Their coverage has included: funding pressures for institutions; rising student debt; creativity battling with accountability; political interference in university business; mental health struggles; anger among academics; fears about climate change; public criticism and distrust of higher education; and unpredictable AI outcomes.

Alexander (2020) foresees radical changes, campus closures, tighter budgets, fewer students and difficult reinventions for institutions whose identity has for so long been highly stable, bringing much pain and stress to their staff. His overall prognosis is one of decline. It looks like higher education institutions are set to continue in 'an on-going state of crisis of purpose' (Salisbury and Peseta, 2018, 245).

Pessimism about higher education and its prospects can, however, be over-emphasised. A visit to a university campus usually encounters a high level of energy, enjoyment and fulfilment. Alexander (2020) is quick to recognise the positive story about higher education, drawing attention to its attractiveness, the demand and respect for it and its research discoveries. The study of academic staff at the University of York found their lives to be not just frustrating but also varied, rich, challenging, energising and motivating (Blake and Gallimore, 2018). Even Connell, whose book expresses a range of concerns, observes that 'In the wider society, despite "post-truth" politics, there is a continuing demand for knowledge, and respect for the people who produce and teach it' (Connell, 2019, 170). Altbach and de Wit (2023) emphasise the centrality of universities to the global economy and praise their durability and adaptability to changing circumstances. On a similarly optimistic note, 'the university is actually the most hopeful community that has ever existed, filled with young people who are looking to the future, and clever souls who are opening up new scientific horizons; a community that has shown for the last eight hundred years that it has the resilience to survive' (van der Zwaan, 2017, 14–15).

As was noted regarding academic libraries at the end of Chapter 1, longevity is a source of strength for higher education alongside high levels of demand, continued achievement and contribution. While acknowledging a multitude of challenges, higher education is in a stronger position than many people think. Returning to where this chapter began, higher education shapes academic libraries whose strengths, weaknesses, opportunities and threats are the subject of the next chapters in this book.

PART 2
SWOT Analysis

Introduction to Part 2

Part 2 marks a change of direction, moving away from a primarily outside-in perspective in the opening chapters which emphasised external, historical and positioning factors and their influence on academic libraries. The second part of the book switches to an inside-out view in which the focus is on the nature and significance of the strengths, weaknesses, opportunities and threats linked to academic libraries and how they experience them. Its framework is SWOT analysis, an established and commonly used technique for strategic planning (Panagiotou, 2003; Helms and Nixon, 2010; Sarsby, 2016). The chapters in Part 2 expand on two earlier articles by the author about how their strengths, weaknesses, opportunities and threats combine to shape the position and prospects of academic libraries (Cox, J., 2023a; 2023b). The book format allows deeper coverage of the significance and strategic implications of each factor in the analysis, as well as its linkage to the external environment.

Why do the strengths, weaknesses, opportunities and threats associated with academic libraries merit analysis in a separate part of the book? It is because they exert such a strong influence on academic library identity, situation and potential. The areas in which it excels or struggles shape the identity of the academic library in terms of what it is, what it does and how others see it. Those activities and engagements it emphasises or from which it is largely absent contribute to the position it inhabits. They in turn impact how its future situation may advance or decline. An understanding of common academic library strengths, weaknesses, opportunities and threats in terms of their significance, overlap and the interplay between them is therefore vital. It underpins positioning approach and strategy development. The ultimate goal is to leverage strengths, address weaknesses, take opportunities and mitigate threats, thereby advancing position and prospects.

A separate chapter covers each SWOT analysis dimension in Part 2, beginning with strengths and progressing through weaknesses and opportunities to threats. Four factors have been selected for exploration in each chapter according to the following criteria:

1 long-term influence on academic library strategy and positioning;
2 broad significance and operation at a macro scale across the whole library;
3 reflection of key global and higher education developments identified in Chapters 3 and 4;
4 prominence in the library literature.

The literature suggests many candidates for inclusion and the factors selected are open to challenge and debate, but the common ground for each one featured in this analysis is that it exerts significant long-term influence on the status and strategic positioning of academic libraries. Although the analysis treats academic libraries as a collective, it must be understood that the factors chosen are by no means universally applicable. Each academic library has its own characteristics and influences, shaped among other things by geographic considerations, local circumstances and the traditions and priorities of its parent institution. Many of the selected strengths, weaknesses, opportunities and threats are likely, however, to be familiar to readers. Another point to note at the outset is that the four SWOT analysis dimensions are far from mutually exclusive. There is frequent overlap between them and therefore across the next four chapters. The longevity of academic libraries can, for example, be both a source of strength and weakness.

The coverage of each factor in the analysis, 16 in total from Chapters 5 to 8, includes: a description of the factor and its evolution; its impact, supported by examples of it in action; the mix of positive and negative influences it exerts, recognising that impact is typically nuanced and no factor is entirely favourable or unfavourable; why the factor is significant for academic libraries, along with its implications for library strategy, thereby feeding into the focus on positioning strategy in Part 3. Context is added for each factor by highlighting linkages with the coverage of history, positioning strategy, global developments and the higher education environment in Chapters 1–4. None of the strengths, weaknesses, opportunities or threats identified operates only internally; its interaction with factors in the outside world contributes to shaping academic libraries.

CHAPTER 5

Strengths of Academic Libraries

Overview

This chapter examines a selection of four strengths for academic libraries: centrality, values, collaboration and reinvention. Coverage of each includes its context, how it is manifested, the advantages and counterweights associated with it and its strategic significance.

Introduction

Strengths are areas in which an organisation performs especially well and may distinguish itself from its competitors. Four strengths commonly enjoyed by academic libraries emerged for analysis when the selection criteria outlined in the Introduction to Part 2 were applied:

1. the central place the academic library occupies in the institutional mission, as well as physically and socially, on campus;
2. the enduring relevance and resonance of library values and the trust they engender among the campus community;
3. a predisposition towards collaboration and partnership with others and with each other to positive effect;
4. the ability to adapt to an evolving, predominantly digital, environment by reinventing the role and value proposition of the academic library.

Centrality

Academic libraries benefit from a position of centrality to the academic mission of the institution, usually complemented by a physical location in the middle of the main campus. This is a natural advantage, conferred to some extent by their longevity as an established presence early in the history of universities from the 13th century onwards. The phrase 'heart of the university', ascribed to the library by Charles William Eliot, President of Harvard University in the late 19th century, is often quoted as the clearest reflection of its centrality. The 1921 annual report of the University Grants Committee was even more emphatic in declaring that 'The character and efficiency of a University may be gauged by its treatment of its central organ – the Library. We regard the fullest provision for library maintenance as the primary and most vital need in the equipment of a University' (University Grants Committee, 1921, 8). Today's academic library is viewed as 'ubiquitous, enduring, and ever-present in the reality of institutions' (Salisbury and Peseta, 2018, 247).

The mission-critical centrality of academic libraries has evolved and expressed itself over time in three ways: scholarly, physical and social. As discussed in Chapter 1, local printed collections were for long integral to and strongly associated with scholarship (Ratcliffe, 1980). Writing about the first half of the 20th century, Atkins (1991) noted the recognition of linkage between the quality of libraries and that of their universities. He cited the view of a Yale professor that the size and quality of the library were vital to attracting and retaining scholars and students. There may be a tendency today to take the digital library for granted but anyone who has worked at an institution subject to a cyberattack will know that the restoration of access to online information resources delivered via the library is a top priority and that academic work is massively disrupted in its absence.

Library buildings have tended to stand out physically, easily identified by their size and mid-campus location and typically attracting large numbers of users from across the institution as a place not only of scholarship but also community. The onset of the COVID-19 pandemic served to underscore the enduring sense of attachment to the library building on campus. Individual academics wrote passionately about how much they missed it, highlighting its uniqueness as a campus space of community, collegiality, contemplation and democracy, home to a unique sense of collective academic enterprise (Chambers et al., 2020; Moran, 2020).

The social dimension of academic library centrality is now its most rapidly expanding element. New or reconfigured buildings emphasise social learning, while the longstanding characterisation of the library as a neutral and interdisciplinary space on campus offers opportunities for its staff to play a vital role as social connectors across the institution. Schlak, Corrall and Bracke (2022) have identified a social, participatory turn in the world at large, referenced in Chapter 3 and reflected also in higher education. They note that academic libraries are well connected at the centre of many social networks and urge their staff to prioritise deeper relationship building. Library engagement with digital scholarship offers a template following some notable successes in leveraging established relationships to bring together people from different disciplines, to host digital scholarship centres and digital humanities labs and to participate in projects on a partnership basis (Cox, J., 2016a).

Being of no specific discipline but available to all disciplines is helpful for library staff. Their effectiveness in linking faculty with each other and with students is already recognised (Fagan et al., 2022a), with ample scope for further development. The social connector role can be maximised by building on the advantages of central and neutral space via event programming which promotes conversation between disciplines and with local communities (Kasten, 2018) and through the attractiveness of library makerspaces as places of experimentation.

Centrality in its traditional and newer forms represents a valuable asset for academic libraries. The associations with scholarship are positive, as is the sense of close proximity to the institutional mission. Chapter 2 highlighted the importance of perceptions for positioning and the library occupies to its benefit a position of centrality in the minds of many in the campus community. Longevity is a factor in this and is helpful in affording a level of brand recognition and an understanding that the library plays a significant role in campus life. Space at the centre of any campus is at a premium but the library building is usually one of its occupants, helping it to attract other entities which can enhance its service offering. These include a range of learning supports, discussed further in Chapter 7, and also at the University of Rhode Island the first-ever library-based AI Lab (Kim, 2019). Physical centrality gives library staff a unique vantage point, enabling them to understand their audiences better, potentially developing a greater awareness than others of students' learning needs, preferences and behaviours by observing these at close quarters.

Making the most of this natural asset is a strategic imperative and this can take many forms. These include an ongoing effort to promote the value of the library as campus epicentre, maximising and advertising the social connector role, attracting local communities, sharing insights based on observations of activities in the library, providing a platform for debate and participating in such debate with the authority that centrality brings. Complacency and competition are obstacles to academic libraries seeking to leverage fully their centrality. Positive commentary about the library can lead to an assumption of support. However, the campus environment is now far more competitive than in the earlier history of higher education and other, often newer, units are claiming centrality as institutional priorities evolve.

The centrality of academic libraries has been increasingly contested in recent decades. Grimes' (1998) interrogation of the 'heart of the university' metaphor, found it to be at odds with reality in terms of resourcing and inclusion of the library in key decisions in the institution. Some of the academic leaders she interviewed considered the metaphor to represent an exaggeration, a finding endorsed by participants in a similar study a decade later (Lynch et al., 2007). Her conclusion was that libraries needed to bypass symbolism and prove their worth through a highly practical definition of centrality focused on enabling user success through service, access and tradition. Oakleaf (2010) later relayed a similar message, observing that many libraries had been too passive and assumed that stakeholders understood their importance. She urged that academic libraries demonstrate their impact and value relative to a range of imperatives for higher education institutions.

The nature of academic library centrality has evolved and the level of resourcing and influence to which it translates may be reduced, but it retains strong scholarly, physical and social elements. Perceptions of centrality endure. These include the use of language such as 'engine' and 'nerve center', by university leaders in the UK and Canada (Robertson, 2015, 500; Baker, D. and Allden, 2017, 14) as well as agreement by 85% of students participating in one survey that their fees should be used to fund library resources, the highest score among 15 options for spending presented (Office for Students, 2018). The centrality of the academic library to the institutional mission, through its role in enabling access to and creation of knowledge, its valued contributions to teaching, learning and research, its mid-campus location and its ability to connect people and disciplines, is a prized asset. Even in very different times for higher education and knowledge production, this traditional level of recognition gives academic libraries a benefit which other departments may envy.

Values

A value system has been defined as 'a set of those beliefs and ideals that has been adopted and/or has evolved within a group as a system to guide actions, behaviors, and preferences in all situations' (Gorman, 2015, 1). The values of academic libraries are therefore significant in framing what they do, as well as how and why. Chapter 2 cited them as an important element in positioning the academic library, helping to shape its identity, adding to its authority and generating approval among stakeholders.

The range of these values is extensive. At its centre are those stated in the ACRL *Standards for Libraries in Higher Education* as 'intellectual freedom, intellectual property rights and values, user privacy and confidentiality, collaboration, and user-centered service' (Association of College and Research Libraries, 2018, 10). A sixth, academic integrity, is added in the accompanying notes of that publication. Academic libraries supplement these with values from the wider library profession. Sources include the *Core Values of Librarianship* published by the ALA, listing five values with some additions to those identified by the ACRL, specifically access, equity, public good and sustainability (American Library Association, 2024). Michael Gorman's (2015) book, *Our Enduring Values Revisited: Librarianship in an Ever-changing World*, includes some overlap in the nine values it identifies but adds literacy, rationalism and stewardship. Individual libraries may emphasise other values, for example creativity and openness at Stanford University Libraries (n.d.) or community and innovation at the University of Toronto Scarborough Library (n.d.). Amid this range of values, three have been identified as pivotal: 'ensuring free and open access to knowledge, serving the public interest, and protecting the intellectual freedom of users' (Rubin and Rubin, 2020, 550).

Academic libraries live their values in a multiplicity of ways, including:

- welcoming use by a diversity of communities;
- striving for social justice through actions supportive of DEI and via the growth of critical librarianship (Drabinski, 2019);
- committing strongly to open access to information and more broadly to open scholarship;
- prioritising the search for objective truth in the face of misinformation and disinformation;
- investing continuously in the long-term preservation of documentary sources from the recent and distant past;
- collaborating successfully with each other and with many parties on campus and externally.

Service as a value underpins everything else and is recognised as a particular strength, indeed a 'mantra' (Koehler, 2015, 31). Gorman (2015) also highlights a commitment to the greater good. Academic libraries are cognisant of a higher purpose to which their values propel them, variously expressed as social responsibility (Fister, 2015b), education as a public good (Nicholson, 2015) and building knowledgeable communities (Heseltine, 2020).

The values of academic libraries generate positive perceptions, most importantly of trust. They are seen in research support as 'a trusted partner for sustainable services, not just short-term projects' (Bryant, Dortmund and Lavoie, 2020, 24). Their trusted status enables them to navigate and help alleviate academic concerns about the use of bibliometrics to measure research performance (Givens, Macklin and Mangiafico, 2017). Ovenden (2020) highlights much greater public confidence in libraries' commitment towards the long-term preservation of information compared with that of technology companies motivated by short-term gain. Academic library values, notably intellectual freedom, intellectual property rights and academic integrity, resonate strongly with their campus communities. They align well with the overarching mission of higher education in preparing students for active citizenship and the advancement of society (Makoe, 2023).

These values are very much of their time too. Many higher education institutions are emphasising their contributions to the public good, as discussed in Chapter 4 where Connell (2019) included the terms democratic, truthful and sustainable in her characterisation of the good university. She and Fitzpatrick (2019) both emphasise the importance of rebuilding a relationship of trust with the public. It is striking how closely aligned the language used is with that of library values and how generating trust, a strength for academic libraries, has become a major focus for many of their parent institutions. Furthermore, the values of academic libraries appropriately represent an antidote to issues in the wider world of polarisation, fake news and the misuse of AI.

Upholding such a demanding set of values is a challenge and Ettarh (2018) expresses concerns about 'vocational awe' which can overwhelm library staff. They also create some dilemmas, notably at institutions which continue to adhere to the tenets of marketisation. Academic library ideals run counter to the emphasis on competition and consumerism and the imperatives of the bottom line. This conflict has caused unease for some library staff (Pinfield, Cox and Rutter, 2017). It has also been a topic of concern for a number of writers. Nicholson (2015) laments an uncritical obsession with accountability, standards and value, representing an acquiescence with neoliberalism which she believes undermines the real purpose of academic libraries in helping to make higher education a transformative experience. Fister (2015c) identifies a tension between value and values and between specific local and wider global needs. The dangers of confusing impact with purpose preoccupy Heseltine (2020), while Gorman (2015) sees values as compromised by too great a focus on technology and management. Clashes can also occur between the values themselves. Examples are between protecting intellectual freedom and combating fake news (De Paor and Heravi, 2020), enhancing service through AI and potential privacy issues (Griffey, 2019) and supporting student progression via learning analytics in the face once again of concerns about breaches of privacy (Oliphant and Brundin, 2019).

Despite the challenges and dilemmas they pose, their values are a significant source of strength for academic libraries. Trust is a highly valuable commodity for position and positioning, earned and owned to the same extent by few other departments on campus. These values translate to actions which are beneficial for libraries and their parent institutions. They are strong, laudable, difficult to argue against and compatible with the interests and perspectives of campus audiences, especially at institutions which prioritise higher education as a public good. Although most of these values are not espoused exclusively by libraries, they comprise a potent and distinctive combination. They have proved durable and relevant throughout times of major change in the world at large, anchoring academic libraries in the face of ongoing instability and uncertainty. As mentioned in Chapter 2, they offer a valuable bridge between the traditional and newer elements of the evolving library value proposition.

In terms of strategy it seems important to create a wider awareness of the values of academic libraries specifically and those of the library profession at large. Library strategy documents often include a statement of values but they may remain largely hidden from view if there is a deficit in explaining on a regular basis their significance and positive impact. This involves explicitly linking values-based actions such as the promotion of information literacy and open scholarship to the academic mission and institutional goals. Their values also provide a lever for academic libraries to influence strategy in areas such as the academic reward system, sustainability and service standards. Within the library, Stoffle et al. (2003) correctly stress the importance of keeping values centre stage and ensuring that they guide decision making as it happens rather than as an afterthought. This should include acknowledging and debating the dilemmas raised by library values and the occasional conflicts between them. The values of academic libraries are fundamental to their distinctiveness, identity and higher purpose and deserve to be given maximum exposure.

Reflective journal extract 5.1
Living academic library values

From the author's journal: 7 November 2020

The most positive meeting of all was probably the Library Strategy Committee – fantastic recognition of what the Library has done in COVID-19 and I certainly feel proud to be at the head of such a committed team. Sometimes I wonder if we are being recognised but that definitely happened on Wednesday last. In fairness, our staff have been tremendous – not only are we the main service consistently open on campus, but everyone has done a great job in responding to loads of needs and committing to a very strong service.

Collaboration

Their positive mindset towards collaborating with other departments on campus and with each other has served academic libraries and their parent institutions well. Although Neal (2015, 317) has observed that 'Cooperation is part of the professional DNA of academic libraries', this has only manifested itself on a far wider scale in recent decades. Collaboration occurred during the era of print-only collection building, notably between libraries through interlibrary lending and cataloguing co-operatives as automation advanced but, as Chapter 1 noted, library participation in campus life was limited. The same chapter also charted a major shift in outlook when the advent of digital information mandated a new value proposition with collaboration and partnership at its centre and this is strongly reflected in professional guidelines and other writings.

The ACRL includes collaboration as one of the values listed in its *Standards for Libraries in Higher Education* (Association of College and Research Libraries, 2018). Gwyer (2015, 280) identifies it as a 'meta-trend' overarching a range of developments impacting academic libraries, while its importance is evident in Saunders' (2016) study of 63 academic library strategies, almost 80% of which mentioned collaboration. One study (Bryant, Dortmund and Lavoie, 2020) emphasises cross-campus partnerships as a necessary condition for building research support services, while another sees the building of strong relationships and partnerships as an essential foundation for successful engagement by libraries in the institution (Jaguszewski and Williams, 2013). Alignment with the priorities of the institution is both a driver and an outcome of collaboration and partnership is highlighted as effective in this context (Pinfield, Cox and Rutter, 2017).

The broad remit of academic libraries alongside their physical and social centrality on campus and the trusted status they enjoy afford multiple opportunities for connection, partnership and contribution. A majority of library directors in the triennial Ithaka library survey (Hulbert, 2023) has identified student success as the top priority for their library and 80% of respondents indicate close collaboration with other campus units towards this end. Partnership with academic units around information and digital literacies is central but has increasingly extended to other service providers, including collaboration on the first-year experience and disability support (Fister, 2015a). Institutional focus on student retention has intensified and Allen (2014) maps out library initiatives in partnership with IT, diversity, student affairs and institutional research units. Academic libraries have typically been more generous than others in sharing physical space and have in many instances hosted student support services from elsewhere on campus in their buildings (Blummer and Kenton, 2017). They have also proved willing to embrace students as partners in service development, notably as co-designers of space (Salisbury, Dollinger and Vanderlelie, 2020; Weaver, 2020).

Partnerships to advance the research mission have also flourished. Multi-partner engagement is key to advancing open scholarship, research data management, digital scholarship and bibliometric analysis. The range of parties with whom academic libraries work is illustrated in stakeholder maps for research information management (Bryant et al., 2017) and research data management (Pinfield, Cox and Smith, 2014). Among those involved are the research, registrar and communications offices, records management, legal advice and human resources. Engagement with digital scholarship projects has increasingly moved academic libraries beyond support roles and into deeper, sometimes co-funded, research partnerships (Posner, 2013; Cox, J., 2016a).

Although competition between higher education institutions has become more intense, interlibrary collaboration remains strong and highly productive. Dempsey's (2018a) study of library consortia identifies a focus on scaling influence, learning, innovation and capacity via organisations such as the ACRL, SCONUL, LIBER, OCLC, the Council of Australasian University Librarians (CAUL) and the Coalition for Networked Information (CNI). Outcomes include collective advocacy, evidence and narrative about library value and positioning, shared training and development and the pooling of expertise through trusted networks, thereby enabling early innovation at times of uncertainty. Cost savings are realised via the procurement and management of shared infrastructure such as library systems, digital resources and collaborative storage of print archives. It has been observed that 'library consortia have brought cooperation to a level that is not seen in most other areas of the academy' (Machovec, 2017, 582).

Many of the benefits of collaboration which strengthen academic libraries are evident in the preceding paragraphs and Atkinson (2018; 2019) summarises them well. They include:

- the ability to address complex issues at scale;
- access to financial, human and infrastructural resources beyond the means of any individual library;
- innovative solutions through the sharing of expertise and multiple perspectives;
- enhanced service provision;
- additional influence in and beyond the parent institution via multi-party alliances.

Collaboration brings numerous challenges too. It requires a substantial and ongoing level of investment, whether across national boundaries or within the decentralised environment of the typical university campus, characterised by a preference for autonomous, independent and sometimes competitive action by individual actors (Bryant, Dortmund and Lavoie, 2020). There may be a need to navigate different organisational cultures among partners and a level of compromise is common, usually involving some loss of local or professional control. Embracing space or service co-design with students is a case in point. The library contribution may be hidden or diluted in a multi-party collaboration and therefore underappreciated. Outcomes do not always match inputs and Corrall (2024) notes a mixed record of success for academic libraries, citing as inhibitors skills deficits and an overly transactional approach, both of which feature in the consideration of strategic implications at the end of this section.

Collaboration is at the very least significant for academic libraries because of the benefits and effort it generates. It represents a point of distinction for them, advantageous in terms of profile and a source of credit from above (Robertson, 2015; Atkinson, 2019). Collaboration broadens the library network, embeds the library more deeply in the campus community and makes valuable contributions to the institutional mission, adding to the sense of its staff as committed campus citizens. The importance of collaboration is likely to increase. Multi-stakeholder involvement is more common than sole library ownership in the newer areas of engagement around student success and research described earlier. Higher education institutions are placing more emphasis on social and collaborative approaches to address major global challenges, often involving communities beyond the campus (Corrall, 2022a). The imperative towards optimal use of resources on economic and sustainability grounds will also foreground collaborative effort.

Library strategy will continue to emphasise collaboration but leveraging it fully as a traditional strength will involve aligning resources with it, not only in terms of staff deployment but also by paying particular attention to the skillsets required in an evolving social, participatory and networked environment. Gwyer (2015) has identified six areas for skills development, including networking, influencing and negotiation, community building and cross-sector working, while boundary-spanning capabilities are a focus for Keene and Downes (2020) alongside a deeper understanding of the context and values of partners. Corrall (2024), in advocating a rethink of how libraries work with others, highlights network competence and a prioritisation of relationship management skills as part of a shift from the transactional to the relational library which promises a step-change in the approach to collaboration. In the immediate term it is important to assert the library role and identity in partnerships of multiple entities, claiming credit where due and highlighting the benefits for the institution. Regularly weighing up the value of each collaboration, whether with campus partners or other libraries, is also appropriate, given the investment required and to ensure that academic libraries remain well placed to make the most of a key strength.

Reinvention

Academic libraries have successfully reinvented themselves and their value proposition since user access to digital information achieved critical mass from the late 20th century onwards. This brought into question their future role and relevance and Chapter 1 described the library reaction as the winds of change began to blow stronger. It was clear that the library monopoly of access to scholarly publications was under threat and that greater user self-sufficiency, with faster access to more information, was on the horizon.

James Thompson (1982), Librarian of the University of Reading, contributed to the debate with a book bearing the ominous title *The End of Libraries*. In it he emphasised that survival depended on major change, not just due to the potential power of the digital library but also because print-based libraries had become 'unusable' (Thompson, 1982, 7). He exposed some serious limitations. Among them were that collections had become too large for ready consultation while typically continuing to double in size every 16 years (Rider, 1944), books were difficult to find, extensive training was needed to use catalogues, libraries could never achieve local self-sufficiency and yet 40% of their books were unused in one study (Kent et al., 1979). The key issues were that libraries based on printed collections were neither user-friendly nor sustainable, with Yale University projected to reach 200 million volumes by 2040, requiring 6,000 miles of shelving (Rider, 1944). The disruptions technology promised were as much to be welcomed as feared, with significant benefits for library staff and users if a positive response, indeed a reinvention, could be mobilised.

Today's academic library is hugely different from that of the 1980s, driven not just by the proliferation of digital information. Major changes in higher education have been influential, including a much larger, more diverse and demanding student population as well as new modes of teaching and research alongside the advance of globalisation and the heightening of accountability. Certain themes are evident in the library response. The overarching emphasis has been on embedding the academic library in the teaching and research activities of its parent institution in a multiplicity of ways, adding value through a range of involvements going well beyond the provision of access to local collections. Library engagement now runs across the whole student journey, contributing to student well-being in addition to learning, and permeates the whole research cycle, concerning itself with the processes as well as the products of research. The library fits into the life of the user (Dempsey, 2016), inserting itself into the workflow of researchers and facilitating a shift from consumption to creation through makerspaces and other creative spaces in reconceptualised library buildings. Partnership with other departments, complemented by an enterprising approach to sharing library space, is now key to institutional support and service enhancement. Academic libraries play to a global as well as local audience through their role as publishers, as well as their advocacy for change in the scholarly communication system.

Library staffing reflects the reinvention in outlook and value proposition. Structures and positions are increasingly oriented towards engagement, outreach and alignment with institutional strategy (Schonfeld, 2016). New roles focused on areas such as first-year support, user experience, data visualisation and marketing have emerged, often staffed by personnel from professions other than librarianship. Growth in research support is reflected in an increase from six to more than 30 staff between 2011 and 2018 at the University of Queensland (Brown, S. et al., 2018). The language describing academic libraries is radically different from the past, characterised by new metaphors such as those proposed by Guthro (2019) which include café, brain, commons and town square. These sit alongside those of laboratory and incubator advanced in another paper, which cites highly active library staff roles 'as scholarly collaborators, co-teachers, co-PIs, and consultants' (Mathews, Metko and Tomlin, 2018, 52). A fundamental repositioning has occurred under the broad umbrella of shifting from collections to services. Collections, printed and digital, continue to be important but as a support to a much broader range of activities through which academic libraries measure their contribution to the institutional academic mission.

Their reinvention has benefited academic libraries by delivering for them a far more diversified, versatile and evolving value proposition, appropriate to the dynamic environment of higher education in recent decades. They are much more embedded and integrated with teaching, learning and research, enjoying multiple points of connection to them and to a range of partners on campus. This has greatly strengthened their support base relative to the somewhat isolated position they occupied previously, as outlined in Chapter 1. Their alignment to the academic mission is more open and active, whether through the variety of activities taking place in their buildings or the social connector roles of their staff. Digital libraries proved vital during the COVID-19 pandemic and epitomised the role of the academic library as a digital leader in the institution and a progressive unit capable of handling major ongoing change.

Challenges have also accompanied reinvention. The diversity of the library contribution makes it less solid and identifiable, sometimes intangible or hard to measure and often shared with others. Legacy commitments to the maintenance of printed collections remain strong and resource-hungry. Material in printed format has an enduring popularity, especially for the assimilation of detailed information, with a majority of more than 10,000 students in a global survey reporting a preference for printed over digital sources (Mizrachi et al., 2018). This mandates a continued sensitivity towards print and efforts to reduce access to materials via the stacks at the University of Virginia Library (Zahneis, 2018) or to transition to an all-digital library at Vermont State University (Jesse, 2023) have encountered vociferous protest, contributing to the resignation of the institution's president in the latter case. The conservatism of academic and library staff, coupled with escalating resource and skills demands, can also put a brake on transformation.

Reinvention has been highly significant for academic libraries and enabled them to keep pace with user and institutional expectations. It has become apparent that the tight focus on building and managing local printed collections was limiting their potential contribution, while leading them towards an increasingly unsustainable service offering. At a minimum, reinvention spared academic libraries the extinction predicted for them by James Thompson (1982) if they failed to evolve. In fact, they have far exceeded the roles envisaged for them in the late 20th century, which were rooted in the prevailing practice at the time and would not have anticipated the development of digital scholarship partnerships, learning commons facilities or digital literacy roles. Change has become business as usual and the approach to positioning the library in its parent institution is now much more consciously active and varied than before.

In terms of strategy, an ongoing priority is to communicate clearly the benefits of the changed value proposition. Chapter 2 noted the challenge of achieving a full understanding of newer value when there is still a strong association among many stakeholders with the traditional role of the academic library. Balancing new and traditional areas of emphasis is important. Finding ways to contain resources directed towards legacy commitments is desirable, ensuring that they are met while maximising capacity to leverage emerging opportunities such as those outlined in Chapter 7. This may involve a tighter deployment of resources, noting the observation that 'many academic libraries have not shifted their staffing, facilities, and infrastructure with nearly as much alacrity as they have shifted their spending towards digital formats' (Schonfeld and Wolff-Eisenberg, 2020). Reinvention should be regarded as never complete and will require ongoing effort. Overall, however, academic libraries have not only adapted to major changes in their circumstances but also successfully reinvented themselves. The end of libraries looks to be some distance away.

Reflective journal extract 5.2
The challenge of change

From the author's journal: 19 May 2018

If I was a soccer manager just now I might be under a bit of scrutiny – our LibQual [survey] score is down for the first time . . . The LibQual rating drop is a worry – some of our changes of structure and focus won't always be popular but I believe in them fully as we need to prepare for 2020 as well as make the journey there. That means taking some hits on more traditional areas of expectation but building capacity in newer areas of digital engagement – not easy . . . That's why I'm analysing the LibQual comments in detail to ensure we can see beyond the numbers and see what it is people actually <u>want</u> and <u>need</u>.

Conclusion

Centrality, values, collaboration and reinvention combine to strengthen academic libraries and Table 5.1 summarises their influence ahead of a collective discussion of strengths, weaknesses, opportunities and threats included in Chapter 9.

Table 5.1 *Academic library strengths and their influence*

Strength	Positives	Counterweights	Significance	Strategy implications
Centrality	• Mission-critical contribution • Mid-campus location • Vital connector role	• Risk of complacency • Support not guaranteed • Others vying for centrality	• Established position in institution • Recognition of role • Unique vantage point	• Emphasise value of connectedness • Maximise social capital • Share insights
Values	• Engender trust • Public good alignment • Compatibility with campus community	• Demanding to uphold • May generate conflicts	• Enduring relevance • Bridge from past to present	• Promote values • Link values to institutional goals • Influence policy and strategy
Collaboration	• Strategic alignment • Institutional citizenship • Broad base of partnerships	• Big investment needed • Risk of diluted recognition	• Point of distinction • Increasing importance • Cost-effectiveness	• Communicate benefits • Assert identity and credit • Cultivate new skillsets
Reinvention	• Evolving value proposition • Versatile contributions • Range of connections	• Value less tangible, exclusive • Legacy commitments endure	• Broader institutional alignment • Active, varied positioning	• Balance new and traditional agendas • Contain legacy functions • Sell the change

CHAPTER 6

Weaknesses of Academic Libraries

Overview

Chapter 6 analyses four academic library weaknesses. Conservatism, stakeholder misperceptions, economic struggles and diversity deficits are the weaknesses chosen. The analysis in each case includes context, what the weakness looks like in action, its negative impacts and some mitigating factors alongside its wider significance and possible library strategic responses.

Introduction

Weaknesses are deficits or limitations inhibiting the progress of an organisation. The following four factors have been identified as weaknesses for academic libraries using the selection criteria listed in the Introduction to the current section of the book and are further explored in this chapter:

1 an overly conservative and cautious approach, limiting agility towards new opportunities, slowing the discontinuation of unviable activities and curtailing external engagement;
2 underestimation by stakeholders of actual and potential library contributions, compromising academic library influence and resourcing;
3 an economic situation in which often static budgets chase sustained rises in expectations and costs, while library value is difficult to measure;
4 a significant deficit in the diversity of academic library staffing and collections, negatively impacting service development and user experience.

Conservatism

The mindset in academic libraries tends towards conservatism and caution, which, while often judicious, can hold them back from realising their full potential. Gorman (2015, 34) characterises library conservatism as a preference for 'steady evolutionary change, order over disorder, and standardization', while Jantz (2017a) observes an adherence to rules and processes. A few factors influence this conservatism. Preservation of previous documentary heritage is a key function, rooting libraries in tradition and bringing many ongoing obligations to the past. In addition, academic libraries typically aim to satisfy the needs of a very wide audience across multiple disciplines, generating a pressure to 'be everything for everyone' (Bryant, Dortmund and [illegible], 2020, 25). This range of commitments and users makes large scale change difficult. Higher education institutions are often slow to change too, with academic staff enjoying considerable power and many holding conservative views of library functions and scholarly communication (Blankstein, 2022) which can place a brake on change.

Conservatism in academic libraries manifests itself in a variety of ways. These include a slowness to recognise major change at an early stage, one example being the beginnings of the shift from printed to online information in the late 1970s. Although some appreciated its implications, one leading scholar viewed the overall library response as myopic and observed that 'The profession seems to have its head in the sand' (Lancaster, 1978b, 357). More recently, academic libraries have been slow to embed AI in their strategies (Huang, Cox and Cox, 2023). Letting go can be difficult and there continues to be a library comfort with print, seeing digital librarianship as 'a nice add on' in some quarters (Marcum, 2016, 4). Collections remain at the core of the academic library offering, reflecting 'a materials-centric, or artefact-centric, view of the world' (Heseltine, 2020, 12) among many library staff. Schlak (2022a) notes that library value associated with digital information has for long largely resembled that for print, namely organisation of materials and support in their use. He summarises the library role as 'the guide on the side who arranges the information into a seamless platform and can provide timely assistance as needed' (Schlak, 2022a, 156).

Peter Drucker (2017) advocated planned abandonment of unjustified activities as a way of freeing up resources to take on new ventures. Although a volume of case studies has been published, its editors noted that this concept had featured rarely in the library literature, as libraries find discontinuing past activities hard, hesitating even over services for which there is only one user (Evangeliste and Furlong, 2014). Abandonment in some of the case studies was more forced by changed circumstances than planned. Conservatism is evident, too, in approaching new opportunities. Research data management is an example, offering potential for a significant shift in library interaction with the research process. Academic libraries have, however, tended to focus their engagement on consultative rather than technical services (Tenopir et al., 2017) and to limit themselves by fitting activities in this domain to their traditional functions and existing knowledge base (Cox, A. M. et al., 2017). Incremental rather than radical change is a feature of library conservatism.

Academic library conservatism promotes an inclination to prioritise internal business over external engagement. The use of director time is a consequential instance. The 2022 Ithaka survey of library directors in the USA generated an estimate that 49% of time was spent on administration and leadership of the library, three times the estimate (16%) for campus engagement outside the library (Hulbert, 2023). This represented a wider gap than had been reported in the 2019 survey (Frederick and Wolff-Eisenberg, 2020b). An analysis by Saunders (2016) of 63 academic library strategic plans found an inward focus on library functions such as collections and space, with only 27% of them making explicit connections to the strategy of their parent institution.

Salisbury and Peseta (2018) have expressed concerns that library staff may be seen as talking primarily among themselves. Three decades ago Atkins (1991) urged that participation in the debate about the future of academic libraries should be extended to include the academic community, but more recent commentary has pointed out that such discussion 'often proceeds without reference to the universities of which libraries are a part' (Dempsey and Malpas, 2018, 67). The need to cast a wider net for feedback and engagement around change has been noted elsewhere (ACRL Research Planning Review Committee, 2019).

Negative impacts arising from conservatism include limited innovation, seen as essential but inhibited by the prevailing culture (Weaver and Appleton, 2020) and by a sense of fear (Bieraugel, 2015). Simons (2017) points out that academic libraries have put more emphasis on providing places of creativity for their users than for their staff. Incrementalism and 'watchful waiting' (Orzech, 2020, 16) may result in opportunities bypassing libraries. Digital humanities demands an adventurous mindset but timidity has held back libraries (Vandegrift and Varner, 2013). The academic library response to internationalisation has also been more cautious and less holistic than ideal (Lombard, 2022), while a more opportunistic stance towards AI could have given libraries a valuable head start there.

By way of mitigation, it is important to remember that conservatism is the dominant *modus operandi* in higher education institutions. Radical change is uncommon and often not well received. A degree of caution is therefore appropriate and many on campus may even welcome the constancy of the traditional library in times of instability. Academic libraries have overcome various constraints, including conservatism, to achieve the successful reinvention of their value proposition described in Chapter 5.

Conservatism and caution carry significance for academic library positioning. Chapter 2 emphasised the importance of an assertive approach to positioning amid dynamic change and intensified competition. This is difficult to execute if the library acts with too much restraint and with its agility limited by a lengthening range of commitments in the absence of regular discontinuation of activities (Jantz, 2017b). Any tendency towards inward focus and hanging back from full institutional engagement risks a loss of influence and a failure to leverage the advantages of centrality. This is especially so in a campus environment characterised by distributed authority where progress often depends on the quality of relationships formed. Worryingly, institutional leaders have commented on the need for stronger library engagement with campus-wide priorities in separate studies (Baker, D. and Allden, 2017; Cooper, Hill and Schonfeld, 2022), while there is a perception by researchers of a lack of library urgency in another investigation (Bryant, Dortmund and Lavoie, 2020).

A conservative and inward-focused mentality may also inhibit effective strategy development and positioning. Budd (2018) observes a librarian tendency towards risk aversion, linear thinking, seeing events in isolation and failing to connect developments in the outside world to the local environment, while Neal highlights 'too much strategic planning and not enough strategic thinking and action' (Neal, 2015, 314).

Two priorities for library strategy stand out: encouraging creativity and maximising outward engagement across the campus. Creativity needs the right environment in which to flourish (Copper, 2023). This includes greater freedom within staffing structures, allocation of resources towards exploration and a supportive culture which promotes curiosity, tolerates failure and avoids perfectionism while rewarding innovation and recognising that reinvention is never complete. Specific actions may include establishing a research and development department (Jantz, 2017a), or at least a role focused on researching influential developments (Jantz, 2017b), and a proactive approach to discontinuation in which saved resources are specifically assigned to new ventures rather than propping up existing activities (Lewis, 2019). External engagement calls for even greater emphasis than currently, breaking free from any library-centric worldview in order to approach relationships from the perspective of the needs and priorities of other parties (Bryant, Dortmund and Lavoie, 2020). Successful engagement beyond the library will benefit greatly from a full appreciation of events and trends in the wider world, a central tenet of this book. A proactive mentality, getting involved instead of waiting to be asked (Davies, 2020) and projecting a confident attitude to the campus community, will also help to combat stakeholder misperceptions of the library, the next weakness discussed.

Stakeholder misperceptions

Key stakeholders often have a limited understanding of their academic library, typically resulting in an undervaluing of its actual and potential contribution. This has negative consequences for the library in terms, for example, of its visibility, appreciation, recognition and resourcing. As Gorman (2015, 40) puts it, 'though libraries are almost always viewed positively, they are not always understood and prized for what they are'. The underestimation of academic libraries comes from a variety of sources and for different reasons.

Chapter 1 noted that institutional leaders and administrators in higher education historically displayed little knowledge of, and interest towards, the library, with one of them labelling it as 'one of those academic sleeping dogs' (Munn, 1968, 52), requiring only rare attention. Academic library engagement with the campus has strengthened greatly in more recent times but a SCONUL study on *The View from Above* (Baker, D. and Allden, 2017), based on interviews with 12 higher education leaders, continues to paint a depressing picture. The academic library, while typically seen as well run, emerges as the object of much indifference, neither a strategic concern nor a risk, low-profile and generally 'not a problem' (Baker, D. and Allden, 2017, 15). A further SCONUL study (Pinfield, Cox and Rutter, 2017) found similarly, noting a perception of the library as fundamentally reliable and unchanging. The perspectives of institutional leaders are often coloured by their own experience of libraries as students and many of them project dated perceptions onto the contemporary library. Surveys of provosts in the USA and Canada have shown a continuing tendency to frame the library contribution according to space and collections (Robertson, 2015; Murray and Ireland, 2018). Of even greater concern for libraries, the 209 provosts in the USA survey most commonly considered them to be only 'somewhat involved' in institutional priorities such as retention, student academic success and faculty research productivity (Murray and Ireland, 2018).

Academic staff also take a traditional view of the library. Its role as buyer of scholarly content has consistently occupied first place in the rating of library functions by importance within the triennial survey of faculty in the USA conducted by Ithaka S+R since 2003 (Blankstein, 2022). Research support has surprisingly been ranked bottom since its introduction in 2009. There is also a noticeable gap in how library directors and faculty score the library's contribution to student learning via the development of information and digital skills. The rating by academic staff is lower than that of directors by between 20% and 40% across three statements pertaining to this role in a comparison included in the 2019 Ithaka survey of library directors (Frederick and Wolff-Eisenberg, 2020b).

The student perspective on libraries is influenced by limited exposure to their range of services. Studies have shown a lack of student knowledge about librarian qualifications, staff roles and duties, perceiving clerical work as most common. Also evident was a disinclination to ask for help on the grounds that support was not needed but also due to doubts that library staff could assist with academic queries (Bickley and Corrall, 2011; Fagan et al., 2021). Such doubts may be linked to unawareness of staff qualifications, while one study (Fagan et al., 2022b) has also highlighted a tendency to associate library staff primarily with books. This tendency is not helpful in shaping comprehensive perspectives by their stakeholders on what academic libraries can offer.

Close association with books is hard to avoid but other factors generating limiting or unclear stakeholder perceptions represent own goals by libraries. A tendency to over-use 'service' terminology has been noted by provosts as unhelpful, in that it looks reactive and fails to convey the full range of library activities (Connaway et al., 2017). The conservatism already noted in this chapter creates avoidable problems in how libraries are seen. This is especially true of the tendency to hang back from full engagement with the campus agenda and to look inwards, thereby reducing influence with stakeholders.

The misperceptions of stakeholders have negative consequences for academic libraries. They may find themselves battling with inattention from above and struggling to get their messages heard. Being taken for granted can feel like being penalised for being a well-managed department (Gwyer, 2018). Ignorance of the challenges, problems and risks facing academic libraries may feed a view that they are getting by successfully and are able to cope with anything thrown at them (Harland, Stewart and Bruce, 2017). Unawareness of their expertise and service offering means that uptake falls short of its potential level. They encounter a lack of credit for their overall reinvention and for work in specific areas such as digital humanities (Posner, 2013) and research information management (Bryant et al., 2017). Failure to recognise their potential impact, for example on retention initiatives (Murray and Ireland, 2018), closes doors to important campus contributions.

There are, however, counterweights to this negativity. Appreciation for academic libraries remains widespread and has begun to expand in scope. Institutional leaders have praised their customer focus, recognised their role in teaching and learning and acknowledged their successful navigation of challenges (Fister, 2015a; Baker, D. and Allden, 2017; Connaway et al., 2017). Faculty tend towards loyalty to the library (Atkins, 1991). They value its role, including as a conduit between themselves and students (Fagan et al., 2022b) and they are becoming more aware of the range of ways it supports student learning, for instance through access to technology and informal study space

(Blankstein, 2022). Students similarly are now more cognisant of the teaching role of library staff and their support for using information effectively, with positive impact on grades (Fagan et al., 2021), while viewing the library as the place on campus to get work done and with the tools they need (De Rosa et al., 2014).

In terms of wider significance for academic library positioning, perceptions matter and so do misperceptions. It is worth recalling the focus in Chapter 2 on the link between positioning and what is in the minds of stakeholders. Unfortunately for academic libraries, stakeholder perceptions of their role and offering are incomplete and represent an underestimate. There are risks that if outputs and benefits are not fully understood, the focus of administrators, especially, may turn towards inputs and costs. Weaver and Appleton (2020) list some provocations arising from preconceptions about libraries, including that they are outmoded, unsustainable and unnecessary when everything is on the internet. Chapter 3 highlighted how lazy soundbites can gain credence and shift opinion in today's world. Misperceptions contribute to the threat to academic libraries, discussed in Chapter 8, of a declining position in the organisational hierarchy as other units and functions emerge in a competitive campus environment. They can limit the library to a service designation (Baker, D. and Allden, 2017; Connaway et al., 2017) and promote a view of the library director as unsuited to a place at the top table of the institution (Gwyer, 2018). Ultimately, the challenge for the library in securing the resources it needs is made even harder.

Communication and engagement with institutional priorities are central to a strategic response for libraries. Securing attention on busy campuses is difficult and effective messaging needs careful thought. A clear, concise and strategic approach to communication is needed, not just to cultivate understanding of the library offering but also to raise expectations. Language is important and will gain from being active and not rooted in 'service' positioning, but strongly focused on value, outcomes and solutions, while resonant with what institutional leaders are talking about. Linkage to institutional priorities, not only in communications but also through active and confident engagement, is important. Davies (2020) offers excellent advice on the range of campus projects to which library expertise can be applied; perceptions can be changed by putting the library forward and inserting it proactively into areas where help is needed and welcomed. It is not surprising that a correlation has been identified between higher institutional valuation of the library and stronger director engagement with campus priorities (Frederick and Wolff-Eisenberg, 2020c).

Reflective journal extract 6.1
As others see us

From the author's journal: 23 January 2016

He [institutional leadership team member] seems to equate the Library primarily with archives. . . . More interesting was his perception that libraries need to make clear their changed role in the digital era – I feel he and [another leader] see us as still doing traditional things and falling behind the curve. Maybe we haven't articulated clearly enough what we will do in the future, despite all the vision work. The timing of all this could actually be good as we are introducing our staff restructuring in the coming week and I will be going around the Colleges and Schools in the next month or two.

Economic struggles

Chapter 4 recounted a tough economic situation for higher education. This includes increased demand but tight funding as governments have emphasised stricter accountability, a highly competitive environment for resources and a series of shocks, notably the 2008 global economic recession, the COVID-19 pandemic in 2020 and a subsequent spike in inflation. The future may not bring any improvement in some regions either, with revenue from student enrolment expected to decline as demographics shift. This has provided an unfavourable backdrop for academic libraries and they have endured economic struggles over a long period, as recorded in Chapter 1 where the headline figure emerged as a halving of their share of institutional expenditure since the 1980s, bringing it below 2% now (Rauf, 2017). Increased competition on campus for institutional funding has been a contributory factor (Jantz, 2017b). Costs have increased significantly in that period and it is unsurprising that over 80% of participants in a triennial survey of US academic library directors consistently identified lack of financial resources as their primary constraint (Frederick and Wolff-Eisenberg, 2020b). The absence of a consistent approach to funding academic libraries across institutions is also unhelpful, typically resulting in static budgets based on tradition rather than evolving needs (Rauf, 2017; Budd, 2018).

Academic libraries face a range of economic pressures whose severity shows no sign of abating. Static budgets are a blunt instrument against rising costs and demands. Students are not only far more numerous but also increasingly consumerist, especially when paying expensive fees, and have high expectations in terms of library services, opening hours, collections and responsiveness (Cox, J., 2021). The needs of academic staff continue to evolve and new library roles in publishing, digital scholarship and infrastructural support bring additional costs on top of ongoing legacy commitments. Technology accounts for a growing share of library expenditure and its cost model has become increasingly recurrent through cloud computing. Library buildings also bring significant capital and maintenance costs.

Beyond staffing, the largest element of library spending is scholarly content, especially recurrent subscriptions to journals. A dysfunctional journals market has long been an economic thorn in the side of academic libraries. Björk (2021) applies Porter's Five Forces framework (Porter, 1979) to an analysis of this market and confirms both low competition and threat of substitution alongside limited bargaining power for suppliers and buyers. This combination of circumstances puts publishers in control and has enabled them to keep prices high, well above annual inflation rates over many years. Academic libraries find themselves locked into expensive subscriptions due to a high dependence by faculty both on access to these journals and on publication in them to advance their careers. When content subscriptions are coupled with staff costs and ongoing IT infrastructure or cloud computing commitments, the majority of library expenditure is typically recurrent. This leaves very little capacity for new purchasing other than via substitution. Some potential exists for income generation, notably through attracting philanthropic donations, winning grants, leasing spaces and charging for services. Such opportunities are limited, however, and may bring their own administrative costs, while library retention of income received is not guaranteed at every institution.

A further challenge, discussed in Chapter 2 and elsewhere, is that the academic library value proposition, or in some eyes its return on investment, is less solid and more diffuse than previously, when the focus was mostly on physical collections and space. The library contribution is often delivered in partnership with others or mediated via technology or third parties and may be less immediately visible to end users (Wales, 2018). One obvious example is the access to online journal articles made possible via the library but not necessarily credited to it. The influence of the academic library on student success is likely to be a matter of correlation rather than direct causation, due to the range of parties involved. Directors when surveyed found it much easier to associate the library contribution with the holistic concept of creating community for students than with specifically increasing their retention or graduation rates (Frederick and Wolff-Eisenberg, 2020b). A later iteration of the same survey found that fewer than 60% of directors participating believed their library had clearly articulated how it contributed to student success, with 65% considering that senior institutional leadership recognised that contribution (Hulbert, 2023). Higher scores would be important in both cases.

The negative consequences of their economic situation for academic libraries are evident. Keeping up with new demands is challenging and making discretionary investments in potential areas of engagement is extremely difficult. Inflation continues to reduce spending power when budgets are static. The cost of maintaining access to journals seriously depletes the amount available for book purchases needed by undergraduate programmes. Proof of library value in specific terms across a multiplicity of involvements can be elusive. Furthermore, libraries may not be helping themselves, through a lack of emphasis on assessing student learning outcomes (Saunders, 2016).

There are some mitigating factors too. Academic libraries have achieved notable economies of scale through their strength in interinstitutional collaboration and consortial purchasing initiatives, as described in Chapter 5. Open scholarship has promoted a questioning of the cost of journals by others, including research funders and governments. Professional bodies have published helpful resources for communicating library value. The ACRL has led a range of projects and publications (Oakleaf, 2010; Brown, K. and Malenfant, 2017; Connaway et al., 2017; Association of College and Research Libraries, 2018), supported more recently by the Research Library Impact Framework from the ARL (Baughman et al., 2023). The emphasis throughout has been on sharing methods for linking library activities to value and positive outcomes in relation to institutional priorities such as student success and researcher productivity.

Strong, aligned resources are important for effective positioning but academic libraries are in a difficult economic situation and are vulnerable globally and on campus. Chapter 3 outlined how a sudden crash in the world economy could happen, while government funding for higher education competes with priorities in health and housing. Locally, the academic library occupies an awkward funding position. Budd (2018) points out that, although it has a very broad constituency, it does not 'own' any students for inclusion in funding formulas in the way that academic departments do. As a result 'the library belongs to everyone and to no one' (Budd, 2018, 213). This contributes to the lack of a standard funding approach and means that libraries are commonly 'funded according to how much money is available rather than what it costs them to provide their services' (Rauf, 2017, 49). The difficulty of demonstrating value in neat and concrete terms alongside high recurrent costs and low income can encourage administrators to view academic libraries primarily as cost centres, a dangerous tendency when allied to the stakeholder misperceptions of the library contribution already described in this chapter.

Money looks set to remain tight in higher education, so academic libraries will want to continue to stretch funding as far as possible via consortia and shared services, while taking a more agile approach to discontinuing less viable activities. The pursuit of more economically supportable scholarly communication models via open scholarship will also make sense, as will monitoring the impact of AI on library costs. There is merit in engaging with stakeholders to cultivate a deeper understanding of the costs and choices academic libraries confront over the longer term. Fundraising may need greater emphasis in the absence of additional local funding. The importance of demonstrating value in terms of impact and outcomes bears repetition, noting a preference by provosts for demonstrations of correlations linked to strategic priorities (Connaway et al., 2017; Murray and Ireland, 2018). This mandates a greater effort towards assessment and a stronger investment to increase library proficiency in rigorous impact research methods (Cheng and Hoffman, 2020).

Diversity deficits

The manifestations of its predominantly White, colonial heritage are readily evident in higher education. They include limited ethnic diversity in the staffing profile of institutions, failure to recognise fully knowledge systems from all parts of the world, curricula infused with subjects shaped by their colonial origins and the dominance of scholarship originating in the Global North and in the English language. An intensified societal focus on equality, inclusion and social justice, along with the expectations of an increasingly diverse student population, has applied pressure on higher education institutions to address these deficits. The emphasis has been on recognising instances of racism in their history and working through a process of decolonisation towards the inclusion of all voices, writings, knowledge systems and philosophies. Academic libraries, as longstanding and central entities on campuses, have been very much in the spotlight too, primarily regarding deficits in the diversity of their staffing, collections and spaces. This is the case despite diversity being one of their core values, adding to the sense that their failure to live up to their ideals in practical terms constitutes a very significant weakness. Although diversity has many dimensions, ethnicity is the focus of this section.

Academic library staffing profiles are predominantly White and out of alignment with the composition of the student population as their largest user constituency. A US study drawing on data from 98 responding ARL institutions recorded 71% of library staff as White, rising to 82% for professionals and 89% for leaders (Schonfeld and Sweeney, 2017). Analysis of a more recent dataset for the UK generated by 81 SCONUL institutions resulted in a figure of 84.8% for White staff whose percentages also increased according to seniority of role (Whyte and McLaren, 2023). Although data for the library profession at large in both countries (Deards and Puente, 2020; Reddington, 2023) showed academic libraries as more diverse than the average, the key issue is that their staffing is unrepresentative of an increasingly diverse student body. One study, based on 2016 data, calculated that US college and university students were 1.6 times as likely to be Black and three times as likely to be Hispanic as academic library staff (Alburo et al., 2020). White domination of academic library staffing can alienate students and staff from other cultures, inhibiting interaction, full service uptake and a sense of belonging (Brook, Ellenwood and Lazzaro, 2015; Bucy, 2022).

Reports of the lived experience of minority ethnic staff in academic libraries are a cause for serious concern. A UK study, based on interviews and a focus group, found consciousness of ethnicity, a sense of being monitored or singled out, experience of microaggressions, a lack of strong human resources procedures or management intervention and limited career progression opportunities (Ishaq and Hussain, 2022). Minority ethnic staff consistently experienced and observed racial microaggressions to a substantially greater extent than non-minority respondents in a US survey (Alabi, 2015). This lack of observation and awareness is part of a pattern of blind spots in the profession. These include perceptions by US library directors of external factors rather than internal culture as the main barrier to attracting more diverse staff and of their own libraries as more equitable regarding race and ethnicity than the rest of the library community (Schonfeld and Sweeney, 2017). The latter trend was in fact more pronounced among respondents from less diverse ARL institutions in this study.

The collections built over time by academic libraries are biased towards the majority culture favoured by their parent institutions, a situation exacerbated by the dominance of a relatively small number of major publishers in terms of output and budgetary consumption. A survey of three collections at the London School of Economics, where collecting practice would likely have been more diverse than average, yielded a figure of over 90% in each case for materials published in the Global North (Wilson, 2022). A lack of appropriate, modern and objective terminology or grouping of subjects in universal systems for organising knowledge, notably the Library of Congress Subject Headings and the Dewey Decimal Classification System, has preoccupied library staff in correction and updating work (Appleton, 2020; Crilly, 2024). Beyond collections, the architecture, imagery and décor of library spaces, especially in older buildings, has the capacity to alienate through association with traditionally dominant or exploitative cultures (Brook, Ellenwood and Lazzaro, 2015; Beilin, 2017; Everitt, 2022; Cox, A. M., 2023).

The foregoing deficits paint an unfavourable picture for academic libraries. The mismatch with their value of diversity is damning and there is nothing to celebrate in the unrepresentativeness of their staffing profile relative to their main users. Collections may fail those seeking the alternative perspective of marginalised groups on a particular subject. Negative workplace experience for minority ethnic staff is unacceptable, as well as a barrier to retention and future recruitment. Progress is slow and there is criticism of a perfunctory, low-priority approach to actioning, assessing and resourcing DEI initiatives (Alburo et al., 2020; Frederick and Wolff-Eisenberg, 2020d). This may be reflected in only 8% of US library directors selecting the ability to foster DEI as a valuable leadership skill in a 2022 survey, which also reported their decreasing confidence in library DEI strategies and collections diversity policies (Hulbert, 2023).

By way of counterweights, societal and institutional pressure are stimulants for change. The critical librarianship movement (Drabinski, 2019) has brought momentum to challenging traditional paradigms and aligning practices with DEI frameworks in areas such as collection development, information literacy, cataloguing and classification (Appleton, 2020; Crilly, 2024). This has spawned productive collaborations with academic staff in updating reading lists to help diversify curricula and with users and local communities to bring new voices into library collections (Clarke, 2022; Wilson, 2022; Crilly, 2024). There is a recognition that libraries occupy a powerful position in knowledge creation and can use their centrality to influence improved DEI in the institution (Dewey, 2014; 2017; Drabinski, 2019; Appleton, 2020).

Nevertheless, the stakes remain high. Deficits in diversity are a major issue and attract scrutiny at a time of focus on DEI. Academic outcomes for students who feel alienated may be adversely impacted. Libraries do not want to contribute towards the student attainment gap identified in the UK between White and Black, Asian or minority ethnic students regarding the number of first- or upper second-class degrees awarded (Universities UK, 2022). Service quality and decision making are likely to suffer if staffing is homogenous and lacks a wide range of perspectives (Brunner and Osorio, 2017). Although the profile of new Master of Library Science graduates in the USA is more ethnically diverse than the current composition of academic library staff there, the numbers are well below those needed to have a significant impact on the workforce by 2033 (Kendrick, C. L. and Hulbert, 2023). The slow rate of progress towards improved diversity already noted is therefore likely to continue. Blind spots in the profession, allied to limited confidence in existing strategies and a lack of prioritisation of DEI-related coverage in library and information science education (Gibson, Hughes-Hassell and Threats, 2018), point in the same direction.

Measures to address diversity deficits will have a long-term presence in academic library strategies. Strong leadership will be vital, expressing more intent and confidence than the evidence to date has indicated. This will entail proper resourcing of formally assessed strategies and a determination to learn from other sectors as exemplars of inclusive recruitment, talent development and mentoring practices alongside systematic diversity tracking (Alburo et al., 2020). A long road lies ahead in diversifying collections and an activist and interventionist rather than neutral approach has been identified as important, supported by clear and well communicated policies with multiple parties involved in their creation and execution (Bledsoe et al., 2022; Clarke, 2022; Wilson, 2022). Space design should likewise benefit from the inclusion of diverse perspectives (Brook, Ellenwood and Lazzaro, 2015). Strong engagement with critical librarianship, especially by leaders, can energise necessary change and help the library to leverage its position of centrality and influence on campus (Appleton, 2020).

Conclusion

Conservatism, stakeholder misperceptions, economic struggles and diversity deficits represent areas of weakness for academic libraries and Chapter 9 will consider them collectively alongside strengths, opportunities and threats. Table 6.1 provides a summary of the influence exerted by the weaknesses discussed in the current chapter.

Table 6.1 *Academic library weaknesses and their influence*

Weaknesses	Negatives	Counterweights	Significance	Strategy implications
Conservatism	• Slow reaction to change, opportunity • Reluctance to discontinue activities • Inward focus	• Parent institutions also conservative • Successful reinvention achieved	• Opportunities not fully leveraged • Barrier to optimal positioning • Less contribution to institution	• Support creativity, experimentation • Maximise outward engagement • Be proactive
Stakeholder misperceptions	• Dated, narrow views • Library taken for granted • Administrator indifference	• Positive sentiment as default • Appreciation widening in scope	• Underestimated • Challenges, resource needs misunderstood • Viewed as just a service	• Communicate value compellingly • Emphasise institutional priorities

Continued

Table 6.1 Continued

Weaknesses	Negatives	Counterweights	Significance	Strategy implications
Economic struggles	• Declining % of institutional expenditure • Static budgets • Dysfunctional journals market	• Consortium purchasing • Others querying high journal costs	• Difficult to keep up with demand • Value can be hard to prove • Global and local vulnerability	• Maximise collaboration • Explain costs and value • Invest in impact research skills
Diversity deficits	• Staffing unrepre-sentative of user population • Collections miss perspectives • Workplace hostility	• Societal and institutional change • Critical librarianship momentum	• Alienation of users, impacting uptake, success • Very slow progress • Library value of diversity not upheld	• Commit at leadership level • Prioritise intentional diversity plans • Work with, learn from others

CHAPTER 7

Opportunities for Academic Libraries

Overview

Four opportunities identified for academic libraries are the subject of this chapter: open scholarship, artificial intelligence, learning space and openings in the wider world. Discussion of each opportunity encompasses its higher education and societal contexts, potential for academic library advancement, positive and inhibiting factors, overall importance and strategic impact.

Introduction

Opportunities in the operating environment offer the potential for advancement and positive development. The application of the selection factors outlined in the Introduction to Part 2 of the book resulted in four opportunities for academic libraries being chosen. The current chapter examines these openings, identified as follows:

1. the potential of open scholarship to change the scholarly communication system, culture and marketplace fundamentally;
2. artificial intelligence, promising transformation of library operations and new, higher-value contributions;
3. reconceptualised and versatile library buildings as a major asset for institutions, enabling new approaches to learning;
4. developments in the wider world, realising greater agility and promoting academic libraries as difference makers on campus and in society at large.

Open scholarship

Increasing concern with long-entrenched flaws in the scholarly communication system, allied to the rise of the open scholarship movement as a source of solutions, has created an opportunity for academic libraries to advance their position. Scholarly publications have traditionally remained behind paywalls, inaccessible to the wider public which largely funds them. A perverse workflow prevails whereby authors write papers and sign away their rights to publishers who then levy charges for access on the institutions whose staff have provided them with content for free. The lack of competition in journal publishing means high costs for academic libraries (Björk, 2021). It has also created an excessively powerful position for the largest publishers, who have further expanded their sales to higher education via products which provide data on publication output and impact at many layers of granularity.

This 'platformisation' of scholarly information (Ma, 2023a) feeds an academic reward system hugely reliant on metrics related to the number of papers published and how often they are cited to dictate hiring, promotions, funding awards and global rankings. The resultant race to publish in high-impact journals has generated negative effects. These include an emphasis on publication venue rather than coverage and a hypercompetitive, less collaborative research culture which has created issues of integrity through falsification of data, predatory publishing outlets and the bypassing of less citation-friendly topics (Sayre and Riegelman, 2018; Ma, 2023b). The focus on metrics and competition also reduces consideration of equality and diversity in knowledge production, often leaving minority voices excluded and unheard (Ma, 2022).

Open scholarship, sometimes called open science or open research among alternative terms, offers an antidote to many of these flaws. It is a global movement and set of principles and practices based on the idea that 'knowledge of all kinds should be openly shared, transparent, rigorous, reproducible, replicable, accumulative and inclusive' (Parsons et al., 2022, 314). Its broad scope includes open research, open access, open data, open educational resources and community participation, often termed citizen science. Vandegrift (2023, 351) observes that 'all the opens participate in creating a more just, equitable, diverse, and welcoming system of knowledge'. The emphasis is on collaboration and sharing scholarship openly as it progresses rather than only at the end. Open scholarship involves a significant change in culture for higher education institutions and their academic communities, calling for shifts in behaviours and practices, including how the academic reward system operates. It brings many challenges but offers much promise and fits well with institutional emphasis on the public good and academic library values of equal access to information, diversity and truth.

Academic libraries are highly active across open scholarship. Examples are promotion of open access, research data management services, embedding of open educational resources, provision of infrastructures for open publishing and roles in policy development (Liu and Liu, 2023). They also provide a range of supports to academic staff, leaders and administrators, including advice on open access policies, publishing venues, copyright and licensing provisions, rights retention and responsible use of research metrics. More recently, they have negotiated transformative agreements with publishers, usually via consortia, which integrate open access publishing of articles by corresponding authors from participating institutions alongside subscription costs. These agreements are intended to transition publishers towards making their journals openly accessible.

A huge positive for academic libraries is that such a transition is now expected by a range of other stakeholders. Many higher education institutions have published responsible metrics policies, along with signing the Declaration on Research Assessment (DORA, https://sfdora.org) or committing to broaden the evaluation base by joining the Coalition for Advancing Research Assessment (CoARA, https://coara.org). Research funders have mandated that the outputs of the research they enable should be openly accessible, a prominent example being Plan S (www.coalition-s.org), supported by a group of national and international bodies. Governments have called for change, notably the mandate from the United States Office of Science and Technology Policy (2022) that by the end of 2025 all publications and supporting data from federally funded research should be publicly and immediately accessible.

Open scholarship has established a momentum for systemic change in scholarly communication. Libraries were formerly almost on their own in advocating for open access but multi-stakeholder support has created a far more favourable climate for change. Transformative agreements have contributed towards improved global rates of open access, encompassing 50% of journal articles and conference papers published since 2010 (Curtin Open Knowledge Initiative, 2025). Research assessment is taking more factors into account, while open educational resources are providing welcome savings for students, estimated at $57,000 for one class at the University of California Los Angeles via its library's Affordable Course Materials Initiative (Steel, 2019).

Proponents of open scholarship are, however, swimming against a very strong tide. Change is slow, with closed access similarly accounting for 50% of post-2010 publications (Curtin Open Knowledge Initiative, 2025). Transformative agreements have attracted criticism for keeping annual costs high, being inaccessible to many authors, squeezing out smaller publishers and hindering bibliodiversity or choice of open access publishing channels (Farley et al., 2021; Ma, 2023a; Brayman et al., 2024). Surveyed US library directors see open access as more likely to increase than reduce costs in the long term (Hulbert, 2023). Conservatism towards the traditional publishing system abounds. One report estimates that it would take 70 years for the biggest five publishers to switch their journal titles to open access at current rates of progress (Brayman et al., 2024). US academic staff in one survey continued to emphasise journal impact factor over open access when choosing where to publish (Blankstein, 2022). The need to invest time in learning new tools and developing different practices is another barrier (Teplitzky, 2023). Culture change does not happen easily.

Despite many obstacles, open scholarship represents an important opportunity for academic libraries. Participating in a transformation of the scholarly communication system is time well spent and can make a major difference for society at large, as evidenced by the role open access to 85% of relevant articles played in the early delivery of COVID vaccines (UNESCO, 2023). Universal open access, albeit some distance in the future, is a prize worth fighting for, as is a more robust, trusted, inclusive and fair approach to scholarship. A more economically sustainable system for publishing scholarly outputs is an ongoing library aspiration which open scholarship can help to realise, alleviating the budgetary pressures experienced for decades under the current system. A significant library repositioning from neutral adviser to activist advocate, thought leader, policy shaper and partner with multiple stakeholders is happening. This includes a changed relationship with publishers as libraries, with wider support, demand more and are willing to provide leadership in discontinuing access to content unavailable on the right terms, for example at the University of California (ACRL Research Planning Review Committee, 2020).

Embedding open scholarship and realising its benefits will be a long haul for academic libraries, meriting prominence in their strategic thinking. Ma (2023a; 2023b) emphasises the importance of educating faculty and administrators about a complex and evolving landscape of policies and practices. Targeting early-career researchers makes sense, given their greater willingness to question traditional approaches (Teplitzky, 2023). Infrastructural support for global open scholarship is fragmented and needs collaborative investment to improve interoperability, discovery, linkage and preservation (Bergstrom, Rieger and Schonfeld, 2024). Academic libraries can make a difference by allocating funding to support collective infrastructure, noting a recommended figure of 2.5% of their overall budget (Lewis et al., 2018). Alternative, community-owned publishing models have been proposed to deliver large-scale open access (Technopolis Group, 2020; Brembs et al., 2023) and academic libraries are well placed to shape their planning and development. Open scholarship calls on academic libraries to act both locally and globally. Harrison (2018) is justified in identifying scholarly communication support as the future of academic librarianship and a vital professional concern.

Artificial intelligence

Artificial intelligence featured prominently in Chapters 3 and 4, attracting huge attention in society at large and in higher education for its role in data-driven problem-solving, prediction and decision making and, more recently, generation of text or other media. There has been a mixed reception for AI. Excitement has surrounded its speed, capability and promise of productivity, economic growth and elimination of routine work. Concerns are widespread, however, about biased data and algorithms, invasion of privacy by over-powerful technology companies, generation and spread of false information and unemployment as intelligent machines take over jobs. Higher education has similarly welcomed opportunities to expand computational research, support student progression and reduce administration, while fearing a loss of academic integrity and rigorous learning through generative AI.

The implications of AI have been part of the academic library discourse for some years too. Its significance has been recognised in commentary identifying it as 'a significant challenge to the future position of the library and information profession(s)' (Cox, A. M., Pinfield and Rutter, 2019c, 433) and predicting that 'the near future of library work will be enormously impacted and perhaps forever changed' (Griffey, 2019, 8). Yet Appleton (2024) observed that even in more recent times the academic library sector was struggling to make sense of AI and to take a considered and strategic position regarding it. Views have ranged 'from techno-optimism to the fear of machines surpassing librarians and eradicating human values' (Gasparini and Kautonen, 2022, 20). Artificial intelligence could easily be categorised as a threat but this book favours seeing it as an opportunity for academic libraries, encouraged by evidence of their strengthening engagement with and increasingly positive disposition towards it (Lo and Hudson-Vitale, 2025).

Artificial intelligence offers many opportunities for academic library operations, services and positioning. Labour-saving possibilities include smart buildings monitoring and usage prediction (Cox, A. M., 2021), robot-based automatic storage and retrieval systems for library collections (McCaffrey, 2021), chatbots for answering routine enquiries and the availability of machine-generated metadata (Griffey, 2019). Efficiencies in some areas can support service expansion in others. Data are central to AI. Existing library work in research data management therefore offers a basis for roles in procuring, licensing and curating datasets as well as monitoring quality and checking AI training data (Cox, A. M., 2021). The presentation of collections as data alongside AI-enhanced information retrieval and the automatic transcription of handwriting in historic documents can create new research possibilities (Cox, A. M. and Mazumdar, 2024).

Space is a key element of library service, enabling the building of communities around the practical use of AI. One example is the Collaboratory at Ryerson University, which has focused on connecting AI practitioners across disciplines (Wang, Tucker and Seo, 2022). Another is the uniquely library-located AI Lab at the University of Rhode Island, where there has been a particular emphasis on supporting debate around the ethical and societal implications of AI through programming and community outreach (Dekker, Ferria and Mandal, 2022).

The pros, cons, complexities and opportunities of AI have promoted a realisation that some level of literacy is needed to use it effectively. Artificial intelligence literacy has been recognised as a separate skillset, defined early on as 'a set of competencies that enables individuals to critically evaluate AI technologies; communicate and collaborate effectively with AI; and use AI as a tool online, at home, and in the workplace' (Long and Magerko, 2020, 2). The rise of generative AI has called for an expansion in scope, outlined by Zhao, Cox and Cai (2024) and including the ability to choose the correct tool, prompt it effectively, interpret its output critically, understand issues of privacy and bias and reflect on the impact on one's skills and learning.

For academic libraries AI literacy is a natural extension of their role in information and digital literacy and opens the door to campus leadership in skills identified as essential for staff and students (Burress et al., 2021; Pelletier et al., 2023a). Their commitment to values such as privacy, transparency and objectivity ensures that they provide a welcome emphasis on the ethical dimensions of AI, generating debate instead of uncritical acceptance. As described in Chapter 5, academic library values are a strength and engender trust among library users. This enables them to position themselves as trusted guides and partners in advising on how AI might be most appropriately applied to teaching and research amid ongoing uncertainty, unpredictability and conflicting views.

There is a definite potential for AI to be a good news story for academic libraries. It can bring efficiencies, reduce time spent on less rewarding work, support the development of new services valued by users and facilitate a fuller exploitation of their collections. Artificial intelligence plays to library strengths, notably knowledge of information structures, collections access, data management and literacy development alongside trusted status and aptitude for collaboration (Cox, A. M. and Mazumdar, 2024).

Viewed through a different lens, however, numerous counterweights to successful academic library engagement with AI are evident. Conservatism, already identified as a source of hesitancy towards new opportunities in the previous chapter, inhibits experimentation and has contributed to a somewhat cautious adoption of AI by libraries (Huang, Cox and Cox, 2023; Cox, A. M., 2025). Related to this may be a lack of confidence, with only 16% of surveyed US library directors believing that their library had a clear vision for futureproofing that takes into account technological and sociopolitical trends (Hulbert, 2023). Artificial intelligence may be viewed as a difficult and uncertain space for academic libraries, with commercial entities likely to dictate the pace and libraries struggling to attract data scientists and developers (Cox, A. M., Pinfield and Rutter, 2019c). Early-career researchers in one study have expressed uncertainty about the role of academic libraries in ten years' time in the face of AI (Nicholas et al., 2025). Resistance from library staff is inevitable to some degree in the face of concerns about ethical issues running counter to their values, radical change in service models and potential job losses (Lo, 2023; Cox, A. M. and Mazumdar, 2024). The gap between perceptions of AI as a threat and AI as an opportunity is not wide.

The high volume of media coverage about AI indicates its significance. It represents a major moment for the world and for academic libraries too. Cox, A. M., Pinfield and Rutter (2019c) have captured this well in linking the impact of AI to fundamental issues such as what a library is, what a collection is, how services are delivered, user expectations, staff skills needs and the identity of users, including machines as clients. What they wrote in 2019 remains valid today and AI has the capacity to shape academic library position and positioning. Academic staff, students and administrators are grappling with AI and keen to avail themselves of relevant library services, guidance and sense-making. There are opportunities to move up the institutional value chain but equally risks in omitting to engage fully. Such risks include bypassing by vendors, flawed AI tools for library operations and services, failure to develop necessary staff skills and a loss of competitiveness and relevance as users become more self-sufficient and act independently of libraries.

Artificial intelligence has been slow to figure in academic library strategies (Huang, Cox and Cox, 2023) but this is changing, with faster momentum evident since the launch of ChatGPT popularised generative AI (Lo and Hudson-Vitale, 2025). An open mentality towards AI will serve libraries well, recognising its challenges while maximising its potential for efficiency and effectiveness. Prioritising AI will facilitate a deeper understanding of community needs, greater staff experimentation and skills development as well as engagement with vendors to influence product development in line with library values and user preferences (Griffey, 2019; Lo, 2023). Leveraging strengths such as collaboration and trusted broker status will be important in ensuring library contributions towards shaping institutional AI policy. The risks inherent in AI should not prevent academic libraries from embracing its opportunities.

Learning space

Four developments in higher education have combined to drive reconceptualised library buildings as versatile and dynamic spaces, key to effective learning and providing academic libraries with opportunities to foreground their vital contribution to the academic mission. The first and foremost of these has been a change in direction from the didactic lecture to constructivist teaching, shifting from passive information consumption towards active knowledge creation. The emphasis is on experiential and collaborative learning, placing a premium on participation, interaction and independent activity, for which accessible, flexible and technology-rich spaces in libraries have become essential (Cox, J., 2024). Secondly, advances in technology enable new forms of learning and are vital to creativity. Students expect access to the best digital tools, not only for their academic progress but also to develop proficiency in their use for their future careers (Alexander et al., 2017).

The latter point links to the third development, which is the increased influence of marketisation within higher education. This drives on the one hand an intensified competition between institutions for students, with a focus on the student experience, and on the other a more consumerist outlook by students whose expectations of facilities like libraries are elevated by high tuition fees in many cases and for whom value for money and future employability are vital considerations (ODonnell and Anderson, 2022). Finally, the student body has diversified greatly and new needs have come to the fore. These include access to a wider range of academic supports, commonly hosted in libraries (Blummer and Kenton, 2017). Pressures on students have increased, generating effort by institutions to support well-being and a sense of belonging, with the library as a key communal space able to play an important role (ODonnell and Anderson, 2022; Bruxvoort, 2023).

Today's academic library usually has a radically different look and feel in response to the changes just described and their attendant opportunities. Until the late 20th-century collections and a single type of reader space for their consultation dominated buildings. Access to digital information has dramatically reduced the footprint occupied by printed collections and library space is now much more versatile. A transformation has occurred, with a mix of technology-enhanced spaces to accommodate different learning styles and preferences. These include social areas, group study rooms, makerspaces, visualisation labs and multimedia production studios (Lippincott, 2022). There is generous provision for active, collaborative learning, with a particular emphasis on supporting digital creativity and experimentation for which the library acts as a platform (Mathews, Metko and Tomlin, 2018; Raschke, 2022). Spaces for quiet, individual study remain essential, however, recognising that library support for concentration and contemplation is even more valued in a busy, high-transaction, digital environment.

The learning commons concept has influenced the reconceptualisation of library buildings since the mid-2000s (Blummer and Kenton, 2017). Its thrust is to organise spaces, technology and staff primarily around the delivery of wider learning objectives, supported through partnerships among academics, librarians and other parties (Cox, J., 2024). The emphasis on high-quality human support is appropriate, as this is a key factor in realising effective use of transformed spaces. Staff expertise and skills have been highlighted as 'the most important ingredients in making library-centered capital projects a success' (Raschke, 2022, 24). Library staff provide essential support, including the cultivation of digital literacy. Additionally, library buildings often play host to other campus services to support student learning success. These include academic writing, mathematics, first-year experience, assistive technology and careers, representing valuable supports for students and important partnerships for libraries.

The community role of the library building has been of increasing importance for students especially, a trend accelerated by the pandemic experience. As campus populations have grown and social interaction has become increasingly digital, more students are at risk of feeling isolated, contributing to the rise in mental health issues in higher education described in Chapter 4. The library building is strongly positioned to offer a place of community and well-being through its central location, long opening hours, high occupancy and the trusted interactions between its staff and the student body (Brewerton and Woolley, 2016; Walton, 2018). Supportive spaces may include sensory rooms, relaxation zones, self-help collections, cafés and food pantries or preparation areas alongside a range of programming designed to relieve stress, especially at exam times (Ramsey and Aagard, 2018; Bladek, 2021; Terrile, 2024). Students also appreciate the library as a third place, distinct from home and academic spaces, where they can be themselves and study or rest in the company of their peers, experiencing a sense of belonging as part of a creative commune (Mathews, 2014a; Lewis, 2017; Bruxvoort, 2023).

The ongoing transformation of their space for learning represents a positive opportunity for academic libraries. It leverages their centrality on campus and emphasises their key role in student life, with much to offer their institutions as 'places for possibility' (ODonnell and Anderson, 2022, 232). This includes promoting the development of student skills such as critical thinking, communication, teamworking and creative use of digital technologies, often in collaboration with other partners. Usage is strong, with one study identifying ten factors driving this, thereby reflecting a highly diversified value proposition (Cox, A. M. and Benson-Marshall, 2021).

On the downside, achieving the necessary capital investment to transform an existing building or to construct a new one is extremely difficult in the face of intense competition for limited funding. Large capital projects are relatively rare, reflected in a calculation by Lewis (2017) that only about 10% of the academic library buildings in the USA were replaced or significantly redeveloped between 2000 and 2015. Even when funding has been secured, inflexibility may pose a substantial barrier where the choice is made to renovate an existing building. Other issues to note are that learning space in new or reconfigured library or learning commons buildings may be inefficiently used or may lack distinctiveness from that provided in other parts of the campus (ACRL Research Planning Review Committee, 2022; Lippincott, 2022).

Taking a broader view, the reimagined library as dynamic learning space emerges as a significant institutional asset, adapting flexibly to shifts in higher education and contributing vitally to meeting student expectations as they evolve (Hickerson, Lippincott and Crema, 2022). Academic libraries feature regularly in university marketing, especially when investment has been made in distinctive buildings and programming, realising a competitive advantage in student recruitment, retention and learning experience (Raschke, 2022; Everitt, 2024). Less tangibly, academic library space can offer something unique as a statement of scholarly values, a place of community for all disciplines and a physical embodiment of the shared enterprise of the campus as a collective (Chambers et al., 2020). A further opportunity exists to leverage library experience to inform and sometimes lead the design of learning spaces across the campus at large, capitalising also on the unique vantage point, mentioned in Chapter 5, that library staff enjoy as observers of student learning behaviours (Appleton, Stevenson and Boden, 2011; Matthews and Walton, 2014).

The major strategic challenge for many academic library leaders is to persuade their parent institutions to make a substantial investment in transforming or replacing any library buildings which have become outdated relative to current needs and expectations. Patience, persuasion and persistence are essential in addition to political sensitivity and advocacy can take many years before yielding success (Cox, J., 2024). Pitching the argument in the wider context of trends in higher education and benefits for the institution is key, while also bringing into play the unique advantages of the library as a campus space (Lippincott, 2022). There is scope to build a broad constituency of support across academic disciplines, service departments and students as beneficiaries of a new or transformed facility. Engaging the student body in advocacy is vital, as is working with students in co-designing space (Weaver, 2020). The journey towards transformed learning space can be lengthy and challenging but has tended to be worthwhile, helping academic libraries to realise the opportunity to position themselves as an essential and multidimensional locus of learning on campus.

Reflective journal extract 7.1
From agony . . . to ecstasy

From the author's journal: 19 August 2017 and 30 August 2019

19 August 2017: From agony . . .
There is very little tangible support from the rest of the campus [towards library building transformation] and meeting on Monday was truly depressing . . . Staying hopeful is a bit of a challenge when you have been knocking on the door for so long, but I hope the effort is not in vain and maybe the investment will translate to a project. Maybe the darkest hour is before the dawn!

30 August 2019: . . to ecstasy
What a week! There is only one place to start this week – the amazing news that we have been successful in our bid for €15M matched funding for the Library building transformation! Hard to believe that this has happened finally after so long, so many campaigns, so many false dawns, so many presentations, so many position papers, so many visits to admire other libraries and return to our own tired building. At last, we now have the opportunity to change all that.

The wider world

Chapter 3 outlined a global environment marked by rapid change and a sense of radical shakeup through the rise of identity politics, the advent of a post-truth society promoting alternative facts, the stalling of globalisation and the increasing replacement of human work by AI. To these can be added the COVID-19 pandemic, a major world event whose disruptive effects are still being felt. It demonstrated how adversity in the wider world can bring opportunities for many sectors, including academic libraries. The first part of this section reflects on these as they continue to play out, before exploring ways in which academic libraries can act to turn some unpromising developments in today's world to their advantage.

The COVID-19 pandemic brought disaster and misery for many, while the suddenness of its onset mandated disruption, new ways of thinking and an accelerated pace of change in most walks of life. Academic library leaders quickly sensed the opportunity for a fundamental shift in their operating model (Frederick and Wolff-Eisenberg, 2020a; Lutz and Schonfeld, 2020), the most obvious manifestation of which was an immediate switch to exclusively digital access to library resources and services. Christopher Cox (2020) summarised this as 'e-everything', as academic libraries moved to a digital-first approach which has endured since the pandemic, not only for collections but also for services. Digital ways of delivering printed items, online consultation and hybrid programming have become commonplace, saving user time, enabling more flexible scheduling and increasing library audiences (Greenhall, 2020). The effectiveness of their digital response brought reputational gain for academic libraries and a new appreciation of their value which has helpfully challenged previous perceptions (Frederick and Wolff-Eisenberg, 2020a; Greenhall, 2020).

Open access enjoyed a boost as the search for a vaccine prompted publishers to lift some paywalls temporarily and encouraged researchers to work differently, collaborate more and share findings earlier. Preprint publication increased significantly in 2020, gaining in attention, impact and influence as a recognised channel for open dissemination of research results (Fraser et al., 2021). The profile of open educational resources in teaching has also increased. Hybrid working has become an established practice in academic libraries, with hiring less tied to geographical location. Overall, the COVID-19 pandemic provided an opportunity to implement major and ongoing change in academic libraries far sooner than would otherwise have happened.

Today's world is troubled in many respects but there are three areas which, although difficult, offer opportunities for academic libraries if they can strengthen their profile and contribution.

First, the toxic combination of polarisation, culture wars, anti-DEI legislation and fake news calls on academic libraries to emphasise the higher purpose in society at large to which their values propel them. The tendency is to foreground the library as a campus rather than societal entity but 'the first purpose of librarians is to improve society, not to be neutral bystanders' (Heseltine, 2020, 13). Academic libraries share the common mission of higher education, identified in Chapter 4 as 'to prepare citizens to contribute to society through knowledge, understanding, critical thinking, and innovative ideas' (Makoe, 2023, 303). The trusted position of libraries on campus can be leveraged to good effect in helping their communities to make well informed judgements about the many viewpoints expressed in the wider world. Information and other literacies are vital (De Paor and Heravi, 2020) but it is clear that more can be done, with only 17% of surveyed US directors confident that their library has a clear vision for redressing the influence of disinformation and misinformation among their community members (Hulbert, 2023).

Secondly, as mentioned earlier in this chapter, the world of research has also suffered from falsification and fraud, leading to a loss of public trust. Practices compromising research integrity include fabricated data and results, false claims to authorship and gaming of research metrics such as citation counts (Biagioli and Lippman, 2020; Ma, 2023b). Reproducibility of research has been a particular concern, with over half of 1,576 respondents in one survey citing a replication crisis in science and 70% unable to reproduce another scientist's experiments (Baker, M., 2016). Researchers want stronger action to support research integrity and there is an opportunity for academic libraries to be more active in this space. Sayre and Riegelman (2019) have highlighted the close match of library skills in data management, open scholarship, systematic reviews and computational research support with guidelines for reproducible research from funders, publishers and learned societies. A deeper engagement with reproducibility and other research integrity issues looks like a natural and welcome extension of library effort (Quan, 2022; Schmidt et al., 2024).

Sustainability is the third area identified for more concerted action, with rising urgency as climate change advances. Academic libraries are already active here and are often commended for their sustainability initiatives, while their roles as exemplars, advocates and educators in green literacy have been highlighted (Hauke, 2018; Mathiasson and Jochumsen, 2022; Hamad et al., 2024). It has, however, been observed that sustainability policies have been rare (Khalid, Malik and Mahmood, 2021), academic libraries tend to follow rather than lead in this area (Appleton, 2022) and more detailed planning is needed across all operations (Corrado, 2024). Another study, albeit of only 15 US academic libraries, found mostly limited initiatives, focused on the environment rather than holistically in combination with the social and economic dimensions of sustainability, along with a lack of assessment of existing efforts (Tribelhorn, 2023). Appleton and Woolley (2023) challenge academic libraries to exert more influence on sustainability by using their trusted position to operate as a cross-disciplinary platform for debate, learning and influencing.

The COVID-driven opportunities described earlier mostly represented new directions or accelerated changes with positive impact on library users and staff alike. Stronger appreciation of the contributions of academic libraries during and after the pandemic provided a platform for improved positioning. The same should be true with activation of the three proposed areas of opportunity in this section, each of which resonates well with campus concerns and is recognised as requiring support. Counter thrusts to leveraging these opportunities include conservatism, the costs and licensing challenges involved in digital-first access (Greenhall, 2020) and inequities or practical difficulties in hybrid working (Bergenäs and Dorthé, 2021; Hosoi, Reiter and Zabel, 2021). The sheer power of the global forces involved cannot be overestimated, with information literacy struggling to counter fake news, for example (Sullivan, 2018). Furthermore, in addition to providing opportunities, global developments generate uncertainty, one of the threats discussed in Chapter 8.

The embedding of changes opened up by the COVID-19 pandemic is ongoing, with 'significant opportunities for future operation, positioning, contribution, and identity' (Cox, J., 2023a, 382). Taking a highly active stance in relation to issues such as polarisation, fake news, research integrity and sustainability recognises their importance for wider society and shows academic libraries living their values. In doing so they position themselves as pillars of stability, responsibility and trust, acting as difference makers both on campus and in the world at large. Trusted status is a major underpinner in the case of each of the three opportunities identified for further activation. It is notable that libraries have retained public trust while others, including higher education institutions, have attracted negative public perceptions. This adds to the sense of the academic library as a major reputational asset to its parent institution.

Finally, regarding strategy, academic libraries can benefit by emphasising their wider social mission regularly and activating it in the face of immediate campus pressures and the limiting effects of stakeholder misperceptions. The fallout from the COVID-19 pandemic should be viewed as unfinished

Reflective journal extract 7.2
Global versus local

From the author's journal: 6 April 2013
I need to keep my horizons broad and to develop my networks to the max. . . . I'd like to have more time for ideas, reading, thinking, travel, people, visits – all important to developing a broader perspective, to see the wood for the trees and to lead the Library forward, in new directions. I may be my own worst enemy by 'doing' so much, engaging promptly with emails, having lots of meetings. There is a fair bit of travel coming up in the next few weeks, all to be welcomed.

business if desired changes are to stick. Monitoring of developments in the wider world and in higher education needs ongoing attention, seeking opportunity in adversity. In that context it seems appropriate to end with the words of Rahm Emanuel, formerly chief of staff to President Barack Obama: 'Never allow a good crisis go to waste. It's an opportunity to do the things you once thought were impossible' (Emanuel, 2020).

Conclusion

Open scholarship, artificial intelligence, learning space and opportunities in the wider world provide openings for academic libraries to advance their position. Chapter 9, which opens Part 3 of the book, will include a collective examination of the significance of the strengths, weaknesses, opportunities and threats identified in this part. Table 7.1 distils how these opportunities impact academic libraries.

Table 7.1 *Academic library opportunities and their influence*

Opportunity	Positives	Counterweights	Significance	Strategy implications
Open scholarship	• Pressure for systemic change • Broad base of support • Libraries at centre	• Academic and publisher conservatism • Slow pace of progress • Few savings yet	• Greater economic sustainability • Positive societal impact	• Seize moment of opportunity • Educate, advocate, influence policy • Act locally and globally
Artificial intelligence	• Higher-value roles • Library as trusted, ethical guide • Leadership in AI literacy	• Bias, privacy concerns • Threat to academic integrity • Possible job losses	• Massive global attention • Potential for fundamental change	• Adopt open, experimental mentality • Develop skills • Influence commercial products
Learning space	• Library central to learning • Holistic support via hosted partners • Vital place of community	• Major capital projects costly • Lengthy period of advocacy • Older buildings hard to adapt	• Alignment with priority needs • Reputational asset • Strong user engagement	• Lobby for space transformation • Emphasise learning trends and benefits • Build broad coalition
The wider world	• Post-COVID agility • Opportunities via instability • Truth and sustainability openings	• Conservatism • Strength of negative global forces • Pressure on costs, time	• Stronger appreciation • Trusted status heightened • Difference-making roles	• Embed helpful pandemic-driven changes • Promote wider social mission • Don't waste a crisis

CHAPTER 8

Threats to Academic Libraries

Overview

The final chapter of Part 2 focuses on threats to academic libraries. Four threats have been chosen, namely decline in position, identity blurring, competition and uncertainty. For each threat there is an examination of its context, how it is present for academic libraries, the challenges it brings alongside some counterweights, why it is significant and how library strategy might take account of it.

Introduction

Threats in the operating environment bring the possibility of damage or other negative impact. Applying the selection criteria outlined in the Introduction to this part of the book, namely long-term influence, impact across the whole library, reflection of key external factors and prominence in the library literature, yielded the following threats:

1. a decline in position in the institution, locating the library further down the hierarchy, with less independence and a smaller share of institutional expenditure;
2. less clarity of identity and unique value proposition in the digital world, coupled with reduced visibility and recognition in increasingly complex institutions;
3. competition for influence and resourcing from within the institution and for service provision to users from outside it;
4. global uncertainty and political, economic, social and technological disruption, resulting in very challenging and complex operating conditions.

Decline in position

Academic libraries have experienced a series of ups and downs across the centuries, charted by the historical overview in Chapter 1. It is difficult to identify a golden era but the 1960s may come closest. The library position was strong, its importance to the academic mission speaking for itself through the local printed collections it assembled and curated. Its place at the heart of the campus was assumed, funding was in a positive cycle, the director commonly reported to the head of the institution and the library enjoyed a high level of independence, with administrators unlikely to interfere much, albeit sometimes due to indifference (Munn, 1968; Gwyer, 2018).

A series of major changes from the 1970s onwards proved unfavourable, however, resulting in a decline in position for academic libraries. Funding tightened and accountability became a key focus. The priorities of institutions shifted as higher education expanded and competition increased. Growth within institutions meant larger management teams, pushing the library further away from the centre. New or expanded departments emerged, spawned by evolving strategic imperatives or increased requirements for regulatory compliance. Many of these departments were administrative, providing competition for already limited funds. They also stimulated lots of organisational restructuring to link related functions together, impacting the library. The most influential change of all for libraries exerted itself when digital information began to encroach on the established primacy of printed collections.

The academic library value proposition in the digital era is more versatile than before, characterised by partnerships, projects and engagements dispersed over many fronts, but also less solid, obvious and easily explainable than when buildings and collections largely represented the library contribution. Faculty and students are more self-sufficient, with less dependence on the library as alternative routes to information and related services are available. Materials freely accessible online are almost as important as library collections according to a survey of US faculty (Blankstein, 2022). The onus is on academic libraries to fit into the workflow of their users rather than vice-versa (Dempsey and Malpas, 2018). They are significantly hindered in that effort by the halving in recent decades of their share of institutional expenditure reported in Chapter 6. That share now typically stands at less than 2%, a situation interpreted as a 'not-so-subtle message that administrators now value library contributions less and increasingly reallocate portions of the library budget to other units' (Jantz, 2017b, 226).

The proliferation of new or expanded departments has not only spread funding more thinly but has interposed layers between the academic library and the top of the institution. Management teams have been enlarged and the creation of new co-ordinating roles such as Chief Operating Officer has displaced others, including the academic library director, from the top table (Gwyer, 2018). Only four of 88 UK library directors surveyed in 2017 and ten of 662 in a US survey in 2019 reported to the head of the institution (Gwyer, 2018; Frederick and Wolff-Eisenberg, 2020b). While reporting to the provost or registrar as the most senior academic leader remained most common in these instances, the UK study also found that in some institutions the director was 'at least two tiers down in the senior staff structure' (Baker, D. and Allden, 2017, 22). As institutions have grown, new organisational configurations have emerged. A grouping with other professional services removes the library from the academic management structure, thereby de-coupling it from the most influential part of the organisation. Alternatively, the library may be grouped with, and indeed lead, student-facing services but with a risk of losing influence with the research community. Arrangements which may appear to make administrative sense can harm the position of the academic library (Dyer, 2024).

Two further concerns are evident in the triennial Ithaka S+R survey of US library directors. Only half of the directors surveyed in 2022 strongly agreed that they were perceived as a member of the senior academic leadership of their institution, compared with over 64% in 2013 (Hulbert, 2023). There has also been a steady decline, from over 70% in 2013 to below 60% in 2019, in respondents strongly agreeing that they shared the same vision for the library with their direct supervisor (Frederick and Wolff-Eisenberg, 2020b).

The situations described above contribute to a decline in position for academic libraries, with negative consequences. One of these is a reduction in influence on campus, reflected in a survey of UK library staff in which only 40% of respondents believed the library was involved in institution-wide decision making (Pinfield, Cox and Rutter, 2017). As noted throughout this book, positioning impacts the recognition, resourcing and prospects of academic libraries. The loss of purchasing power over time has made it difficult to keep up with emerging demands. Diminished visibility in organisational structures can feed into the stakeholder misperceptions and tendency towards underestimation of the library contribution described in Chapter 6.

Nevertheless, academic libraries still enjoy a position of centrality in the institution, as Chapter 5 highlighted. The newer value proposition includes many thriving elements, among them vibrant learning space, a diversity of points of connection to the academic mission and greater influence beyond the institution, all founded on an enduring high level of trust in the library. Organisational alignment with academic structures is the most favourable model and continues to be much more common than recent alternatives. Inclusion in larger groupings can also add resilience as institutions grow, while library directors have been able to expand their influence at the head of newly converged departments (Bulpitt, 2012; Gwyer, 2018).

Overall, however, decline in position carries threat not only in terms of resourcing, influence and perceptions but also mentality. Gwyer describes ongoing concern among library directors about the position of the library they lead, citing 'a lot of soul searching (and some doom and gloom)' (Gwyer, 2018, 433) linked to a feeling of slippage in the organisational hierarchy. Pessimism and a sense of decline are not limited to directors and an amount of agonising permeates other library staff. In some cases, 'a rhetoric of crisis' (Williams, C. A., 2025, 125) can prevail. While this can sometimes generate urgency and determination, it is more frequently a source of insecurity and defensiveness. A deficit mindset emerges, with others considered to be doing better. This can further hold back the library and does nothing to improve its position actively. While academic libraries have contributed to some extent to their own decline, especially through the conservatism and inward focus outlined in Chapter 6, they have little control over many of the forces described earlier in this chapter and will profit more from a positive approach to positioning.

The strategic response to a decline in position is neither simple nor straightforward. Starting with optimism and a celebration of the many successes arising from reinvention is important, alongside continuing to leverage fully the increased recognition of the library for its strong performance and adaptability during and since the COVID-19 pandemic. A willingness to experiment served academic libraries well during the pandemic and this merits ongoing encouragement (Copper, 2023). Responding to the exhortations of university leaders that directors prioritise the needs of the institution over those of the library also makes sense (Baker, D. and Allden, 2017; Cooper, Hill and Schonfeld, 2022). A reminder that 'the wider contribution was why the librarian was there at the top table when the university opened' (Davies, 2020, 232) remains relevant. Strategy should be continuously informed by the positioning components identified in Chapter 2, namely clarity of identity, distinctiveness from competitors and an intimate understanding of audience needs, all supported by impactful communications and aligned resources. It is no coincidence that library directors with a well-developed strategy to meet changing user needs more commonly feel part of their institutional leadership (Frederick and Wolff-Eisenberg, 2020b).

Identity blurring

An accumulation of factors noted in separate contexts throughout this book has combined to blur the identity of academic libraries and generate attendant risks. Developments in technology and in higher education have again proved influential.

Chapter 2 highlighted clarity of identity as a key component of positioning strategy, impacting 'the extent to which the marketplace understands what the library is and has to offer' (Walters, S. and Jackson, 2013, 11). Prior to the digital era, there was a relatively clear and straightforward understanding of what academic libraries represented. Typically, printed collections dominated a large library building at the centre of the campus, essential to the academic enterprise and symbolising a cumulating scholarly record (Dempsey and Malpas, 2018). The gradual overtaking of print by digital information disrupted, extended and dispersed the academic library offering as new user needs, expectations and possibilities emerged. The winds of change blowing through higher education also impacted the library identity. The institutional agenda broadened and spawned new units operating in areas close to libraries, notably learning and research support. Boundaries became more porous, encouraging partnership and more fluid approaches to project work and distributed service delivery. One effect of all these forces for academic libraries has been a less distinct identity, increasingly blurred with other entities.

There are many manifestations of a more diffuse library identity. The reinvention of academic libraries has scattered their involvement across the student learning journey and the research cycle. Buildings are very different, with collections far less prominent amid a mix of spaces which includes support for creativity and well-being. Library staff are often not the only service providers in the building, as other units may also be hosted, delivering academic and technical supports under the umbrella of student success (Lewis, 2016). A previous trend, known as superconvergence and operational in England primarily, expanded the scope of such library-hosted services to encompass areas such as registry, finance and counselling (Appleton, 2010). This meant a convenient co-location of more services for students but reduced clarity of scholarly and professional identity for academic libraries (Melling, 2013; Cox, A. M. and Brewster, 2019). Furthermore, the previous section of this chapter noted that, as institutions grapple with increased structural complexity, academic libraries may find themselves grouped in new organisational configurations with professional services rather than reporting to the academic leader of the institution. From a user perspective this merges their identity with that of other service units.

Blurring with other providers is also at play in many newer areas of academic library engagement such as digital and open scholarship, research data management, digital literacy and institutional research. These are multi-partner ventures and services are not exclusively owned by or associated with academic libraries, whose contribution may not always be obvious. Another feature linked to library identity is that emerging roles have generated new posts requiring specialist skills often only available by hiring staff from professional backgrounds beyond librarianship. Examples include software developers, statisticians, instructional designers, learning technologists and publishers (Gwyer, 2015; Adams Becker et al., 2017; Harrison, 2018). The library staffing profile is therefore far less uniform and distinctive than previously.

As academic library roles diversify it becomes harder to identify a core skillset. A report of the responses of 830 qualified academic librarians to a 2017/18 survey revealed that only ten of 53 skills, aptitudes and knowledge areas were identified as core by more than 50% of the respondents (Saunders, 2020). Only three of the ten were specific to academic libraries, with the other seven comprised of generic skills such as communication and customer service. Many definitions of professional identity emerged from another survey of over 700 information professionals (Campbell-Meier and Hussey, 2018), suggesting that library staff are challenged to project a consistent and distinctive identity even among themselves, much less to their user communities. A further source of identity confusion applies in the USA, where professional librarians hold faculty status at some institutions but not at others, with variations in implementation even where operational (Freedman, 2014; Walters, W. H., 2016).

This range of roles, staff backgrounds, hosted services and co-delivery with other providers, coupled with a lack of clarity among library staff themselves, means that people are unsure about the identity of the academic library. Interviews with senior stakeholders at UK institutions revealed disagreement about what a library is and does (Pinfield, Cox and Rutter, 2017), while Freedman (2014) has noted the absence of a clear and consistent understanding of staff roles as a daily reality. This represents a threat along similar lines to the consequences noted for stakeholder misperceptions in Chapter 6, including lower visibility and less recognition for the library alongside a tendency to underestimate its contribution. Credit may be diluted or given to others, especially when services are experienced on screen rather than in person, with potential for negative impact on library resourcing. An unclear identity may also breed insecurity and lack of confidence among library staff.

There are mitigating factors, however. Academic libraries are not alone in experiencing changed and less solid identities. Chapter 4 noted major shifts for academic staff, including increased specialisation of employment and unbundling of functions (Macfarlane, 2011). The student body has diversified hugely, while universities themselves have long remained unsettled (Barnett,

2022). Demarcations between academic and other staff have been dissolving, creating a Third Space for cross-campus collaborations in learning support and other areas where libraries can leverage their connectedness (Whitchurch, 2008; 2013; Salisbury and Peseta, 2018). Reinvention and collaboration have realised many benefits for academic libraries, including a much more versatile value proposition and skills profile via multi-professional teams.

Identity is important for academic library positioning and a lack of clarity and distinctiveness is disadvantageous. The idea of a 'brand crisis' is unwelcome (Walters, S. and Jackson, 2013, 11), but the reality is that the library identity is more blurred today. Metaphors, running to 26 in one list (Salisbury and Peseta, 2018), diverge greatly in what they convey, reflecting a difficulty noted in Chapter 2 in packaging academic library identity and value for concise and impactful communication. There is a risk of stretching the library agenda beyond core business and diluting its longstanding association with scholarship. Programming for student well-being is an area highlighted in this regard (Cox, A. M. and Brewster, 2019). The danger of being '"jack of all trades, masters of none"' has been voiced (Wales, 2018, 454). Chapter 2 highlighted a hazard which academic libraries would wish to avoid but to which identity blurring exposes them. This is confused positioning, whereby 'frequent changes and contradictory messages may simply confuse customers about a company's positioning' (Hooley et al., 2020, 175).

With regard to strategy, cultivating and communicating a clearer identity, focused on distinctiveness, merits attention. There is plenty of scope for accentuating features unique, singly or in combination, to academic libraries. These include enabling social and scholarly community, offering places of welcome, inclusion, contemplation, collective academic enterprise and 'soul', as well as living a set of constant and resonant values with service excellence and trust at the forefront. Heseltine (2020) is right in urging clarity and confidence of purpose. He identifies building knowledgeable communities as core, emphasising what the library is for more than what it does. A focus on what academic libraries can deliver uniquely or best is sensible (Lewis, 2016), while always remaining open to new involvements. Longevity on campus can be leveraged, too, as a solid basis for contemporary identity. Adapting continuously to a changing campus environment is important and this includes working successfully with an expanding range of partners while also maintaining distinctiveness from them. Davies helpfully encourages academic libraries to acknowledge, embrace and navigate more complex organisations, including their '"blurred" areas' (Davies, 2020, 232), in a spirit of confidence and reciprocity.

Reflective journal extract 8.1
An identity dilemma

From the author's journal: 2 April 2021
The other 'political' dimension in play this week was [hosting] the Student Success Hub. I was glad of the opportunity to socialise this among Library staff on Wednesday and could sense a dilemma I also feel – let's be generous in supporting student success by inviting others in to provide services, but let's not compromise the identity of the Library. A balancing act . . . and we need to proceed with good judgement, but to avoid insularity as this [Library building transformation] is a University project.

Competition

Chapter 4 characterised higher education as a highly competitive environment, with institutions striving against each other for funding and vying with other providers, all fuelled by an increasingly consumerist and discerning student perspective. This translates within these institutions into a similarly competitive 'internal market for resource, visibility and attention' (Appleton, 2018, 209). Money is tight and the challenge for academic libraries is to be not only essential but to be 'seen by our stakeholders as *more essential than the other essential programs and projects that are competing for the same resources*' (Anderson, 2016, 3). As recently as 1991 Atkins commented on a lack of jurisdictional challenge to libraries from other parties but a major shift has occurred since then, generating intensified competition from within and, even more so, from without.

Atkins (1991) identified the computer centre as the major on-campus rival for libraries from the 1960s. Others emerged with the expansion of higher education institutions, as outlined already in this chapter. Partnerships, but also overlaps, have developed between academic libraries and these departments around services, infrastructure, advice, space and information management (Dempsey, 2015). There can be a fine line between collaboration and competition in partnerships, for example with the research office in open access and research information management, with the IT department in relation to research data management and with the teaching and learning development unit to advance digital literacy and open educational resources. It has been observed that others could provide some services offered by libraries or assert primacy and leadership in newer areas such as open scholarship and managing research data, with implications for resourcing and position (Verbaan and Cox, 2014; Pinfield, Cox and Rutter, 2017).

Jurisdiction is at stake also in the expanding range of engagements spawned by Third Space working, highlighted as an opportunity earlier in this chapter but also carrying some threat. The Third Space is defined as 'an emergent territory between academic and professional domains, which is colonised primarily by less bounded forms of professional' (Whitchurch, 2008, 377). It involves a range of collaborations, including learning skills development, student well-being and institutional research. The risk for academic libraries lies in the regular contestation for leadership posed by unbounded actors who may assert themselves more strongly and leave library staff trailing or unrecognised in areas where they have much to contribute, for example bibliometric analysis and study skills.

The toughest competition comes from beyond the campus where well-resourced commercial entities have developed systems and services not only to rival academic libraries but also to capture user traffic from them. Obvious examples are the popular and easy-to-use discovery tools provided by Google and the rapid supply of publications by Amazon. Publishing companies, notably Elsevier, have acquired or developed services to support academic workflows, including writing, reference management, publication and data storage (Kramer and Bosman, 2015; Dempsey, 2016). Scholarly social networks such as ResearchGate and Academia.edu enable authors to facilitate open access to their publications. Research information management represents another significant area of campus penetration for publishers and other providers. Artificial intelligence is an emerging source of competition, likely to encourage further self-sufficiency in areas currently supported by libraries.

The key threat for academic libraries is disintermediation as users bypass their offerings in favour of those available elsewhere. There is ample evidence of this. The 2021 Ithaka S+R US faculty survey indicates that twice the proportion of respondents, 29%, began their searches on Google Scholar compared with the 14% starting with their library's website or catalogue (Blankstein, 2022). Another survey of 1,600 early-career researchers recorded a figure of 39% using Google Scholar to a great extent, probably an underestimate (Nicholas et al., 2020). Other studies of different cohorts of early-career researchers in the same project are discouraging for libraries. The general finding in one is of a limited role and visibility for libraries in discovery, with their systems seen as cumbersome relative to Google (Nicholas et al., 2017). More recently, strong uptake of ResearchGate, Academia.edu and Sci-Hub is reported based on their convenience and regardless of copyright issues (Herman et al., 2023). Returning to faculty, cloud-based or commercial services emerge as far more favoured than library solutions for research data storage and preservation in one survey (Blankstein, 2022), while only one of eight researchers interviewed in 2019 about ways of keeping up with the literature mentioned the library (Archer et al., 2019).

Disintermediation is a major negative by itself, but it creates others too. It helps to feed a perception, consistently supported via strong agreement by a fifth of respondents to a triennial survey of US faculty, that the role of the librarian is becoming much less important because of easy access to academic content online (Blankstein, 2022). Furthermore, a slightly lower percentage strongly agreed that for the same reason money spent on library buildings and staff should be redirected to other institutional needs. Within the campus, competition from other departments, often astute at promoting and positioning themselves for credit, has been a factor in the halving of the library's share of institutional expenditure.

There are counterweights to the threats that intensified competition brings. Chapter 2 emphasised the positive associations for positioning of having been the first provider in any space, as libraries can claim for access to information. It is notable in one study that early-career researchers in the USA and UK make little use of alternative providers if library collections are strong and easily accessible (Herman et al., 2023). Competition is not new and the reinvention of academic libraries shows how they have been able to navigate it over time. Like collaboration, competition can stimulate innovation and improved services.

Competition represents a significant positioning challenge for academic libraries, however. Distinctiveness from competitors emerged in Chapter 2 as one of the key components of positioning. One of the issues it raises is where to compete and invest or cede to others and divert resources elsewhere. An example is discovery, traditionally a library stronghold but now operating at network level and increasingly 'routed around, rather than through, the library' (Schonfeld, 2014, 5). There are also some notable brakes on academic library competitiveness. Economic weakness inhibits investment, while conservatism obstructs innovation and legacy printed collections absorb resources. Perceptions of library competitiveness relative to other entities are a concern, especially in the case of early-career researchers as likely long-term library users and influencers.

Ensuring maximum competitiveness is a key consideration for academic library strategy in a highly competitive operating environment. Academic libraries can punch considerable weight as one of the largest departments on most campuses and Chapter 2 proposed an assertive approach to positioning. How this looks will vary per institution, but it may include claiming leadership proactively in areas such as open scholarship and contributing to institutional competitiveness by fully leveraging library assets, including archives and special collections, institutional repositories and transformed buildings (Cox, J., 2021). Optimising the use of resources to maximise support for innovation focused on providing solutions in areas of pressing need for users is also important (Mathews, 2014a).

Actively monitoring competitors and learning from them is a priority, as is differentiating from them through local knowledge, personal service, relationships and trust. Finding an appropriate balance with local partners between collaboration and competition for recognition and resources is challenging but important (Pinfield, Cox and Rutter, 2017). It is difficult to handle competition from providers operating at scale beyond the campus. Often it may make more sense to complement and add value to the services of such entities than to compete with them, while seeking out opportunities where effective collaborative solutions across institutions can be realised selectively, for example around shared infrastructure (Dempsey, 2018b).

Uncertainty

Volatility both at global level and in the higher education system has manifested itself repeatedly throughout this book. The global landscape features political tensions and polarisation, economic vulnerability, climate change as an existential threat and the increasing power of technology, all adding up to a potent cocktail of instability. Areas of uncertainty for higher education include funding, student enrolment numbers, skills for future employment, evolving pathways to qualifications and increasing levels of government intervention. In combination these can create concerns about their ongoing viability for some institutions. Speculation about the future of the world strikes an ominous tone, notably the previously referenced calculation in one publication of a 41% chance for a potentially catastrophic event to occur within five years (Peston and Koria, 2023).

Academic libraries operate in this unstable environment, as an examination of the recent biennial top trends identified for the sector by the ACRL reflects. Fake news first appeared in 2018, as did AI and machine learning in 2020, followed by COVID-related trends in 2022 and politicisation linked to anti-DEI legislation in 2024 (ACRL Research Planning Review Committee, 2018; 2020; 2022; 2024). The current section of this chapter is a mirror image of that about opportunities in the wider world in Chapter 7. Uncertainty resulting from the instability generated by forces in that same environment is the opposite side of the coin. A close connectivity between opportunities and threats is evident in the consideration which follows of academic libraries' experience of uncertainty.

Staff in academic libraries exhibit a cognisance of uncertainty as a reality in their working lives. Over 250 UK academic library staff respondents were offered a list of 30 political, economic, social and technological trends in one survey but reached no consensus on the major ones and considered each to have some potential to transform their libraries (Pinfield, Cox and Rutter,

2017). In a related study, directors were also unable to come to a common view when asked in interviews to identify three key trends impacting academic libraries in the next decade. The authors saw this finding as reinforcing 'the sense of a profession in a state of uncertainty' (Cox, A. M., Pinfield and Rutter, 2019a, 504). Twelve directors interviewed in another study identified increasing uncertainty via uncontrollable external factors as a major challenge, highlighting impacts on budgets and changes in institutional strategic focus (Harland, Stewart and Bruce, 2018).

That sense of uncertainty carrying threat has proved well founded in the current decade. The most obvious instance has been the onset of the COVID-19 pandemic in 2020, which closed academic libraries for periods of time and wrought lasting change in user behaviours. The year 2022 has attracted less comment but is highly instructive due to the combination of factors involved with little forewarning. The outbreak of war in Ukraine, energy shortages, inflation, stock market turmoil, climate events and cybercrime joined forces to cause major disruption (Roubini, 2023). Academic libraries experienced change across a broad spectrum, including damage or destruction, reduced purchasing power, curtailed opening hours and loss of access to digital resources. The recency of these experiences and fears of any repetition cast a shadow of uncertainty over future thinking.

Two specific areas of unpredictability for academic libraries are of note. The first is AI, identified as an opportunity in Chapter 7 but also simultaneously referenced as a potential threat. A further event marking the significance of the year 2022 was, as previously noted, the launch of ChatGPT. This brought generative AI into the mainstream, with ongoing uncertainty regarding user behaviours and implications for academic library roles. Other areas of unpredictability for libraries are the extent to which AI will impact cataloguing via automatic metadata generation, the match of staff skills to emerging roles, competition from other professions and possible domination by commercial operators alongside the potential for job losses (Griffey, 2019; Cox, A. M., 2021). Furthermore, the nature of library digital collections could change fundamentally if they are seen as data, able to be searched and mined collectively without any need for differentiation by document type (Cox, A. M., 2021).

The future of scholarly communication is the second sphere of uncertainty highlighted. Academic libraries have strongly promoted universal open access but appear to have given less consideration to how its full realisation would impact their own operations, notably staff deployment. This could diminish their buyer role, with which faculty most commonly associate them (Blankstein, 2022), as well as the extent of their own collection control and curation activities. Organisational and role changes in a core area of activity for academic libraries would seem to be in prospect but how and when these will happen is far from certain. In the interim a lack of local policies relating to open access issues has been identified, raising concerns regarding readiness for change (Scott, Harrington and Dubnjakovic, 2021).

Uncertainty represents a threat with downsides for academic libraries. It denies them a stable long-term base into the future. There is a sense of striving to keep pace with moving targets as institutional priorities and user behaviours shift, while technology keeps changing the game. Funding is insecure for libraries and their parent institutions in the face of competition and economic unpredictability which keeps the risk of a global crash in the offing. Roles can feel unsettled, while polarisation, populism and fake news threaten library values. Being at the mercy of events in the outside world beyond their control is difficult as staff in academic libraries wonder what is coming next. On the upside, an unstable world also generates opportunities. Chapter 7 identified greater agility and other gains arising from the COVID-19 pandemic, as well as roles for the academic library in creating knowledgeable communities to combat disinformation, supporting research integrity and acting as an exemplar of sustainability practices. A further mitigation is that uncertainty is far from exclusive to academic libraries and is a shared experience throughout and beyond the campus.

Stock market investors dislike uncertainty. It is problematic for academic libraries, too, and poses a significant threat to their current and future work. The nature of the threat lies in the difficulty it creates for immediate operations and long-term planning. This in turn makes it hard to take decisions on investment or indeed disinvestment, to commit to definite organisational changes, to communicate effectively and to position the library clearly in its parent institution, which itself is typically also experiencing a lot of instability. It is perhaps unsurprising therefore that only a third of US library directors surveyed in 2022 strongly agreed that their library had a well-developed strategy to match evolving user needs and research habits (Hulbert, 2023). The reality is that academic libraries 'need to rebuild the airplane while it is in the air and we get to do so without the aid of blueprints' (Lewis, 2016, xiii).

Academic libraries have experienced uncertainty across their history, notably through two world wars, various economic recessions and the emergence of digital information, while Neal (2015) has observed an intensification of anxiety and urgency since the 1990s. They can expect that it will continue to be a fact of life and the best strategy would seem to be to embrace it as part of 'a permanent process of ongoing realignment' (Cooper, Hill and Schonfeld, 2022, 23). This will call for agility, creativity, risk and a willingness to change direction, sometimes at short notice (Stoffle and

Cuillier, 2010). User behaviour drives library roles and staying close to the changing needs of their audiences while continuously researching the external environment will be a worthwhile investment (Jantz, 2017b). Shaping change is possible through dialogue with suppliers and adapting local funding models towards an evolving open access environment (Lewis et al., 2022). The values of academic libraries also offer a vital anchor amid instability alongside previous experience of navigating uncertainty.

Reflective journal extract 8.2
The shock of the COVID-19 pandemic

From the author's journal: 21 March 2020

We are all in a different place this week with the spread of the coronavirus which I'd mentioned towards the end of last week's entry . . . It's also been said that it feels like the outbreak of world war must have done – total uncertainty and normal living suspended. It really is a worry in so many ways – will we all survive this? . . . It's going to be a bit strange trying to keep some level of library service going from off campus, but I'm impressed with the effort everyone is making around that. . . . I'm finding that each day is long and full of new situations to be addressed as well as lots of online meetings . . . it's all very intense and working online so much, including vast swathes of email about all kinds of topics, e.g. copyright, is really tiring.

Conclusion

Decline in position, identity blurring, competition and uncertainty are threats to academic libraries with the potential to damage their position and positioning. Table 8.1 encapsulates their impact and implications, while the next chapter includes a collective analysis of the strengths, weaknesses, opportunities and threats identified in Part 2 and looks for points of interaction, overlap and contradiction.

Table 8.1 *Academic library threats and their influence*

Threat	Negatives	Counterweights	Significance	Strategy implications
Decline in position	• Lower position in hierarchy • Reduced budget, influence	• Usually aligned with academic units • Still central, well connected	• Less noticed, more under-estimated • Insecurity, pessimism	• Prioritise institutional agenda • Capitalise on COVID gains

Continued

Table 8.1 Continued

Threat	Negatives	Counterweights	Significance	Strategy implications
Identity blurring	• Brand less distinctive • Credit diluted • Unclear professional identity	• Longevity • Productive partnerships • Blurred identities of other groups	• Users unsure of library identity • Potential for confused positioning	• Emphasise unique value • Communicate distinct purpose • Work across boundaries
Competition	• Service ownership unclear • User traffic captured by others • Struggling to compete	• First provider recognition • Ongoing library reinvention	• Library bypassed • Resourcing questioned • Perceived as insufficiently competitive	• Maximise competitiveness • Assert position • Balance local collaboration and competition
Uncertainty	• Volatile operating environment • Aiming at moving targets • Sudden disruption	• Instability creates opportunities • Previous resilience and adaptability	• Catastrophic events possible • Long-term planning compromised	• Be agile and embrace uncertainty • Scan the environment • Use values as anchor

PART 3

Position and Positioning Strategies

Introduction to Part 3

The final part of the book builds on earlier coverage across its four chapters. The combination of external influences in Part 1 and of strengths, weaknesses, opportunities and threats in Part 2 underpins the assessment of the contemporary position of academic libraries in Chapter 9. It aims to make sense of complexity, recognising that any such assessment is challenging and needs to avoid the temptation to deliver a neat, over-simplified summation. The reality is that many factors are at play, some helpful and others unfavourable towards the library position. A collective review of the SWOT analysis comprising Part 2 finds contradiction alongside linearity. The future looks equally multifaceted, as portended by three intensifying trends explored.

Chapter 10 draws upon the messages emerging from the overall analysis to date to identify ten positioning strategies aimed at advancing the academic library within its parent institution. The first strategy, position the library actively, serves as a base for the other nine, which emphasise leveraging natural advantages assertively while addressing deficits and approaching the operating environment with a positive mentality. This chapter has a practical focus and the same is true of Chapter 11, which incorporates a selection of resources to support academic libraries in their positioning work. The concluding chapter provides a reminder of the learnings emerging from a deeper understanding of the external and internal worlds of academic libraries and what these mean for their future position and positioning.

CHAPTER 9

The Position of Academic Libraries Today: Making Sense of Complexity

Overview

Chapter 9 offers an assessment of the position academic libraries currently occupy, comprising:

- an introduction to the complexity, variables and constants inherent in any evaluation of academic library position;
- a reminder of the key influencing factors in the world at large and in higher education;
- consideration of academic library position across multiple dimensions;
- a summary of the library profile on campus;
- how own goals by academic libraries have contributed to their position;
- collective analysis of the strengths, weaknesses, opportunities and threats identified in Chapters 5–8, including some parallels with the experience of professional services in higher education;
- discussion of some intensifying trends with potential to shape future position;
- conclusions on current position and vital juncture in relation to the future.

Introduction

This chapter attempts to summarise the position of academic libraries today – a challenging task, as there are so many variables at play. It is necessary at the outset to acknowledge the complexity of the wider global and higher education environments alongside the long and lengthening agendas of academic libraries and their parent institutions. Higher education institutions make choices according to scale and resourcing about where they can differentiate and be most competitive. Their libraries in turn differ from those at other institutions due to a multiplicity of local factors, including funding, leadership, quality of skills and personnel, location in the organisational hierarchy and the institutional areas of emphasis and priority to which they align (Dempsey and Malpas, 2018). Generalisation about the position of academic libraries in a collective sense is therefore difficult.

There are, however, some constants amid their ongoing evolution and variety of experience. The key drivers of academic library development cited for the 1980s endure today, namely: 'changes in higher education; budget cuts, variations in management and governance, changes in scholarly communication; changes in technology; changes in disciplinary and individual scholarly interest; changes in the ways services and resources are provided' (Simons, 2017, 3). To these can be added many newer factors, but one longstanding and vital influence on library position is notably absent from the list. This is user perspective, which in turn drives behaviour. Anderson (2011) points out that perception matters more than reality and that how users perceive the value offered by libraries will determine their future, a point echoed by Mathews in his observation that 'Our future will be defined by how well we understand our users' (Mathews, 2014a, 21). One further constant is that academic libraries continue to preoccupy themselves with their own position as a matter of great importance. This manifests itself in debates in the library literature about relevance and potential obsolescence (Salisbury and Peseta, 2018), while 'library directors are eternally concerned with discerning their role and function within the changing organization and sector' (Gwyer, 2018, 433).

The consideration of current academic library position in this chapter takes a multidimensional approach, cognisant of variations but also continuities and common features, while informed by a summary in the next section of the most influential factors in the operating environment.

Influences in the external environment

The global and higher education environments provide essential context for understanding the position of academic libraries. Chapters 3 and 4 respectively described a range of factors in each case and this section selects a number of these as a brief reminder of their significance. Some of them represent uncomfortable territory for higher education institutions and academic libraries.

Globalisation is an overarching factor, facilitating high connectivity between people, services and resources but also vulnerability to events, trade disruption, diseases and natural disasters. Politically, polarisation of opinion has been on the increase, often with contestation over social justice issues and a hostility towards expertise and authority fomented by the rapid spread of fake news and alternative truths. Conditions foreshadowing a global economic crash exist, notably via exceptional and escalating levels of government and private debt, while increased protectionism brings higher inflation and trade disruption. Climate change is constantly in the news through a mix of destructive events and forecasts of disaster whose mitigation will be difficult and costly. Increased digitalisation is a marked feature of the post-COVID world, while the rise of AI gathers momentum for both good and ill, bringing uncertainty in its slipstream. The 21st-century world has already experienced enough unanticipated events to erode former certainties and serve as a warning of more shocks to come (Roubini, 2023).

Higher education is impacted by the features just described. An underpinning characteristic of its own environment, except for a small proportion of wealthier institutions, is a very tight resourcing climate regardless of whether government intervention is strong or weak. This creates a high level of competition in which survival is far from guaranteed and institutional closures are not uncommon. Although student participation is at record levels in many countries, there is a risky dependence on revenue from international students. A progressively more consumerist outlook among students has raised expectations of flexible course delivery and experiential learning alongside high-quality services and facilities. Institutions are grappling with the optimal integration of AI in teaching and research. Government and public scrutiny of the actions and outcomes of higher education continues to intensify, while campuses have become more politicised, promoting protest, challenges to DEI and greater emphasis on civic literacy (Pelletier et al., 2024). The dynamics of on-campus life also include greater numbers and influence of administrative staff in more complex institutions and a corresponding disaffection among academic staff amid a deterioration in their employment conditions and a more pressurised existence which promotes competitive individualism (Fitzpatrick, 2019). Institutions continue to operate according to a decentralised form of organisation, with many autonomous but often conservative actors in an increasingly competitive atmosphere on campus.

Outline of the position of academic libraries

This section outlines the contemporary academic library position, drawing on previous chapters and taking into account especially the influence of the factors identified by the SWOT analysis in Part 2. Many elements are involved, categorised here as pluses and minuses, while recognising that the overall picture is less simple than such a division might suggest.

Pluses

Longevity is a foundational feature of the academic library as an established and expected campus entity, able to call on a depth of experience in its parent institution and in higher education. It has proved resilient, responsive and adaptable in the face of major change and challenge across eight centuries (Weiner, 2005; Marcum, 2017) and this provides a solid bedrock for engaging with ongoing disruption. Also helpful is its longstanding association with scholarship, distinguishing it from a growing number of administrative units on campus and linking it closely to the academic mission. Writers about the idea of the university have 'recognized the importance of the library as an institutional common ground that . . . continues to resonate with ideas of the university as place for cultural and intellectual pursuits where knowledge is expanded for the common good' (Salisbury and Peseta, 2018, 247).

The collections of academic libraries are at the core of their strong association with intellectual work as a vital, if no longer exclusively offered, source of access to the scholarly record. They represent the most readily identified library contribution to the academic endeavour of its community, ranging from unique historical archives and special collections to mainstream and obscure journals accessible at the touch of a button. As described in Chapter 1, collections dominated the identity and purpose of academic libraries from their earliest days. Increasingly digital, they remain central to their service portfolio today, still foregrounded in the narrative of library mission statements (Heseltine, 2020) and forming the basis of many involvements generated by the more diversified library value proposition. The functions linked to managing collections consume significant staff time, generating concerns, particularly when the use of printed material is declining, about how to resource engagement with newer areas of activity (Anderson, 2011; Lewis, 2016). Within such calculations preservation is, however, acknowledged as a key responsibility (Schlak, 2022a).

In tandem with collections, its building continues to constitute a large part of the library identity and offering, having at most institutions undergone a transformation in which user experience is prioritised over the presentation of collections. Reimagined library buildings represent a strong return on institutional investment, highly frequented, aligned with learning directions and used for a multiplicity of purposes from group collaboration to individual contemplation. Maintaining distinctiveness from similar learning spaces located at a smaller scale elsewhere on many campuses may be an issue (Heseltine, 2020). Nevertheless, communal physical space, usually at the centre of the campus, positions the academic library as an interdisciplinary hub and connector, while an enlightened approach to sharing space and hosting other services has extended the scope of the offering.

The staff of the academic library are key to fulfilling its connector role and indeed to everything else it does. They are typically committed, values-driven, service-oriented and collaborative, with a skills base enhanced by recruitment from a diversity of professions. As a result, they tend to be well regarded and strongly integrated as trusted partners and advisers with valued traditional and new expertise. Academic libraries are, in the main, well run. Williams points to the quality of their management practices and service development methodologies which 'put them in a good position to respond to change however it may be triggered' (Williams, C. A., 2025, 123). This was particularly evident to, and recognised by, their institutions during the COVID-19 pandemic (Frederick and Wolff-Eisenberg, 2020a). Library directors sometimes lead wider campus functions too, including student-facing services, digital education, research or digital scholarship (Schonfeld, 2016; Gwyer, 2018).

Numerous points of distinctiveness contribute to the position of academic libraries. They actively live the values they espouse, promoting generosity, equality and an orientation towards academic freedom and the public good which sits well with their audiences. This helps to ensure that a high degree of trust is invested in them as an excellent foundation for good relationships with their communities. The trust they enjoy positions them well for effective engagement with major issues in today's world, notably social justice, research integrity, sustainability and the ethics of AI. Academic libraries also represent a unique place of community on campus, an egalitarian and welcoming space which is open to all, largely free of charge and a location where people can not only learn but can linger, relax and exchange emotional support (Moran, 2020).

The community role of their buildings is but one element in the general connectedness of academic libraries. They are highly social and relationship-based organisations, operating in an increasingly participatory environment (Corrall, 2022c). People meet through library events and exhibitions and library staff connect members of their community who have shared interests. Staff are well placed to observe and report on trends in learning and other areas of significance for the institution at large. Libraries are effective collaborators and leaders of collaborative ventures, generating goodwill along the way which often opens other doors to contribution and achievement. They are global entities, publishing resources to worldwide audiences, influencing change in scholarly communication and participating in the wider world to support the social mission of their institutions (Corrall, 2022a).

This consideration of positives towards the position of academic libraries concludes with a digest of the ways in which they are an asset to their parent institutions through a combination of traditional and new value. As already noted, collections remain vital to teaching and research, while archives of academic, historic, global, national or regional significance often confer prestige and reputational gain on the institution. The library value proposition has broadened hugely since digital information displaced the centrality of printed collections. A more versatile contribution, embedded across the whole learning and research lifecycle and founded on community and connectedness, is now evident. Libraries act as collaborators, creators, connectors, facilitators and guides, with a focus on student success and positive student experience through information literacy and well-being support alongside deeper engagement with research via partnership in digital scholarship and publishing. They connect strongly with external audiences too, but their primary influence is on campus where, in recognition of their centrality to an increasingly vital sense of community, they have been described as the 'quintessence of our collegiality' (Moran, 2020).

Minuses

Factors unfavourable to the position of academic libraries, sometimes rooted within the positive features just identified as pluses, have also emerged throughout this book. Conservatism inhibits academic libraries from reaching their full potential. While they have adapted to change, their tendency has been to do so on their own terms, accommodating it within existing parameters. Schlak and Macklin (2022) call this 'horizontal development', instancing the ready application to digital resources of the functions, skills and financial models established for printed collections. This example of growing smoothly into related domains rather than seeking out transformative approaches on better terms has helped to trap them in a dysfunctional economic model for journals, which denies them resources to advance their position in other areas. Favouring predictability and well defined processes also obstructs greater experimentation and innovation.

Another inhibiting feature of conservatism is an inclination to prioritise internal business at the expense of fuller external engagement and wider visibility. This has promoted a damaging perception in some quarters that the library could and should be doing more than it is to advance the wider institutional agenda. One study revealed that 'many university leader interviewees felt this prioritization of the university over the library was not really the case under current or recent library leadership' (Cooper, Hill and Schonfeld, 2022, 17). Another report recorded an observation that the library tended to keep itself to itself, also questioning a failure to share its digital expertise for the benefit of the institution (Baker, D. and Allden, 2017). Benign neglect by stakeholders represents a further unhelpful view of the library, leading to it being taken for granted and getting limited attention, partly because it is well managed. The actual or potential contribution of academic libraries is often misunderstood or poorly understood by institutional leaders, commonly resulting in underestimation or lack of recognition.

Understanding the academic library fully has, however, become more difficult due to the diversification of its value proposition and in turn the lengthening of its agenda. Willenborg and Detmering (2024) observe in the context of student success that other units find it easier to define their contribution than the library, because its range of engagements is so broad, making it difficult to present a coherent and resonant summary to the institution. The broadening of library activities beyond their previous core has featured as a positive in the previous section but communicating and measuring their often-intangible value can be challenging. Partnership is generally healthy, but library contributions may be hidden under the broad umbrella of multi-party delivery. Users may struggle to understand the identity of the library, with one academic noting that 'the library's purpose is now in question. Is it just a study hall where students gather to work? A high-tech teaching space? Or merely the physical infrastructure for housing various campus functions, like coffee shops, advising centers or even an honors college?' (Mintz, 2024).

There is a growing sense even among academic library staff of a lack of clarity about core purpose and what the future holds. Heseltine (2020) has pointed out the dangers of confusing impact with purpose and emphasising what the library does as opposed to what it stands for, all reflective of a lack of staff confidence. Baker cites Walton's concerns with the dilution of the library brand through alternative terminology, concluding that 'The key message is not to be afraid of the 'L' word' (Baker, D., 2017, 12). For Mathews (2014a, 17), 'We should constantly be asking *what business are we in*?', offering books, information, learning, content and research as options before settling on 'the business of being intellectual platforms'. When future uncertainty regarding the impact of AI and changes in scholarly communication is factored in, the academic library's sense of its own position feels somewhat unsettled.

Politically, the academic library can find itself distant from the centre of power in the institution. This is not a new situation, highlighted also by McAnally and Downs (1973) and Atkins (1991) more than 50 and 30 years ago respectively. Deficits in the understanding of academic libraries and underestimation of what they contribute doubtless play a part in this, alongside the emergence of new competitors, priorities and complexities in their parent institutions. Very few directors report to the head of the institution today, although the library continues to be most commonly if by no means always located on the academic side of the organisational hierarchy. A perception that leadership of 'problem areas' is required to ascend the institutional ladder and that the library is not one of those is concerning (Gwyer, 2018, 440). Such thinking does not bode well for an increased presence of library directors at the top table.

The economic position of academic libraries is difficult and this too is not a recent phenomenon. It is characterised by typically static budgets which represent a declining share of institutional expenditure and are no match for rising costs. Supporting an expanding agenda is challenging in its own right but much harder when so much of the budget is accounted for by recurrent subscription costs, which have increased at a rate well above average inflation over a long period of time, generating an ongoing affordability challenge. Open scholarship offers an opportunity for significant economic change, but this will not happen quickly and improved resourcing seems unlikely in the interim as higher education institutions are also in a funding struggle.

None of this helps the position of academic libraries in terms of their ability to compete. They operate in an intensely competitive environment both on campus and in the face of powerful, much better resourced, companies operating globally. Libraries are in a fight for jurisdiction across a range of newer areas of activity where leadership by them is not guaranteed. In addition, they are experiencing disintermediation in spheres where they previously held sway, notably discovery and to some extent access. They find themselves in something of a vicious circle, needing to diversify into new areas in response to competition but struggling to resource those new ventures adequately when other recurrent commitments continue, leaving little discretionary funding available.

Reflective journal extract 9.1
A sharper edge

From the author's journal: 13 June 2015

I sense 'benign neglect', a long-time curse for the Library – we are good citizens who deliver the goods with no fuss. . . . There are opportunities and we need to leverage our strengths towards them – we have a good reputation and a track record of achievement but can be taken for granted. Showing a sharper edge may actually help – sometimes we have to say 'no' and be prepared to fight for our share of the action.

Summary profile

The academic library is a constant presence on campus and enjoys a high level of respectability as 'support for the library is still invoked somberly as a bedrock principle of academic seriousness' (Anderson, 2011, 290). It is generally perceived as a decent and trusted campus citizen, emphasising service, mutuality, collaboration and the public good, while striving hard amid stretched resources and keen competition. Although well versed in change, this is assimilated gradually. The library sometimes provides leadership on campus, for example in open scholarship, but it does not often feature as a trendsetter, power broker or high-profile actor. While its contributions now extend to many areas of campus activity and deliver a lot for the institution, it may act in an understated way and be missed out when credit is being given. Underestimation is both consequential and common, while frequently underpinned by a shallow understanding dressed up in platitudes such as '"everyone loves our library here"' (Cooper, Hill and Schonfeld, 2022, 16).

Understatement can be seen as a virtue, however, adding to the authenticity of the library as a counter to marketisation and epitomised by how its buildings 'slip into being a bit shabby in an agreeable way' (Lewis, 2017, 170). The academic library building is in fact a major element in its profile. It is a highly democratic space, socially important as a creator of campus community and valued for this even more during and since the COVID-19 pandemic. Its forced closure provoked an emotional response which highlighted the sentimental place it continues to occupy for many, centred in one outpouring around 'the sounds of its muffled diligence and . . . its less muted gigglings, munchings and canoodlings' (Chambers et al., 2020). The framing of the academic library as a whole is highly varied, from a persistent association with books to a sense that the web makes it redundant in turn to fulsome appreciation that 'Few professions have been so far-sighted, so collaborative, and so forthright in action' (Alexander, 2020, 35). Academic libraries face many challenges, and may not always be known for what they would prefer to be known for, but they retain a strong and multifaceted profile on their campuses.

Own goals in academic library position

Many of the factors shaping the position of academic libraries are beyond their control – for example global political events or developments in technology with consequent shifts in user behaviour. Other influences are, however, controllable, including the deployment of resources, the messages that are projected, how time is spent and what skills and mindsets are developed. Academic libraries have failed in some instances to control their controllables and these failures are characterised as own goals in this section. All have featured in previous chapters and are brought together in summary form here.

- *Inward focus*, already referenced repeatedly in this chapter for its impact on library underestimation, is a longstanding issue. As far back as 1991 Atkins warned of undue emphasis on managing the library efficiently over promoting it to institutional leaders. That admonition remains relevant, as evidenced by Saunders' (2016) finding that only seven of the 63 academic library strategic plans she examined included goals relating to student recruitment, retention or other institutional success factors.
- *Hesitancy*, resulting in slow or limited engagement with emerging technologies, notably AI (Huang, Cox and Cox, 2023; Cox, A. M., 2023), and potentially key areas of contribution such as study skills and virtual learning environments (Heseltine, 2020). A failure to punch their full weight in digital humanities has been attributed to an 'academic inferiority complex' (Vandegrift and Varner, 2013, 76), while feelings of inequality have inhibited interactions with the research community more generally (Bryant, Dortmund and Lavoie, 2020).
- *Ineffective communications*, contributing to reduced impact and user misunderstandings. The need for more compelling communications has been identified elsewhere (Pinfield, Cox and Rutter, 2017) and also at regular intervals throughout the earlier SWOT analysis in this book, including in relation to stakeholder misperceptions and identity blurring.
- *Overuse of service terminology*. While service is a core value for academic libraries and is something they often champion in their communications, it is a term which audiences may view as somewhat passive and reactive (Connaway et al., 2017). This creates an unwanted association and works against the desire to project the academic library as a partner rather than a service provider in many ventures.
- *Blind spots inhibiting greater staffing diversity*. Chapter 6 highlighted a surprising unawareness of racial microaggressions in the workplace, inadequate focus on internal culture and a tendency in one study for more racially homogenous libraries to view themselves as more equitable in relation to ethnicity than the overall library community surveyed (Schonfeld and Sweeney, 2017).
- *Insufficient emphasis on research methods*. A lack of proficiency in data analysis and statistical methods, identified over a long period by Cheng and Hoffman (2020), alongside limited confidence in the quality of research in the library and information science field reported by the academic librarians they surveyed, is problematic. This is especially so when academic libraries increasingly need to rely on rigorous impact research to convince stakeholders of their value.

The key point linking the deficits just outlined is that they are all avoidable and academic libraries have the capacity to address them and improve their position.

SWOT analysis revisited

The Introduction to Part 2 emphasised how much its strengths, weaknesses, opportunities and threats influence the academic library's position, profile and potential for advance or decline. It is therefore timely to return to the SWOT analysis conducted in Chapters 5 to 8 and to consider the factors it identified in collective terms, including patterns, linkages and contradictions between them and some parallels with the experience of professional services staff on campus.

Table 9.1 provides a reminder of all 16 factors for easy reference. One immediately striking feature is the extent to which the emergence of digital information and services has shaped the analysis. It hastened the end of the library's monopoly on access to information, with many effects, including the decline in position, less clear identity and greater vulnerability to competition which have featured as threats. On a more positive note, however, it drove a major reinvention in role and contribution, realising new collaborations and transformed learning space as key elements in a diversified value proposition. Another point of note is the mix of factors either unique to academic libraries or commonly experienced in other sectors. The latter category includes competition, deficits in staffing diversity and uncertainty, especially around the potential impact of AI. Academic libraries can, however, point to some features specific to their world. Among these is the influence of their values on the level of trust they continue to enjoy at a time when so many institutions have lost public confidence. Others are the pedagogical and communal centrality of their buildings and, less happily, the peculiar dynamics and dysfunctionality of the journals market central to their economic situation.

Table 9.1 *Factors identified in earlier SWOT analysis of academic libraries*

Strengths	Weaknesses	Opportunities	Threats
Centrality	Conservatism	Open scholarship	Decline in position
Values	Stakeholder misperceptions	Artificial intelligence	Identity blurring
Collaboration	Economic struggles	Learning space	Competition
Reinvention	Diversity deficits	The wider world	Uncertainty

Connection, contradiction and complexity

One might expect routinely to find a linear progression from strengths and opportunities to positive influences on position and from weaknesses and threats to negative impact. There are many examples of this throughout the analysis both within each factor and in the linkages between them. The latter include the ways in which centrality promotes collaboration and the less favourable connection between stakeholder misperceptions and decline in position as well as economic struggles.

Contradictory effects are, however, surprisingly common. The frequent commentary about the centrality of the academic library to the life and work of the campus stands in marked contrast with the relatively low level of attention it often receives from institutional leaders. The goodwill it attracts should translate into strong resourcing support instead of a halving of its share of the institutional budget. Another contradictory reality, whereby the academic library 'belongs to everyone and to no one' (Budd, 2018, 213), is economically unhelpful, as noted in Chapter 6. Collaboration, although overall a strength, can also contribute to identity blurring and a dilution of recognition for the library, while there may also sometimes be a need to compete with partners. Although habituated towards conservatism, academic libraries have succeeded in reinventing themselves. Even so, they continue to be associated by many with their traditional book brand rather than the diverse elements of their newer value proposition.

Their values represent a source of strength for academic libraries but they, too, harbour contradictions. The most glaring instance is the contrast between diversity as a core value and the homogeneity of the typical library staffing profile. Neutrality has lost its resonance in the face of fake news, the decolonisation of collections, the advance of critical librarianship and library support for social justice. A 2024 survey responded to by 179 Canadian academic librarians identified higher negative sentiment towards neutrality compared with previous international averages and an expressed willingness to act in a non-neutral way in response to a number of the scenarios presented (Jaeger-McEnroe, 2024). Access is another library value, clearly relevant in the championing of change to realise universal open access to scholarly information. Counterintuitively, however, libraries continue through high recurrent payments to strengthen the dominant position of commercial publishers.

The boundaries between the categories in a SWOT analysis are porous and this holds especially true in the current study for opportunities and threats. Artificial intelligence, open scholarship and the wider world are listed as opportunities but could quite easily become threats. The situation is complex, with plenty of scope for AI to have negative impact. A major disruption to the collections function in academic libraries could occur if open access becomes the norm. Equally, the threat of uncertainty is ever-present as the obverse of opportunities in the wider world, depending on how different political, economic, social and technological developments fall.

Some parallels with professional services in higher education

By way of a very brief comparative perspective, it is interesting to note some commonality of experience between academic libraries and professional services on campus. Professional services comprise a diverse group, defined in one instance as 'a large community of university staff who perform administrative, student services, financial, technical and numerous other roles critical to organisational operations' (Veles, Graham and Ovaska, 2023, 127). Although generalisation is therefore hazardous, it is possible to identify some areas of intersection with the academic library SWOT analysis, specifically in terms of stakeholder misperceptions, reinvention and identity blurring.

Issues experienced by professional services staff with stakeholder misperceptions appear to centre on academic staff. The use of the designation non-academic, although largely superseded by the phrase professional services, persists and is seen as a form of 'othering' (Caldwell, 2024, 508) which denigrates expertise and defines staff by what they are not (Caldwell, 2022b). This feeds into a sense of underestimation familiar to academic library staff, alongside a lack of understanding and 'the continued idea that professional services are in the shadow of academic staff and not perceived as equals in terms of their contribution or value' (Caldwell, 2022a, 29). Invisibility has surfaced too, including an almost total absence of professional services from the literature of higher education (Szekeres, 2004), something which has also been observed for academic libraries (Munn, 1968; Weiner, 2005; Salisbury and Peseta, 2018).

Some of the above has been changed and challenged more recently by a reinvention in the roles and influence of professional services staff. This has been driven by changes in higher education which have demanded a different staff profile to support greater complexity, wider global engagement via internationalisation and heightened emphasis on the student experience (Veles, Graham and Ovaska, 2023). New and more specialist professional services roles, often at more senior levels, have emerged in teaching and learning development, student support, widening participation, research administration and quality. A particular feature has been the shift towards delivering in partnership with academic staff, breaking down the boundaries of the previous academic/administrative divide and characterised by Whitchurch (2008) as Third Space working. Many professional services roles have taken on an increasing academic component and have advanced in visibility, autonomy and influence (Szekeres, 2011). Examples are research administrators, academic developers and learning technologists (Veles, Graham and Ovaska, 2023).

Reinvention of value, increased role specialism and frequent partnership working with academics resonate with the experience of academic libraries. They contribute to changes in the identity of professional services staff. Whitchurch (2010, 171) captures some of these conveniently in a summary table which highlights specialisation of expertise, consultancy work, hybrid academic and administrative backgrounds and identities and less precisely defined roles. Caldwell (2022b) refers to an identity crisis for staff arising from so much change, while Henkel (2010) observes an ongoing construction and reconstruction of identities. Fluidity seems to be the norm and identity blurring, like stakeholder misperceptions and reinvention, represents common ground with academic libraries.

Influences on future position: three intensifying trends

The position of academic libraries is subject to ongoing change, especially in the unstable world described throughout this book. This section discusses three intensifying trends, one from each of the global, higher education and academic library environments, in terms of their implications for future position. Each has already been alluded to in previous chapters and now merits further attention as a likely longer-term influence on academic libraries. It is important first to remember one factor overarching everything put forward here, namely the potential for global catastrophe. Destructive climate events, another pandemic or even a third world war are all possible, each of them completely unpredictable but probably sudden in its onset and devastating in its consequences. The hope must be that no disaster will strike and the trends described next can play out in normal circumstances.

Artificial intelligence as a global force

It is impossible to ignore AI as a major factor in all walks of life. There is a recognition that 'we must contend with AI as a political, economic, cultural, and scientific force' (Crawford, 2021, 20). In 2024 for the first time in its history one topic, AI, featured in all five Social, Technological, Economic, Environmental and Political (STEEP) categories in the *EDUCAUSE Horizon Report, Teaching and Learning Edition* (Pelletier et al., 2024). That document summarised the growing influence of AI as follows: 'AI is changing the way we communicate, beginning to reshape pedagogy and student experiences, increasingly impacting the economy and the workforce, and being used to address climate change and sustainability issues. Meanwhile, the potential for using AI in politics is growing' (Pelletier et al., 2024, 6).

This book has also charted the importance and increasing pervasiveness of AI as well as its future potential for society, higher education and academic libraries. It balances promise with fear. Examples include: saving of time and enhancement of productivity but also elimination of jobs; rapid processing of data and generation of content but concerns about accuracy, privacy, bias and over-powerful governments; in higher education, more personalised learning but threats to academic integrity. There is the potential for AI to carry all before it as an irresistible force for change, powerful but also dangerous, especially if it were to surpass the ability of humans to control it.

Artificial intelligence can be expected to impact the future academic library position. It will continue to change user behaviour and expectations, increasing existing levels of self-sufficiency. This will challenge libraries to add new value, but AI will provide them with tools to do so, alongside opportunities to take key roles in inculcating the literacies needed to deploy it ethically and effectively. Collections may be presented and used in very different ways and it has been speculated that generative AI, by using its synthesising and extractive capacities to act as a reading intermediary between humans and scholarly content, could bring into question the need for a formal published record via journals or books (Bergstrom and Ruediger, 2024). Whatever emerges, libraries will continue to rely on their staff to advance their position. The profile and skillset of their workforce will be under pressure to evolve faster than heretofore to keep pace with changing opportunities and requirements.

Demographic challenges for higher education

Chapter 4 noted some unfavourable demographics in the recent past with negative consequences for participation in higher education in certain countries. The future looks bleak in some cases. Having experienced since 2010 a fall of 8.4% in enrolments (Hanson, M., 2025a), the USA needs to brace itself for worse to come. Blumenstyk (2024, 4) uses the term 'demographic cliff' and cites a 10% reduction in the overall high-school-to-college pipeline in the period to 2035, with 524 colleges projected to lose 25% of their current first-time, first-year enrolment. Many others will doubtless suffer too, even if not to the same extent. Elsewhere, while England expects to see a rise in applications of 25,000 (8%) between 2024 and 2030, most of this gain is projected to disappear by 2035 due to a drop of 20,000 applications after 2030 (Bekhradnia, 2024). Experience in other countries is likely to be mixed, as an uneven demographic pattern across the globe has been noted (Altbach and de Wit, 2023). When challenges in maintaining international student recruitment are added, the economic situation for higher education looks difficult and some institutions may not survive.

Different approaches to recruitment and programme delivery could offer some mitigations. The ageing demographic will mean longer working lives which, coupled with AI-driven transformations in work, should enlarge the market for lifelong learning. Online learning, already much more strongly established since the COVID-19 pandemic, enables wider and more flexible access, especially to work-related microcredentials, as described in Chapter 4. Some likely consequences are a greater vocational emphasis in the offerings of some institutions (Blumenstyk, 2024), an even more diversified student body and an increasingly 'phygital' student experience as students alternate between the physical and digital learning environments (Fisher, 2024).

Demographic changes will have significant, if uneven, effects on academic libraries. Where negative, they bode ill for an already stretched funding environment and their impact could even be existential, as some institutions are likely to face closure. Libraries will find themselves responding to a further level of diversification in the student population. Greater numbers of part-time and often time-poor students pursuing microcredentials and other programmes will need to be supported both online and on campus and will have specific needs and vulnerabilities. This will represent a change in scale as much as anything else but could still prove significant. There may also be a tension to resolve in relation to providing access to more vocationally oriented information resources at the expense of scholarly material as tightened budgets force choices to be made. More generally, anything academic libraries can do to attract and retain students, including through the deepening of relationships and strengthening of their social function discussed in the next section, will be valued.

From collections to services to relationships

The changed value proposition of academic libraries has been characterised as a shift in emphasis from collections to services (Dempsey, 2016; Pinfield, Cox and Rutter, 2017; Frederick and Wolff-Eisenberg, 2020b; ODonnell and Anderson, 2022). A further iteration towards relationships is taking shape. Collections and services are and will remain highly significant in the library offering but some uncertainties about the future of scholarly communication, coupled with a heightened social emphasis in higher education, will foreground the importance of building communities and deeper relationships (Schlak, Corrall and Bracke, 2022).

Academic library budgets have long struggled to maintain subscription-based collections due to a combination of price inflation and local funding reductions, leading one analysis to conclude that 'a collections-based approach that relies on external content is an unsustainable model' (Schlak and Macklin, 2022, 120). The same authors also note that such costs reduce the sum available for other purposes, gradually eroding the value the library can deliver. Heseltine (2020) points out that the library's long-term retention of institutional control of campus access to digital resources may not be secure, instancing the potential for changes in publisher business models. As per the discussion of open scholarship in Chapter 7, there is certainly scope for a transition to a fully open access system, perhaps community-owned. Whether or when such changes may occur is uncertain, but they raise questions about the long-central collections role of the library. The same can be said of how AI may reshape the scholarly record, already noted in this chapter and towards the end of Chapter 8. This combination of unsustainable costs, possible changes in scholarly communication and the potential for AI-led disruption is significant. It suggests that academic libraries should ask themselves how safe a bet collections represent at the centre of their longer-term offering and that they should continue to diversify their value proposition by stepping up the emphasis they place on social connector roles.

Chapter 4 highlighted a much more participatory turn in the world at large through which people expect to have roles in co-creation and co-production (Corrall, 2022c). Major global challenges such as those outlined in the United Nations Sustainable Development Goals call for collaborative problem-solving (United Nations, 2015). Technological change spreads the same message that 'students who are capable of creative insights, collaborating in diverse teams, and navigating through global cultural differences will be at an advantage' (Penprase, 2018, 225). All of this has implications for higher education. These include rapid curriculum evolution, more active forms of pedagogy, the involvement of students as partners in areas such as institutional governance and decolonisation initiatives and the inclusion of wider communities beyond the campus in research and teaching (Corrall, 2022a; Penprase, 2018).

Academic libraries have also taken on a more social orientation. They have broadened their roles in the lives and learning journeys of students by assisting the transition to higher education, expanding the range of literacies they teach and supporting student well-being and sense of belonging, while also extending their engagement with local communities (Corrall, 2022b). The building blocks are in place for an intensification of their social function by academic libraries as the key implication of the directions of travel just described. They are well placed at the centre of social networks on and outside their campuses (Bracke, 2022b). This is in addition to high levels of social capital built through multiple teaching and research partnerships alongside the trust and trustworthiness they enjoy (Schlak, 2022c).

The next level calls for a shift from a transactional to a relational approach, prioritising community building and deepening relationships more intentionally by placing them at the centre of library practice and strategy, systematically recorded and evaluated in the same way as established assets (Corrall, 2023b). The tendency is towards putting the social assets of the library on a par with its more tangible collections, spaces and services (Bracke, 2022a). This includes a shift in balance from connecting users to collections to a focus on facilitating conversations between people (Heseltine, 2020). It emphasises a democratic model of 'task-sharing, knowledge-sharing and power-sharing' (Corrall, 2023b), promoting radical collaborations to maximise teamwork in highly active approaches to problem-solving (Corrall, 2024). Working with students as partners can be viewed as key to their success through developing their creativity and ability to collaborate effectively, building on existing support provided via makerspaces and the cultivation of multiple literacies.

Schlak (2022a) sees actively developing and sustaining learning communities which want to come together but might otherwise not do so as a key opportunity for academic libraries and a valuable asset for their institutions. They can pay a vital role by resolving knowledge gaps and facilitating information transfer. If properly measured and communicated, these added areas of contribution may prove even more advantageous as the collections developments already described create uncertainty. This chapter noted early on the importance of user perspectives and behaviours in shaping academic library position and this continues to hold true. Its evolution is well captured in the observation that 'libraries find themselves as dependent on their users as the latter previously found themselves dependent on the former for good information' (Schlak, 2022b, xxix).

Conclusion

The academic library is a complex phenomenon and its position is shaped by a mix of positive and negative forces, contradictions and sometimes own goals. Its value is derived from a blend of traditional and new activities and it means many different things to those who constitute its diverse clientele.

The conclusion to Chapter 1 included a brief consideration of whether the position of today's very different academic library represents a decline or advance relative to its pre-digital antecedents and did not come down on either side. The summary headlines are a loss of monopoly of access to information at one level and a more broadly based contribution to the institution at the other, but the choice between decline or advance is not a simple binary one, as there are so many factors at play. Chapter 8 deliberately used the phrase 'decline in position' rather than 'declining position'. There is plenty of evidence that decline has occurred in recent decades in terms of funding, distance from the top table and loss of ground to competitors, but this does not necessarily mean that academic libraries are at present on a trajectory of decline. The boost in perceptions of their value generated by the COVID-19 pandemic would indicate otherwise. Their strengths remain potent, with centrality a major natural asset, values an enduring anchor, collaboration critical in a socially networked world and reinvention representing a vital capacity for ongoing adaptation. They have averted prophecies of their demise, including their outsourcing (Law, 2010) and the replacement of their directors by IT administrators (Anderson, 2011).

The position of academic libraries nevertheless carries vulnerabilities, including issues of identity, recognition, ability to compete and an unsustainable economic model for journals access, not to mention the many external factors beyond their control. Looking at the intensifying trends just identified, they would appear to be at a vital juncture, with lots of uncertainty surrounding AI, the higher education learning model and the evolution of scholarly communication. Committing further to the social academic library as a strong and meaningful contribution to the institution offers promise. It can leverage strengths and offer a more viable and controllable investment than the longstanding concentration of resources in external content. Striking an appropriate balance between the academic library's social and collections roles requires careful consideration and its next moves will be significant for its future position. Positioning strategy will be the focus of Chapter 10.

CHAPTER 10

Positioning Strategies for Successful Academic Libraries

Overview

This chapter looks at how academic libraries can best position themselves in their parent institutions and incorporates:

- an introductory outline, including the campus positioning environment;
- a reminder of some important messages about positioning, its components and why it is a vital focus for academic libraries;
- ten proposed positioning strategies aimed at advancing the library situation, including: position the library actively; prioritise the institutional agenda; be agile towards opportunities;
- consideration of each strategy, including its context, aims, scope and associated actions;
- discussion of some concepts and practicalities linked to aligning resources with positioning;
- a summary of potential benefits accruing to the well-positioned academic library;
- concluding thoughts, emphasising the ongoing commitments effective positioning requires.

Introduction

Ten strategies proposed for advancing the position of academic libraries in their parent institutions are the primary focus of this chapter. They are offered as a menu from which individual libraries may choose depending on their circumstances, recognising that different combinations may be appropriate per library. The current chapter takes earlier coverage into account, especially positioning strategy, which was the focus of Chapter 2. Positioning academic libraries is influenced by their history and the environment in which they operate. That environment offers challenges, including resourcing, competition and general uncertainty, alongside opportunities, for example institutional focus on the public good, open scholarship, lifelong learning and standing up for the truth.

On the surface academic libraries are well placed for successful positioning on campus. They have a strong platform for contributing to the institutional agenda thanks to their centrality, connectedness with the campus community at large, engagement across all disciplines and accumulation of goodwill. The *modus operandi* of higher education institutions creates a challenging positioning environment, however. A high degree of decentralisation can lead to multiple entities jockeying for position and sometimes jurisdiction, making it difficult to secure influence at the top table in often complex organisational structures. Overall, there is typically a very busy, intense and crowded campus space for positioning and it can be hard even to be heard, much less stand out.

Institutional strategies are far from constant. They are instead dynamic, fluid and subject to frequent change, dependent in particular on government policy, which varies from country to country and within any country, depending on which party or combination of parties is in charge. This impacts the positioning of academic libraries, with stakeholders asking different questions and seeking new value as their priorities evolve (Cox, J., 2018). Libraries seeking to align with institutional strategy therefore need to be flexible in their outlook. Furthermore, there is a sense of radical change being continuously on the agenda for academic libraries, including a need for 'new strategies, and maybe new values and a new culture' (Lewis, 2016, xv). The positioning environment remains challenging and the first of seven principles for survival to 2030 has been identified by one author as to 'Lose sight of the shore' (Guillén, 2021, 282), letting go of the past and accepting fundamental change.

The remainder of this chapter recalls the main points about positioning from Chapter 2 before putting forward ten possible positioning strategies for academic libraries which are followed by a consideration of some resource implications and potential benefits associated with their implementation.

Positioning: some key messages

Definitions of positioning bring two concepts to the fore. First, a highly active approach to positioning, emphasising strengths, emerges as essential to success by contrast with the risks inherent in passivity, including the assignment of an unwanted position (Dunford, 2019). Secondly, there is a focus on influencing the minds of a range of audiences, from users to funders (Kotler, 1997; Ries and Trout, 2001). The position the academic library occupies in the minds of its stakeholders strongly impacts how they perceive it, with positive or negative effects. The five positioning components identified in Chapter 2 are key to the library situation and bear repetition: clarity of identity; distinctiveness from the competition; an intimate understanding of the needs of target audiences; impactful communications; and strong resources. By addressing them libraries aim to carve out a distinctive niche and to bring clarity about their offering to their intended audiences (Walters, S. and Jackson, 2013).

Positioning is fundamental to deciding what to do and what not to do (Porter, 1996) and is intimately informed by an awareness of internal and external factors which seeks to leverage unique strengths fully (Barney, 1991; 1995). The ultimate goal of effective positioning is to situate the library compellingly in the eyes of its stakeholders so that it occupies an advantageous place in the institution with potential for further advancement. The ten strategies proposed in this chapter are therefore targeted towards that end. It is hard to overstate the importance of positioning as a force for good or ill in the fortunes of academic libraries (Cox, J., 2019). Positioning is a source of possibilities or consequences and opportunities or threats, impacting prospects for resource allocation, influence with institutional leadership and location in the organisational hierarchy. Being seen as vital to the interests, strategies and competitive advantage of the institution is key (Penniman, 1997).

Shaping perceptions is crucial. Positioning creates distinctiveness 'less by the specifics of what you do and more by the perceptions that your customers have of what you do' (Walters, S. and Jackson, 2013, 60). Stakeholder misperceptions emerged in Chapter 6 as a weakness for academic libraries, however, which their positioning needs to combat. There is a gap between how libraries and others perceive their contribution (De Rosa and Johnson, 2008) and this represents the biggest positioning issue they face. Despite major changes in their value proposition there is a tendency in many quarters towards dated views of what academic libraries do, resulting in limited perspectives and a general underestimation of their value. Increasing awareness and appreciation of their much broader contemporary value proposition is not as simple as promoting their new agenda exclusively, given the enduring need for printed materials, preservation of heritage and quiet space for concentration and in-depth study. It is necessary therefore to ride both horses when positioning the academic library, since long-established and newer activities each support the library's contribution to the institutional mission.

Positioning is complex, with some elements controllable, including prioritising the use of resources and the approach taken to messaging, but others are at the mercy of external events and technologies shaping changes in higher education. Appleton (2022) advocates that library leaders apply a critical perspective to the position of academic libraries and the same should hold true for their positioning which, given its importance and potential consequences, requires ongoing and focused attention.

Ten positioning strategies

The strategies put forward in the coming pages originate in this book's survey of the history and operating environment of academic libraries as well as its SWOT analysis and assessment of their contemporary position. While there is some overlap with the strategic responses recommended in the 16 sections of the SWOT analysis, the ten strategies in this chapter are consistently pitched at a more generic level. They are aimed, both individually and collectively, at improving the position of the academic library in its parent institution. The intention is that libraries can make a selection, choosing whichever configuration of strategies is most helpful to their situation. It is understood that libraries might already be strong in some of the areas covered and may therefore focus their attention on other strategies which have received less emphasis previously but hold promise for future positioning.

Numbering of the ten strategies is used for ease of identification rather than to represent any ranking in terms of their relative importance.

1. Position the library actively

Chapter 2 advocated an assertive approach to positioning, as this holds far greater potential than passively allowing the library's fate to be decided elsewhere by events, politics, technology or other forces. Conservatism has influenced an insufficiently active approach in the past, as mentioned in Chapter 6, with academic libraries failing to take the initiative and feeding stakeholder misperceptions which in turn have damaged their position. Active positioning is essential in a competitive environment where it has been noted that 'if the library does not move assertively, others, either on campus or off, will do the jobs our students and faculty need to have done and the library will become increasingly less relevant' (Lewis, 2016, 155). There is therefore a need to shake off any conservative outlook, sense of subservience, over-modesty or disinclination towards marketing.

Instead, assertiveness, leadership and proactivity should be the bywords for academic library positioning. The library can shape its own positioning on campus according to the directions it takes and how effectively it communicates its value and identity to stakeholders. There are many opportunities to lead the institution, not just support it. Examples include open scholarship, research data management and learning space design, with AI more recently emerging as a vital and uncertain area for higher education where libraries have much to contribute as trusted brokers. Openings also exist to operate on a broader canvas by taking lead roles in response to global issues of major significance for parent institutions, for instance combating disinformation, promoting informed political judgement and generating debate as well as awareness around climate change.

A proactive mentality is a key component of assertive positioning, with potential for 'influencing stakeholders, shaping users' perceptions of their own needs and even institutional direction of travel' (Cox, A. M., Pinfield and Rutter, 2019b, 324). Library directors are exhorted to 'be in conversations and initiate conversations – not waiting to be invited to them' (Hilton, 2019, 93). Similarly, Davies (2020) urges that library staff should put themselves forward by sharing skillsets which are applicable to many more projects than is typically recognised in the institution. These capacities include understanding user needs, managing information and assembling an evidence base. Libraries are in a fight for resources and attention and should not be shy about communicating their assets and achievements, claiming credit where it is due and making sure that their contribution to the success and competitiveness of the institution is widely known. A highly active stance towards positioning is vital and underpins the remaining strategies in this chapter.

2. Know the territory

The importance for academic libraries of maintaining a strong awareness of the wider environment in which they operate has been a key theme throughout this book. Libraries, like their parent institutions, are shaped by what happens globally and in the higher education sector. They need to prioritise an outward-looking approach and to avoid too much tendency towards inward focus. This may involve a rebalancing of effort such that some of the attention given to enhancing internal processes can be diverted elsewhere in favour of greater strategic awareness, better preparedness for change and ultimately improved positioning. Environmental scanning and research involve not just awareness-gathering but also interpreting developments, appreciating their significance, connecting events and anticipating likely impacts on the institution and the library. This calls for a better capacity for environmental analysis by academic libraries than has been observed heretofore (Budd, 2018).

Self-awareness, including awareness of history, strengths and weaknesses, is important for academic library positioning, but a detailed knowledge of the world beyond the library is even more essential. Understanding a dynamically changing operating environment is key at multiple levels:

- *the world at large*, in terms of political, economic, social and technological developments;
- *higher education*, including government policy, the demographics of student participation and how students learn as well as evolving research priorities and concerns;
- *the parent institution*, notably its pressure points, opportunities and organisational dynamics;
- *individual constituencies*, recognising that staying close to users is vital, for example constantly asking what is happening in the lives of academics and students and how their needs are changing, while striving to understand the perspectives of campus partners in terms of their responsibilities, capacities, priorities, needs and areas of common interest (Bryant, Dortmund and Lavoie, 2020).

A shallow appreciation of the operating environment is insufficient. Attaining a deep understanding calls for ongoing effort and prioritisation, acknowledging complexity and uncertainty alongside opportunity and taking time to discuss and analyse trends. Investment in continuous research should mean that strategy formulation and deployment of resources are better informed, all supporting advancement of library position in the institution. It is nevertheless important to accept that the unexpected and unpredictable may still happen despite any library's best efforts in tracking developments, as exemplified by the onset in 2020 of the COVID-19 pandemic.

3. Be politically attuned

Understanding the politics of the institution is important and is an extension of knowing the territory. Some people frown on political engagement and Atkins (1991) noted a view in academic library circles late in the last century that politics was demeaning. This was at odds with reality at that time and is even more so now for any library seeking to make progress and to get things done in today's extremely competitive campus environment.

Academic libraries commonly find themselves in political situations which require political acumen. Among these are winning resources, selling a new strategy, promoting disruptive change in scholarly communication and asserting service leadership or jurisdiction. Political skills are therefore vital and include 'Knowing who to work with, how to influence situations, when to act, and how to advance an agenda' (Cox, J., 2023b, 280). Foundational to effective political engagement is cultivating a deep understanding of the parent institution – how it works, where different types of decisions are made and who are the influencers, supporters and blockers. It makes sense in positioning terms to invest time and energy continuously in developing an appreciation of emerging institutional priorities and new resources as well as established governance structures and other routes to decision making. It is hard to disagree with the assertion that 'There is no substitute for the effort it takes to understand the workings of the college or university' (Budd, 2018, 215).

Active participation in committees is often significant in building political influence and it is essential to maximise library presence on them and to support their work effectively. Also necessary are working across boundaries, building partnerships, offering to help and strengthening relationships as much with less like-minded people as with natural allies (Davies, 2020). Building up political capital through relationships, alliances, reputation and valued contributions was recognised as valuable in one study of 12 library directors in the State University of New York (SUNY) system, enabling subsequent drawdown on the same resource for library advantage (O'Bryan, 2018). Being politically attuned essentially means being streetwise and recognising that collaborators may also be rivals or vice versa, that competition is a daily reality and that political manoeuvring is normal and indeed essential to making things happen (Bolman and Deal, 2021). Equally, it is important to use the academic library's reputation, trusted status and centrality judiciously as enduring political assets.

4. Prioritise the institutional agenda

Higher education institutions have expanding agendas, translating to a long list of things to be done, so all contributions are welcome and strong participation by all units is needed. The academic library has many contributions to make, but Chapter 9 noted a perception that it could be doing more for the institution. A quote from one of the participants in the SCONUL study on *The View from Above* encapsulates this: 'For the most part librarians don't bring problems; nor do they bring solutions.' (Baker, D. and Allden, 2017, 24). This is concerning in terms of academic library positioning and there is a need to reverse any such perceptions, especially through active, meaningful and impactful participation across the whole campus agenda.

Academic libraries can start from a base of understanding and prioritising engagement with institutional imperatives and establishing how they can support them. A study of 63 institutional leaders found that 'The most important characteristic sought by university leaders was for the library director to act not as the chief manager of the library but rather as a university leader with responsibility for the library . . . working as part of the leadership team of the university to advance the university's interests' (Cooper, Hill and Schonfeld, 2022, 17). This should be the mentality not just of the director but of the whole library leadership team, bringing greater breadth and depth to the library's support for the institution (Dewey, 2014). Harland, Stewart and Bruce (2018) advocate factoring skills and attributes to enable strategic contribution to the institution into the selection criteria applied to building the library leadership team.

Acting as a strong campus citizen and working with others to advance shared priorities is good for both the library and the institution, representing enlightened self-interest from the library perspective. It also leverages aspects of the library's position which are helpful towards outward engagement and valued contributions, notably centrality, broad remit, service ethic, observation of learning behaviours and opportunities to act as convenor (Cooper, Hill and Schonfeld, 2022). The last of these has sometimes translated into the hosting of a range of campus services in the library building as well as wider remits for library directors as co-ordinators of student academic support, IT and digital initiatives (Schonfeld, 2016; Gwyer, 2018).

There are also examples of academic library strategies very explicitly putting university priorities first. The University of Western Australia Library's (2024) *Strategic Plan 2024–26* includes 'Growing Student Enrolment' as one of its five strategic priorities, outlining a range of actions and partnerships to support this. Advancing the reputation of its parent institution via strategic collaborations and innovative library spaces is a focus of the North Carolina State University Libraries (2022) strategy for the period 2022 to 2027. Goal 6 is 'Be recognized as the leading university for innovative partnerships, entrepreneurial thinking and applied problem-solving' and is followed by Goal 7, 'Elevate the national and global reputation and visibility of NC State'.

5. Maximise library connectedness

Enhanced contribution to the institution benefits from the fact that the academic library is a well-connected entity. Its high level of connectedness is also in itself an asset to be leveraged for improved positioning. Academic libraries enjoy some natural advantages, notably their physical centrality on most campuses, proximity to the academic mission across all disciplines, trusted status, community role and global publishing function, generating multiple points of contact with a broad range of constituencies. The position of trust they occupy is fundamental to the quality of relationships academic libraries are able to form and it positions them well as partners, leaders, supporters and influencers. Another significant context and driver for maximising library connectedness is the increased social and democratic focus in the mission of higher education institutions, itself in tune with the social and participatory turn in the wider world (Corrall, 2022a; 2022c).

Chapter 5 identified centrality as a key strength of academic libraries. Their buildings emerged as vital places of connection, convergence and community in that chapter and elsewhere, but the actions of library staff as social connectors are even more important. There are many ways for academic libraries to leverage their connectedness for their own benefit and that of their parent institutions. One example is bringing people together through event programming, which connects the Library at the University of California Santa Barbara with as many people as its instruction programme (Metzger, 2022). Another is fostering creativity at Virginia Tech Libraries through partnerships between staff and students in studios and other active learning spaces whose purpose is 'to nurture and amplify connections among students, technology, and ideas' (Mathews, Metko and Tomlin 2018, 53), recognising that the library is 'situated at the intersection of these three strands'.

Academic libraries can continue to insert themselves into the lives of their communities, providing lifecycle and life-wide support (Corrall, 2022b), while elevating how they engage with their users from a transactional to a relational model marked by deeper co-working and active building of communities, as highlighted in Chapter 9. Potential gains for their parent institutions include increased development of student skills, improved retention as students feel a stronger sense of belonging and better outcomes through the filling by libraries of structural and information holes in the organisation. By maximising their connectedness and building their social capital, academic libraries can advance their positioning and profit from better access to institutional resources (Dillon, 2022). Committing to the relational model across the whole library is key (Corrall, 2023a), as is shifting mentality to build the leveraging of social capital, relationships and connections into strategic planning (Bracke, 2022a).

6. Emphasise distinctiveness

One of the five components of positioning identified earlier is distinctiveness from the competition. Distinctiveness is important in promoting identity, value proposition and niche. It can be harder to demonstrate uniqueness in a busy global and campus environment where so much is happening, change is rapid, there are many players and multi-party delivery of services is common. A strategy of emphasising distinctiveness is proposed as a response to the threats of identity blurring and competition outlined in Chapter 8. Academic libraries offer a multiplicity of services to a diverse range of audiences, putting them at risk of falling into 'the everybody trap' (Ries and Trout, 2001, 60) by trying to be everything to everyone. This breadth of scope makes the library value proposition increasingly diffused, creating vulnerabilities in terms of perceived identity and purpose, as audiences become unsure of what position the library specifically occupies. A focus on measuring impact, while essential in certain contexts, can mean an 'increasing tendency to define the success of the academic library in terms that are unrelated to any core purposes' (Heseltine, 2020, 11).

Academic libraries have several points of distinctiveness on which they should capitalise. These include:

- the library as a special and inclusive place of campus community;
- criticality to the advancement and preservation of scholarship across all disciplines;
- unique archives and special collections;
- commitment to service as well as other lived values which inspire respect and support;
- longevity as an established campus presence since the early days of universities;
- trusted status as a basis for deeper relationships and knowledge of local needs than external competitors.

The above points are common to academic libraries at large but each individual library will have its own unique qualities to add to this list. Other writings have prompted some questions about distinctiveness which academic libraries may wish to ask themselves continuously. Lewis urges consideration of the jobs they 'can do that cannot be more effectively done by others' (Lewis, 2016, 91). The key issue for Gwyer is 'what are the unique values and services that libraries bring to universities; and how are these strategically aligned and effectively conveyed to senior managers?' (Gwyer, 2018, 440). In their book about positioning Ries and Trout ask: 'What position do you want to own?' (Ries and Trout, 2001, 193). Their focus is on the niche any entity, including an academic library, occupies in the mind of actual or prospective audiences. Heseltine highlights the issue of core purpose and mission when he poses the question 'Why do we do what we do?' (Heseltine, 2020, 16). There is scope for fruitful debate among library staff in addressing these questions and the exercise should help to extend and clarify the ways in which the academic library can emphasise how and why it is distinctive from others on and outside the campus.

7. Communicate value and identity

This strategy aims to address stakeholder misperceptions, highlighted earlier as a consequential weakness for academic libraries which can influence underestimation of their contribution, misunderstanding of their role and confusion about their identity. From this emerges a definite need to communicate clear messages to stakeholders about the library's value and identity, emphasising not only what it actually does but what it can potentially contribute beyond this too. Misperceptions may result at least partly from previous messaging failures, with ineffective communications included among the library own goals listed in Chapter 9. Communicating successfully is challenging today and it has been asserted that 'In our noisy times the fight for attention is severe and brutal' (Kendrick, T., 2021, 2). There is also a lot, perhaps too much, to communicate, given the range of areas in which academic libraries are active as their value proposition diversifies. Oakleaf's (2010) Research Agenda for articulating academic library value runs to almost 40 pages across ten areas of contribution.

Academic libraries need to give due attention to what and how they communicate. Concise messaging using active language focused on the needs and interests of the intended recipients has a decent chance of compelling their attention (Kendrick, T., 2021). Mathews urges new language, oriented towards solving user problems and projecting the library as 'a platform for incubating ideas and a catalyst for getting things done' (Mathews, 2014a, 23). Emphasising knowledge creation conveys a far broader and more active sense of the library role than a materials-centric formulation centred on access to knowledge (Heseltine, 2020). Framing messages according to what the academic library enables users to do and with linkage to outcomes important to the institution and its members, such as student success, research productivity and reputation, makes good sense (Oakleaf, 2010). The use of evidence, supported by rigorous impact research and well presented data, will also help to tell a convincing story (Bakkalbasi, 2017). It is important to note that the focus on communicating library value advocated here should be aimed at improving awareness and ultimately on actively increasing value rather than proving it defensively (Lewis, 2016; Oakleaf, 2010).

Terry Kendrick (2021) offers excellent and practical advice for libraries of all types on both messaging and overall approach to communication within a strategic marketing framework. He emphasises working from the outside in, so that libraries can craft engaging and varied messages capable of surprising audiences and aiming to cultivate and maintain two-way conversations instead of simply broadcasting information. The need for a systematic, sustained and long-term strategy, backed up by full staff engagement and by attention to how users actually experience all interactions with the library, is argued cogently throughout his book. There is no magic formula for communicating the value and distinctive identity of academic libraries successfully. Persistence is essential, however, as is the flexibility to keep trying new things, including moving beyond library media to get the message out via higher education channels, for example. It is important also to maintain an awareness that communication happens in a multiplicity of ways, sometimes non-verbally and including the various forms of connectedness and practical support for the institutional agenda outlined earlier.

Reflective journal extract 10.1
Making ourselves heard

From the author's journal: 2 April 2010

Also, we can all (myself definitely included) up our game in terms of engaging the academic community and senior personnel in the university. They don't understand our achievements and evolving roles but we have not done enough to lead opinion in these areas and we need to think how we might change this – getting out there more proactively, I guess, and being confident of ourselves, our services and our staff.

8. Be agile towards opportunities

Combating conservatism, another weakness identified in Chapter 6, is a particular focus of this proposed strategy. Major shifts are in progress, notably in scholarly communication, AI, the relational library and in user habits and expectations among a continuously diversifying clientele. Opportunities are there for the taking by academic libraries and, just as they are helping students to develop skills such as teamwork and creative problem-solving for success in today's world, so they also need to cultivate these aptitudes among their own staff. While conservatism breeds hesitancy towards new possibilities, there can be a cost to not taking a risk, too (Faires, 2017). Establishing a more creative, inventive and agile spirit across the library is key to making the most of opportunities but, like any culture change, is challenging, especially when caution is deep-rooted, as is allegiance to established processes. The point that 'Libraries need to be more enterprising than bureaucratic' (Dempsey, 2012, 214) is well made. This calls for ongoing leadership commitment in the face of conservative tendencies which are typically to be found not just in the library but across the campus (Jantz, 2017b).

Possible steps to be taken include empowering and rewarding innovation, establishing rapid turnaround in project approval processes, looking outwards towards new developments and solutions, recognising less concrete or immediately impactful contributions and investing continuously in organisational development (Lewis, 2016; Marcum, 2016; Simons, 2017). Also relevant to the development of an agile culture is the concept of learning organisations, advanced by Schlak (2022a) in the context of shifting the academic library from a transactional to a relational model. Such organisations are able to adapt and evolve, even transform themselves by continuous learning and exchange of learning among staff to develop their creative capacities (Senge, 2006). The ability to learn faster than others promises a sustainable form of competitive advantage (Hooley et al., 2020).

Perfectionism can be the enemy of early engagement with opportunities and there is much to be said for the mantra articulated at the University of Arizona Libraries some time ago: 'Do not let "perfect" get in the way of "good enough".' (Stoffle and Cuillier, 2010, 139). More recently, one of the underpinning themes in the University of Leeds Libraries' (2022) vision for 2030 is a culture of innovation, including celebrating experimentation and extending beyond comfort zones. Agility towards opportunities involves anticipation and immersion rather than sitting on the fence and waiting for events to unfold. Examples include a revised deployment of collections funds to enable better support of and transition to new open access models (Lewis et al., 2022), continuously experimenting with evolving AI tools and staying close to users to foresee needs beyond those satisfied by the immediate library service offering (Mathews, 2014a).

Reflective journal extract 10.2
Aiming higher

From the author's journal: 5 September 2014

Great motto at North Carolina State University (NCSU) – the libraries are NCSU's competitive advantage . . . shows me how our Library could lead at NUI Galway if we, myself included, are more ambitious and assertive. There is a 'wow' factor at the Hunt Library, NCSU, but it's their thinking that really impressed me – they experiment, are courageous, agile and visionary and they think big. They seem to be prepared to gamble, something that's easier when you have (as we have also) a strong track record of success. I sense that it's time for us to re-energise ourselves, use our strengths and move forward in a way that would make a real difference. What have we to lose?

9. Embrace uncertainty

Embracing uncertainty is closely connected with agility towards opportunity but differs in that it is concerned with the mentality we adopt towards the unknown, with instability at unprecedented levels and uncertainty identified as threat in Chapter 8. This strategy considers the benefits of a changed, more positive, accepting and embracing mindset towards uncertainty. It treats uncertainty as normal, and hardly a new normal at this stage.

It is not uncommon to hear people, including library staff, wishing for an interval of stability after such a sustained period of volatility in recent times but this looks like a forlorn hope. Uncertainty shows no signs of going away any time soon and libraries will continue to undergo disruption, so a positive mentality will be helpful. Bell (2015) sees approaching change with enthusiasm as vital to a successful transformation for libraries, while Guillén (2021) urges optimism instead of loss aversion bias towards uncertainty, with a focus on what can be gained rather than lost. Comfort with uncertainty is identified as important (Marcum, 2016) alongside 'the ability to engage and thrive in the messy and ambiguous' (Jaguszewski and Williams, 2013, 14). These attributes will not come naturally to everyone, but there is more to be gained by actively embracing uncertainty than being passively dictated to by it.

Brian Mathews (2014b) looks at how futurists operate and identifies some principles and practices library staff can follow to change how they think about the future. They include:

- adopting an open and curious mindset to recognise many potential futures rather than a single version;
- focusing on likely impacts rather than what exactly will happen;
- considering possible directions from the perspectives of different parties;
- asking questions about what will shape the environment influencing academic libraries, for example higher education and publishing, rather than about the future of libraries themselves.

These processes can help to identify signposts and to see connections between them, enabling academic libraries to prepare for a range of conditions, actively shape their future and reduce their levels of uncertainty. Mathews urges library staff to cultivate what he terms change literacy as a core professional skill for thinking constructively about the future rather than fearing it.

Difficult times offer opportunities too, as outlined in Chapter 7. By actively living their values and leveraging the trusted position they occupy on and outside their campuses, academic libraries are able to assert their higher purpose, playing significant roles in the fight against polarisation, inequality, climate change, misinformation, disinformation and research fraud. As they confront current and future uncertainties, academic libraries can take strength from their successful response to the crisis suddenly generated in 2020 by the COVID-19 pandemic when they proved themselves adaptable, innovative and steadfast for their communities.

10. Capitalise on longevity

There has been a lot of focus on change, turbulence and uncertainty about the future of academic libraries in this book. This may generate feelings of insecurity among library staff, but they can draw on the longevity of academic libraries as a platform for looking towards the future with optimism. Libraries have played a vital role in universities since the middle of the 13th century and they have enjoyed a natural positioning advantage as the first service provider in their area of activity. Their original functions of collecting, enabling access to information, preserving scholarship and supporting intellectual engagement remain at the core of their offering. The values they espouse are timeless and especially relevant now, notably generosity, openness and a focus on the public good. Their strengths, identified in Chapter 5 as centrality, values, collaboration and reinvention, continue to represent enduring assets. They have experienced frequent foreshadowing of their doom and encountered many threats, especially through the advance of technology, but they have more than survived these and have often turned difficult situations to advantage.

Academic libraries have an imperative to evolve and to keep up with changing needs and expectations, but this does not necessitate knee-jerk reactions to developments, seismic changes of direction, binary choices between their traditional and newer agendas or the abandonment of what they have long striven for and still represent. There is plenty more for them to achieve in areas vital to the academic mission, for example AI, scholarly communication and community building. The campus community expects to have access to a library and it values this as uptake of both the physical and digital components of the library offering continues to be strong. Longevity is a valuable positioning asset. A long-term perspective should therefore underpin strategy and positioning so that further evolution can occur with a confidence based on solid foundations of continuity and change across the history of academic libraries.

Aligning resources with positioning

Four of the five positioning components are addressed by the ten proposed strategies, some implicitly and others explicitly. In the latter category are impactful communications (communicate value and identity), understanding the needs of target audiences (know the territory), distinctiveness from the competition (emphasise distinctiveness) and clarity of identity (communicate value and identity). The component not addressed is the alignment of strong resources, an important factor for realising effective positioning and considered separately in this section, which begins with a reminder of some points made in Chapter 2.

Barney (1995, 50) supports a broad definition of resources to encompass 'financial, physical, human, and organizational assets' and writes of capabilities in addition to resources, while also emphasising the need to factor in the intangible as well as tangible resources at the organisation's disposal. The tangible resources of academic libraries include staff, budgets, collections and buildings. Less obvious, but highlighted regularly in this book for their importance, are intangibles such as trust, values, reputation, expertise, centrality, connectedness, longevity, heritage and community. They represent 'historically developed resource endowments' (Hooley et al., 2020, 145) which need to be evaluated and adapted to match changes in the operating environment (Barney, 1995).

Intangible resources may offer a unique competitive advantage which others find difficult to imitate or to emulate. They conform to the valuable, rare and inimitable elements of Barney's (1995) VRIO framework and academic libraries can capitalise on them as positioning assets. The final part of that framework provides that resources are optimally deployed if they are fully organisation-supported in terms of factors such as budgets, structures and processes. This links to the Resources, Processes and Values (RPV) theory, which promotes the joining up of these three elements. It 'holds that resources (what a firm has), processes (how a firm does its work), and values (what a firm wants to do) define an organization's strengths as well as its weaknesses and blind spots' (Christensen, Anthony and Roth, 2004, xvii).

Many moving parts need to be considered in seeking to align resources with positioning, notably staff, time and space. Staff often comprise the library's most expensive asset and are vital to everything it does or plans to do. Effective staff recruitment and development are key (Hooley et al., 2020). Assembling a diverse workforce supports agile positioning by facilitating a variety of approaches and perspectives. Areas for skills development highlighted in the proposed positioning strategies and in other chapters include relationship management, community building, environmental scanning, impact research and communications.

There are choices to be made in how staff are deployed, especially if institutional priorities are to be more effectively supported and if there is to be a stronger commitment towards the relational library. Both are highly significant for positioning, but achieving the latter brings deployment challenges, in that its measures of productivity are less solid than for more traditional library functions. This is encapsulated in the comment that 'a social future for libraries is not so much a set of problems to be solved as it is a set of communities to create' (Schlak, 2022a, 161). Optimising team and reporting structures is part of ensuring that resources and capabilities are organisation-supported. The trend is away from rigid hierarchies and towards agile structures which enable experts from different functional areas to work together as needed (Adams Becker et al., 2017). As the number of specialist posts and services increases, a particular source of debate for academic libraries has been whether to continue with subject librarian teams or to move towards bringing functional experts together instead or to settle on an appropriate mixture of both (Hoodless and Pinfield, 2018).

How time is spent is a critical consideration and this applies to library directors too, noting that greater engagement with senior institutional leaders on their imperatives can create a virtuous circle by providing more opportunities to demonstrate library value (Frederick and Wolff-Eisenberg, 2020c). Making time for expansion into newer areas of work means examining current commitments, including investigating ways of containing the effort required to support those legacy functions which remain essential. There have also been calls for a greater willingness to discontinue services whose uptake has diminished (Dempsey, 2012; Martin and Sheehan, 2018; Schlak, 2022a). Space, too, has emerged as a vital resource whose utilisation needs to be optimised to provide a platform for effective learning, user creativity, campus community and ultimately library positioning.

The well-positioned academic library

The proposed positioning strategies are intended to advance the academic library so that it is well placed for further progress and benefits in a variety of ways, including:

- an appropriate balance of effort and focus between the institutional and library agendas, with the library viewed as a problem solver and connector across the institution;
- stronger influence on campus and more lead roles for the library through assertive positioning and heightened sensitivity to institutional politics and imperatives;
- better informed perceptions of the library by stakeholders, with the distinctive features of its value proposition understood and appreciated;

- a clear sense of its purpose as the library capitalises fully on its unique strengths;
- fuller recognition of the library's contribution on and beyond the campus;
- improved competitiveness for resourcing and optimal alignment of resources with priorities;
- intensified engagement with and by users, including effective two-way communications;
- greater ability to anticipate opportunities and threats through enhanced awareness of external developments and an emphasis on creativity and learning;
- more control of destiny, embracing uncertainty with greater confidence towards the future, while leveraging past achievements to good effect.

These are desirable outcomes and, while they cannot be guaranteed amid ongoing high levels of instability in the operating environment, academic libraries have a far better chance of success if they adopt an active, assertive and diversified approach to their positioning. It is essentially a matter of taking the initiative and looking outwards, while being strategic towards their assets and aiming high.

Conclusion

The importance of positioning is recognised in the business world and this chapter has highlighted how vital it is for academic libraries. Insufficient library attention to positioning in the past may have contributed to issues such as underestimation, benign neglect, lack of political clout, resourcing struggles and user confusion. There is no universal positioning strategy or set of strategies for academic libraries. Much depends on the existing position of the library and the situation and priorities of its parent institution. These will drive the appropriate combination of positioning strategies for advancing an academic library in the institution.

Academic libraries' operating environment is fluid, but positioning calls for a long-term commitment and the ten strategies outlined in this chapter are all of an ongoing nature. Positioning must be a never-ending effort and preoccupation for academic libraries through which they continuously challenge themselves and keep asking questions about the dynamics of their wider environment, their place in it and what other players are doing and thinking. An element of competition runs through positioning and rivalry is a part of today's campus environment. Academic libraries need to be able and willing to compete, playing to their strengths, especially those unique, natural assets which offer advantages over others and support their essentialness to the institutional mission. Ries and Trout (2001, 201) include a chapter titled 'Playing the Positioning Game' and it is important for academic libraries to be politically informed players on that pitch. Getting on the front foot is essential and perhaps culturally challenging for some, but positioning cannot be left to chance and it is best to approach it with confidence and a positive mentality.

Positioning is about being noticed for the right reasons. Actions in support of the priorities of its parent institution are the most eloquent positioning statement an academic library can make and will have the greatest impact on positive positioning. Published library strategies are an ideal opportunity to make this clear and the examples cited earlier from the University of Western Australia (2024) and North Carolina State University (2022) are powerful in this context. Using resources well is also vital and it is for each library to decide their optimal deployment and alignment with the positioning strategies it chooses. Effective positioning requires significant effort and commitment, but the potential benefits justify the investment.

CHAPTER 11

Academic Library Positioning Toolkit

Overview

This short chapter identifies time-saving resources to guide practical library positioning.

Introduction

Chapter 11 comprises a toolkit which offers a selection of resources to support the practical work of positioning the academic library. It begins with overviews of the operating environment, as well as key readings about positioning strategy. This is followed by guides to a range of techniques encompassing environmental scanning, PEST analysis, the Five Forces framework, futurism and scenario planning, SWOT analysis and the RBV, VRIO and RPV frameworks, which focus on organisational resources. The final section suggests some questions designed to prompt a productive dialogue about positioning with academic library staff and stakeholders. The listing of resources is selective throughout and the aim is to save time for readers by providing a concise point of entry into materials and techniques targeted at effective positioning.

Outlines of the operating environment

The global environment

It is difficult to locate publications assessing the current state of the world and future implications from all of the political, economic, social and technological angles, but three books are noteworthy. *Megathreats: Ten Threats to Our Future and How to Survive Them* by Nouriel Roubini (2023) emphasises economic factors but goes beyond these and is broad if somewhat pessimistic in coverage. In *2030: How Today's Biggest Trends Will Collide and Reshape the Future of Everything* Guillén (2021) identifies eight major trends and is strongest on social and demographic shifts but also includes technology and economics. A longer future horizon is explored by McRae (2023) in *The World in 2050: How to Think About the Future,* which first takes stock of the current situation globally. He then examines forces for change before projecting, often with cautious optimism, how things will look in 2050 for different continents. Each of these works is informative but overtaken by subsequent events and it is necessary to draw on other sources such as newspapers, magazines, television, radio and podcasts for news and ongoing analysis of developments.

Higher education

Edited collections with diverse groups of contributors provide background and analysis of issues in higher education from a multiplicity of perspectives. Examples are *Changing Higher Education for a Changing World* (Callender, Locke and Marginson, 2020), *Higher Education in the Next Decade: Global Challenges, Future Prospects* (Eggins, Smolentseva and de Wit, 2021b) and *American Higher Education in the Twenty-First Century: Social, Political, and Economic Challenges* (Bastedo, Altbach and Gumport, 2023). Perusal of any of these volumes provides a sense of enduring matters of importance on the higher education agenda. Such sources are only current at the time of writing and the annually updated coverage offered by the *EDUCAUSE Horizon Report, Teaching and Learning Edition* is welcome. It highlights social, technological, economic, environmental and political trends, as well as key technologies and practices and future scenarios.

The *Times Higher Education* and the *Chronicle of Higher Education* websites deliver ongoing news, analysis and commentary about the latest developments and hot topics in higher education, primarily focused on the UK and USA respectively. There is substantial international coverage in the *Times Higher Education* too. Each is updated daily online and offers free bulletins emailed daily during the working week, with links to newly published content mostly available only to subscribers but sometimes openly accessible. They both have in addition a range of other e-mail newsletters on specific themes and, in the case of the *Times Higher Education,* geographic regions. *Inside Higher Ed* provides further US coverage. Sources of international coverage include *University World News* and the education section within the multiple geographic editions of *The Conversation.*

- *EDUCAUSE,* https://library.educause.edu/resources/2021/2/horizon-reports
- *Times Higher Education,* www.timeshighereducation.com

- *Chronicle of Higher Education*, www.chronicle.com
- *Inside Higher Ed*, www.insidehighered.com
- *University World News*, www.universityworldnews.com
- *The Conversation*, https://theconversation.com

Academic libraries

Readers are probably already familiar with sources of intelligence about changes in this environment, but it is worth noting a selection of resources which update developments at regular intervals. Among these are the triennial surveys by Ithaka S+R of US library directors (Hulbert, 2023) and US faculty (Blankstein, 2022). Coverage in the former includes director relationship with the institution, library role, resourcing, strategic priorities and contribution to student success. The survey of faculty is focused on their evolving information habits and behaviours and perceptions of the role of the library. *College & Research Libraries News* publishes a biennial list of top trends in academic libraries (ACRL Research Planning Review Committee, 2024), including commentary and further sources, while the ACRL issues an environmental scan, also every two years, highlighting trends in higher education and what they may mean for academic libraries (ACRL Research Planning Review Committee, 2025).

Positioning strategy readings

Positioning is one of the overarching themes of this book and Chapter 2 addressed positioning strategy specifically. It drew on literature from the marketing field and in particular the foundational reading, *Positioning: The Battle for Your Mind – How to be Seen and Heard in the Overcrowded Marketplace* (Ries and Trout, 2001). First published in 1981, its coverage is naturally dated in places, but it offers a clear exposition of positioning principles, especially the importance of influencing perceptions about a product or service. Saqib's (2021) literature review affords a perspective on how the concept of positioning has evolved over time.

Turning to library positioning, a helpful bridge between it and the application of concepts from the marketing literature is the book *Breakthrough Branding: Positioning Your Library to Survive and Thrive* (Walters, S. and Jackson, 2013). Although focused on the public library environment, Section II offers advice on positioning strategy which is applicable to academic libraries too. This book also addresses branding, identity and advocacy for libraries. A book targeted at academic libraries specifically is *Positioning the Academic Library Within the Institution: Structures and Challenges* (Appleton, 2021), also published as a special issue of the *New Review of Academic Librarianship* in 2018 (vol. 24, issue 3–4). This comprises 19 contributions, many of which have been cited in this book, representing a mix of thematic articles, case studies and a literature review. Also extensively cited in earlier pages is *The Social Future of Academic Libraries: New Perspectives on Communities, Networks, and Engagement* (Schlak, Corrall and Bracke, 2022). Its thought-provoking contributions on shifting from a transactional to a relational model carry significant implications for the positioning of academic libraries.

Techniques to support positioning

The techniques covered in this section can support the positioning of academic libraries. They are grouped first according to those with a focus on the external environment, followed by those emphasising internal resources. One group looks outwards at signs in the operating environment, while the other is concentrated on understanding assets the organisation owns and can leverage to advantage. The SWOT analysis technique spans both environments.

Environmental scanning

The United Nations has produced a short and freely available publication titled *Horizon Scan User Manual: A Step-by-step Guide* (UN Global Pulse, 2022). This is a practical resource for 'exploring the external strategic environment in a systematic way to identify potential challenges and opportunities' (p. 11). It outlines a clear five-step process for horizon scanning, from getting started through collecting data and filtering to sense-making and reporting. The manual is aimed at government agencies but its principles are widely applicable in other sectors. Enduringly valuable and incorporating a library context is the second chapter of Corrall's (2000) *Strategic Management of Information Services: A Planning Handbook*. This offers lots of practical guidance on environmental scanning and has a broad scope which includes benchmarking, surveys, PEST analysis, scenario building and stakeholder mapping. Its identification of 15 stakeholder groups remains valid in today's environment. Environmental scanning emerges as an umbrella term for a range of techniques, evident also in an overview by Butterfield (2015). It extends to futures analysis, while emphasising the need to keep the scanning process manageable by selectively investing effort in the PEST categories considered to be of most importance to the organisation.

PEST analysis

The PEST analysis framework facilitates the examination of the macro-environment according to its political, economic, social and technological dimensions. It offers some flexibility, for example the extension of PEST to Political, Economic, Social, Technological, Legal and Environmental (PESTLE) analysis. Writing from a business perspective, Makos (2024) summarises what the four PEST dimensions cover and provides a guide to how to conduct and follow up a PEST analysis, while also introducing the additional scope of PESTLE analysis. Substantial introductions to PEST analysis as a technique feature more commonly within books than as the main element of journal articles, whose coverage tends to focus on its application to specific contexts. Martinez and Wolverton (2009) outline the main features of this technique within chapters 2 and 3 of their volume on higher education strategy. They include a list of questions to ask in relation to higher education when carrying out a PEST analysis. From a library perspective PEST analysis provides the framework for a review article examining the higher education environment as the main driver of academic library strategy (Cox, J., 2021). Chapter 3 of this book also deploys the PEST dimensions to identify the main features of the global environment in which academic libraries and their parent institutions operate.

Five Forces framework

Also focused on the external environment is the Five Forces framework devised by Michael Porter (1979). This is a tool for assessing the forces affecting competition in any industry and supports organisations seeking competitive advantage by identifying opportunities, threats and points of differentiation. The forces are competitive rivalry, threat of new entrants, bargaining power of suppliers, bargaining power of buyers and the threat of substitution. Academic libraries may find the framework appropriate for establishing their position and positioning within an area where they are experiencing strong competition, thereby informing plans to ensure that their 'capabilities provide the best defense against the competitive force' (Porter, 1979, 143). Porter (2008) later updated and further elaborated on his framework, providing also lists of steps to take and pitfalls to avoid in using it. Examples of the framework in action include its application to higher education (Penprase, 2024) and the scholarly journals market (Björk, 2021).

Futurism and scenario planning

As described in Chapter 10, Mathews (2014b) makes the argument that library staff can learn from futurists in how they approach what is to come. Drucker

(1997), in an article titled 'The Future That Has Already Happened', emphasises that much can be divined from existing events by investigating more deeply what is visible but has not yet been seen. Cornish (2005) endorses this view in his book on futurism, a broad-ranging guide to skills and techniques for improving foresight and shaping a better future. In his study of possible futures for higher education Alexander (2020) provides in the opening chapter an overview of trend analysis and scenario planning. This incorporated a summary map of trends visible just before 2020 and mostly still prominent today, while also presciently urging readers to 'imagine a future academy after a major pandemic has struck the world' (Alexander, 2020, 23).

Scenario planning is a common tool for envisaging the future. Wade (2012) emphasises the importance for successful leadership of having an orientation towards the future and factoring in the unexpected throughout a well illustrated overview which includes step-by-step guidance and four case studies showing scenario planning in use at different types of organisations. Another source of practical guidance and case studies, this time grounded in a library context, is *Navigating the Future with Scenario Planning: A Guidebook for Librarians* (Giesecke, Cawthorne and Pearson, 2015). It includes advice on how to write up scenarios in a compelling way, as well as providing a convenient summary of previous writings about scenario planning. These include its application by academic libraries, for example in *The ARL 2030 Scenarios: A User's Guide for Research Libraries* (Association of Research Libraries, 2010).

SWOT analysis

All of the tools described so far have been directed at understanding or anticipating the external environment. The SWOT analysis framework is both internal and external in focus. It has been defined as being 'concerned with the analysis of an organization's internal and external environment with the aim of identifying internal strengths in order to take advantage of its external opportunities and avoid external (and possible internal) threats, while addressing its weaknesses' (Panagiotou, 2003, 8). Dunne (n.d.) offers a short practical overview of SWOT analysis, including its scope and how to execute it. A literature review by Helms and Nixon (2010) provides examples of its use and concludes with a critique of the SWOT analysis methodology as well as noting supplementary or alternative tools.

Its simplicity contributes to the popularity of SWOT analysis but also to a range of deficiencies. Cox identifies some of these, noting that it 'carries risks of subjectivity, bias, and over-simplification, sometimes only generating lengthy and unstructured lists of factors which lack the required depth of understanding of context and interconnectivity for strategy development' (Cox, J., 2023b, 264). His two-part SWOT analysis of academic libraries cites previous examples of library use of this framework while providing a basis for an updated and expanded analysis in Chapters 5 through 8 of this book (Cox, J., 2023a; 2023b).

The resource-based view

Over time a school of thought has argued that too much emphasis has been placed on opportunities and threats and that more attention should be directed towards internal assets. The RBV or resource-based view of organisational analysis has emerged, looking unambiguously inwards at the assets, sometimes intangible, owned by an organisation as sources of competitive advantage. It has sought also to enhance SWOT analysis by enabling a deeper assessment of situation, prospects and positioning. Barney (1991) developed the VRIN framework to support the characterisation and identification of valuable, rare, inimitable and non-substitutable strengths unique to an organisation and capable of being leveraged as competitive assets. Four years later another paper by Barney (1995) updated the framework as VRIO, with organisation-supported becoming the fourth characteristic. Also relevant is RPV, another internally focused model introduced in Chapter 10. It advances the alignment of resources, processes and values while also supporting the examination of the agility of an organisation towards disruptive change (Christensen and Overdorf, 2000; Christensen, Anthony and Roth, 2004).

Positioning strategy conversations: some questions to ask

Conversation helps to shape positioning strategy. It includes discussion and reflection both among the academic library team and by it with stakeholders. This section proposes a set of questions, based on issues identified as significant in this book, which can be used or adapted as required to facilitate a helpful dialogue in either situation. The term stakeholder is broadly defined in this context to include institutional leaders, users and potential users and the questions proposed in that category are more generic in nature.

For library team discussion

- What impact might political, economic, social or technological developments nationally and in the world at large have on the current

and future position of the library? Can we anticipate opportunities or threats?
- What is happening in teaching, learning and research? Are there any new trends, policies, behaviours, needs and expectations which we need to research further or to which we should respond?
- What are the university's top priorities in the immediate and longer terms? What is the library doing to help advance them and what more can we do?
- How influential and competitively resourced are we on campus right now? What is the campus political climate and with whom could we work more closely?
- Are we playing fully to our strengths and are any points of weakness holding us back?
- How effectively are we communicating the library value proposition? Is the library accurately perceived?
- Who are our main collaborators and competitors on and beyond the campus and in what areas are they active?
- How is our identity distinctive? What are our unique characteristics and how can we make them count to the maximum extent?
- Are we clear about our core purpose and the ways in which we convey this?
- What will advance our position and how do we want to be seen? What does active positioning require of us in terms of approach and the alignment of our resources?
- What has our previous experience taught us? Have others had similar experiences? Are there routes we should take and traps to avoid?
- With which stakeholders should we meet to discuss our position and positioning?

For dialogue with stakeholders

- What is changing or has changed most in your environment in recent times?
- What is coming down the tracks?
- What opportunities and challenges do you foresee? What will these mean for you and for the university?
- What are your priorities and pressure points at present?
- When you think of the library, what springs to mind?
- How do you perceive the current contribution of the library to meeting the challenges you face?

- Where do you think we can do more to help secure a competitive advantage for you and for the university?
- Are you aware of (concisely described) library activities, expertise, connectivity and values linked to your priority areas?
- Can we advantageously share our experience in cross-cutting areas such as research dissemination, AI, digital literacy and student belonging, retention and progression?
- What do you want the library to factor into its strategy development?
- How best can we partner with you and your colleagues in the future for mutual benefit? Are there groups in which we should participate?
- Who else would you suggest we meet to have this type of conversation?

CHAPTER 12

Conclusion

In the grip of events

A change of Presidency in the USA in January 2025 brought chaos to higher education as the second Trump administration commenced with a blizzard of executive orders and other measures, some with temporary effect, others expected to have longer-term impact. Actions included:

- a threat to pause federal funding while a review of the alignment of expenditure with new government priorities was in progress;
- the suspension of research grant approvals by the National Institutes of Health (NIH) and other major federal funding agencies;
- a policy proposal to curtail NIH funding of research overheads;
- a federal order issued to universities and colleges to eliminate all race-based policies and programmes;
- denial of federal funding to institutions refusing to comply with the administration's demands;
- a major reduction in the staffing of the Department of Education, foreshadowing its possible closure.

These measures represented merely the prelude to a sustained and often hostile federal government challenge to higher education in the USA as 2025 progressed (*Chronicle of Higher Education*, 2025b). They caused alarm in terms of immediate or future funding and costs, academic freedom, implications for any DEI-related initiatives, jobs, teaching and research programmes and potential impact on cross-border collaborations (Blake, 2025; Grove, 2025a; 2025b; Knott, 2025). There was much in these developments to concern academic libraries in and beyond the USA too, including financial uncertainty, information and data access restrictions, independent collection development, effective international engagement and threats to some of their core values. That the position of academic libraries is intimately bound up with external events never seemed clearer.

Key messages and learnings

The central thesis of this book has been as follows. It is essential for academic libraries to have a deep understanding of their history and wider operating environment, as well as a full appreciation of their strengths, weaknesses, opportunities and threats as these interact with external forces, if they are to develop strategy effectively and to position themselves for advancement.

Part 1

Some lessons from history were evident at the outset when Chapter 1 reviewed how the position and positioning of academic libraries have evolved over the centuries. These included, advantageously for their position today, their longer history than most campus units, as well as the constancy of their close association with scholarship and the institutional academic mission. Less positively, the opening chapter showed that academic library struggles regarding funding, recognition, status and influence, as well as stakeholder indifference and their own inclination towards inward focus and conservatism, are not new. Rather they are longstanding and deep-rooted. The advance of digital access to information, increasingly at the expense of printed collections, proved a major turning point and was highly consequential in terms of library roles, value and identity, with a mix of positive and negative impacts on position.

Chapter 2 focused on positioning strategy, outlining what successful positioning encompasses, namely clear identity, distinctiveness, intimate understanding of target audiences and their needs, effective communications and aligned resources. It also explained why positioning is important in the way it affects perceptions, influence, resourcing and prospects. Positioning is also difficult for academic libraries, however, as they strive to balance their traditional and solid value proposition with its newer, far more diverse version in ways that make sense to stakeholders in a constantly changing environment. An active approach to positioning emerged in this chapter as essential in order to match intense competition, shape perceptions of the library and take greater control of its destiny.

The complexity and challenges of a multiplicity of political, economic, social and technological factors in today's world with consequences for higher education and academic libraries were the subject of Chapter 3. Some of these factors are progressive, some negative and some both, as in the case of AI.

They are without precedent in some instances and even existential when it comes to climate change. Some fly in the face of the previously established order, so that everyone is situated in uncharted territory. Their significance for the position and strategic positioning of academic libraries is huge. This includes access to global services alongside exposure to global competition, political instability and contravention of values and principles they hold dear but also opportunities to uphold and promote them. Also important are changes in the demographics of their user population and a mix of technological threat and opportunity in terms of jobs, service development and user engagement.

Higher education, the environment in which academic libraries operate most closely, has experienced major change in recent decades and Chapter 4 examined its current situation. It found a dynamic, globalised, disrupted, often under-resourced, less trusted and more competitive and bureaucratic sector. In combination with a pressurised and demanding academic, administrative and student body, this has created a difficult campus environment which libraries find challenging to navigate and influence. They are operating in a sector which feels increasingly under siege and whose position is uncertain and unsettled, especially since the COVID-19 pandemic and the intensification of technological change through online learning and AI. Despite the ongoing sense of crisis, higher education is still in demand, highly creative and vital to society. It is nevertheless tightly stretched as it confronts new funder demands and user preferences while striving to maximise resources and competitiveness. All of this filters through to academic libraries in various ways, including a constant pressure to do more with less, support new needs, compete for resources and prove their value as a climate of marketisation and accountability prevails.

Part 2

Their strengths, weaknesses, opportunities and threats influence the position and prospects of academic libraries and underpin their strategies as they collide with global and higher education developments. Part 2 of the book, comprising Chapters 5 through 8, conducted a SWOT analysis to understand academic libraries' current situation in greater depth.

The enduring potency of centrality, values, collaboration and reinvention as academic library strengths was featured in Chapter 5. Centrality in terms of institutional mission, physical location and within social networks stands out as a natural advantage to be fully exploited. It provides an excellent platform for positioning progress, marking the library as a recognised campus entity which performs a vital and advantageous connector role. The values of academic libraries represent an undersold positioning asset and source of credit in today's world, offering a welcome counter to disinformation, polarisation, marketisation and individualism. They have promoted the retention of a high level of user trust as a point of distinction relative to many other entities, carrying great significance for academic library position and positioning.

Collaboration is also distinctive regarding the extent of library commitment to it and the range of partners involved. It is an established library tradition and a very positive association at a time of increasingly prevalent competitive individualism. It emphasises generosity and sharing of resources in the cause of mutual benefit, institutional priorities and the greater good. The reinvention of the academic library value proposition is readily evident in the diversity of involvements and contributions across teaching, learning and research, the transformation of physical spaces and the whole user experience on offer. This translates to a more sustainable position than when library value was mainly bound up in collections, providing more options for further development of positioning.

On the negative side of the ledger are four weaknesses which were selected for examination in Chapter 6, namely conservatism, stakeholder misperceptions, economic struggles and diversity deficits. They inhibit academic libraries from reaching their full potential and taking the opportunities available to them.

Conservatism breeds incrementalism, continuity and steadiness, but is this sufficient in the face of external disruption, competition, dynamic and rapid change and unprecedented challenges? Innovation, agility, proactivity and greater outward focus are essential in these circumstances. Stakeholder misperceptions may be the most significant weakness, given that position is so strongly influenced by what is in people's minds. Underestimation, indifference, unawareness and traditional perspectives contribute in many cases to an assigned position which is not favourable for academic libraries.

Economic struggles have long been part of the academic library existence and will persist as higher education institutions continue to experience a tight funding climate. Their libraries are trapped in a dangerous combination of static budgets, increasing costs, reduced competitiveness and sometimes latent value in the digital environment. Questionable economic sustainability is bad for position and positioning. Diversity deficits affect staffing, collections and space, contributing to a sense of academic libraries not being fully in tune with the foregrounding of DEI in most of the contemporary world. There is much ground to make up and impacts may include user alienation, a loss of effectiveness and the missing of opportunities afforded by access to multiple perspectives.

Chapter 7 identified opportunities, specifically open scholarship, AI, learning space and aspects of the wider world, for academic libraries to advance their position and exert new influence. Each of the four opportunities demands some reprioritisation, a reconceptualisation of existing paradigms and a general openness and agility towards rethinking the traditional boundaries of the role of the academic library.

Open scholarship offers a rare and vital chance to reshape scholarly communication and student learning, confronting major flaws and emphasising the library at the centre of academic life. It could also help to address the unsustainable costs of the current academic publishing system. Artificial intelligence might be viewed primarily as a threat but there is more to be gained by focusing on what it promises in terms of operational efficiency, new service potential and higher-value roles moving the academic library up the institutional hierarchy. The trusted status of the library is a major asset which can be realised in leading an increasingly confident campus deployment of AI.

Transformed library space has also proved highly influential in terms of the student learning experience. Academic library buildings have become both technology-rich spaces for interdisciplinary creativity and collaboration and vital places of campus community and belonging. The redefined academic library building provides a real platform for further development and advantageous positioning. The world faces many problems but is also a source of opportunities, as academic libraries proved in their successful response to the COVID-19 pandemic. There are opportunities and indeed responsibilities to promote truth in the face of disinformation or research fraud, even-handedness instead of polarisation, DEI against hostility from multiple sources and sustainability as climate change accelerates. Academic libraries can be recognised as real difference makers on and beyond their campuses.

Chapter 8 completed the SWOT analysis by considering four threats. A decline in the position of academic libraries over recent decades represents an overarching threat, fed by the other three factors, which were identified as identity blurring, competition internally and externally at an intensified level and uncertainty in the operating environment. These threats can jeopardise the position and positioning of academic libraries.

Decline has compromised progress and had a cumulative and residual effect on academic libraries over recent decades, evident in practical terms in their resourcing as a percentage of institutional expenditure, the reporting line of the director and their general position in the organisational hierarchy. This can also shape external perceptions and generate a sense of insecurity within the library. Clarity of identity was emphasised earlier as vital to positioning but it has become a concern for academic libraries. Their value proposition has diversified in the digital era, making it harder to explain their distinctiveness from other units with which they often collaborate. It can be difficult for stakeholders to understand a less concrete and measurable value proposition, potentially diverting credit and funding elsewhere.

Competition pitted against academic libraries is far stronger and more broadly based today. Campus partners such as the research office and the IT department can also be competitors. External competition is even tougher and has captured business in areas such as discovery, publishing and data storage. Disintermediation raises questions about academic library competitiveness and user confidence. The level of uncertainty in their operating environment makes library positioning very difficult as higher education institutions frequently shift priorities or fear for their future viability. Library strategy encompasses shorter time horizons and, having negotiated the COVID-19 pandemic, further disruption looks likely through AI and changes in scholarly communication, not to mention political tensions globally and the existential threat of climate change.

Part 3

The final part of the book began with Chapter 9, which sought to distil the current position of academic libraries from the multiplicity of external factors in their operating environment as well as their own unique combination of strengths, weaknesses, opportunities and threats. The overall picture that emerged is mixed. At one level, the academic library is a long-established, trusted, expected and collegiate part of campus life, vital to the institutional sense of community. It is much esteemed and valued both as essential to scholarship and as a strong partner through its committed and values-driven staff. At another, it tends to be taken for granted, is subject to benign neglect and often underestimated as well as misunderstood, contributing to a diminution of economic and political power despite the goodwill commonly exhibited towards it. There is also a definite sense that the position of academic libraries could be more favourable if they addressed some avoidable own goals, including a tendency towards too much focus on internal operations at the expense of campus priorities.

Position is not static and AI, demographic shifts and a stronger relationship-centred than collections-based emphasis can be foreseen as key influences in the near future. Less foreseeable but far more impactful than any of these would be a global catastrophe, a possibility which everyone must hope will not materialise. Much is uncertain but one thing that is clear is that the academic library is at an important juncture, where it needs to capitalise on enduring strengths in the face of gathering vulnerabilities.

Chapter 10 rooted its menu of ten positioning strategies in the summary developed in the previous chapter of current position and how academic libraries had arrived at it. Common features of the proposed strategies are that they have an external focus on the actualities of the global, higher education and campus worlds and seek to maximise internal library strengths. Taking an active approach to positioning was the first and overarching strategy recommended. Looking outwards was a unifying theme for six of the other strategies, namely: know the territory; be politically attuned; prioritise the institutional agenda; communicate value and identity; be agile towards opportunities; and embrace uncertainty. The other three strategies emphasised leveraging some of the strengths of academic libraries: maximise library connectedness; emphasise distinctiveness; and capitalise on longevity.

It is intended that academic libraries may select from this list of proposed strategies according to their circumstances and priorities. Whatever selection of strategies is made, it is essential to align human, financial, physical, digital and intangible resources with them. The stakes are high and successful positioning promises meaningful rewards for academic libraries, alleviating the weaknesses and threats they confront. Potential benefits include expanded resources, greater influence, intensified user engagement, a fuller valuation by stakeholders of the library contribution and a more secure base in the institution and in the wider world.

Positioning is complex, competitive and challenging. It requires guile, skill and commitment alongside a highly practical approach to enacting strategies based on some level of theoretical knowledge but fully informed by developments in the macro-environment as well as the characteristics of the internal world of academic libraries. Chapter 11 recognised this combination of theory and practice by signposting a selection of resources to support the work of positioning, enabling a better understanding of the environment in which it takes place and of some of the techniques it involves. Conversation is an important element in developing positioning strategies and the chapter concluded with some questions aiming to stimulate a positive dialogue among library staff and with stakeholders.

Ten takeaways

1 The position occupied by academic libraries is complex and multidimensional.
2 Their history is a mix of earlier continuity and more recent disruption.
3 Positioning is important, influential and challenging.

4 Global instability and sometimes lack of precedent have implications for academic libraries.
5 Pressure on higher education transmits itself to them.
6 The campus positioning environment is highly competitive and political.
7 Academic libraries have many competitors, beyond as well as on their campuses.
8 The collision of strengths and weaknesses with opportunities and threats shape the current position and future potential of academic libraries.
9 Their overall position combines positive and encouraging elements with negative and concerning factors.
10 Effective positioning is assertive, looks outwards and maximises the strengths of academic libraries, with promises of advancement and reward.

What next?

This book introduced itself with the story of an academic library under threat at Western Illinois University, but it concludes on an optimistic note. Yes, academic libraries are in a difficult position and the path to improving their situation is not linear or without obstacles. They are, however, endowed with strengths of enduring value and there are some truly transformative opportunities for them to grasp. The book has outlined some strategies to support them in taking the initiative, capitalising on their strengths, mitigating their weaknesses and responding to the threats they face. It has also tracked the historical evolution of their position and positioning and identified the major forces in their operating environment as well as the main features of their internal world, while pointing to further resources for positioning. Armed with these tools and an impressive array of intangible as well as tangible assets, academic libraries should take on the challenge and opportunity to advance their position with confidence. The rewards include stronger resourcing, uptake, appreciation and influence. They are worth fighting for and the key lies in a highly active, informed and assertive approach to positioning. There is far more to gain than to lose, so seize the day!

References

Acemoglu, D. and Johnson, S. (2023) *Power and Progress: Our Thousand-year Struggle Over Technology and Prosperity*, PublicAffairs.

ACRL Research Planning Review Committee (2018) 2018 Top Trends in Academic Libraries: A Review of the Trends and Issues Affecting Academic Libraries in Higher Education, *College & Research Libraries News*, **79** (6), 286–93, https://doi.org/10.5860/crln.79.6.286.

ACRL Research Planning Review Committee (2019) *Environmental Scan 2019*, www.ala.org/sites/default/files/acrl/content/publications/whitepapers/EnvironmentalScan2019.pdf.

ACRL Research Planning Review Committee (2020) 2020 Top Trends in Academic Libraries: A Review of the Trends and Issues Affecting Academic Libraries in Higher Education, *College & Research Libraries News*, **81** (6), 270–8, https://doi.org/10.5860/crln.81.6.270.

ACRL Research Planning Review Committee (2022) Top Trends in Academic Libraries: A Review of the Trends and Issues, *College & Research Libraries News*, **83** (6), 243–56, https://doi.org/10.5860/crln.83.6.243.

ACRL Research Planning Review Committee (2024) 2024 Top Trends in Academic Libraries: A Review of the Trends and Issues, *College & Research Libraries News*, **85** (6), 231–46, https://doi.org/10.5860/crln.85.6.231.

ACRL Research Planning Review Committee (2025) *Environmental Scan 2025*, www.ala.org/sites/default/files/2025-04/2025_ACRL_Environmental_Scan.pdf.

Adams Becker, S., Cummins, M., Davis, A., Freeman, A., Hall Giesinger, C., Ananthanarayanan, V., . . . Wolfson, N. (2017) *NMC Horizon Report: 2017 Library Edition*, New Media Consortium, https://library.educause.edu/~/media/files/library/2017/12/2017nmchorizonreportlibraryEN.pdf.

Alabi, J. (2015) Racial Microaggressions in Academic Libraries: Results of a Survey of Minority and Non-Minority Librarians, *Journal of Academic Librarianship*, **41** (1), 47–53, https://doi.org/10.1016/j.acalib.2014.10.008.

Alburo, J., Bradshaw, A. K., Santiago, A. E., Smith, B. and Vinopal, J. (2020) Looking Beyond Libraries for Inclusive Recruitment and Retention Practices: Four Successful Approaches. In Hines, S. S. and Ketchum, D. H. (eds) *Critical Librarianship*, 85–109, Emerald Publishing, https://doi.org/10.1108/S0732-067120200000041009.

Alexander, B. (2020) *Academia Next: the Futures of Higher Education*, Johns Hopkins University Press.

Alexander, B., Adams Becker, S., Cummins, M. and Hall Geisinger, C. (2017) *Digital Literacy in Higher Education, Part II: An NMC Horizon Project Strategic Brief*, New Media Consortium, https://library.educause.edu/resources/2017/8/digital-literacy-in-higher-education-part-ii-an-nmc-horizon-project-strategic-brief.

Allen, S. (2014) Towards a Conceptual Map of Academic Libraries' Role in Student Retention: A Literature Review, *The Christian Librarian*, **57** (1), 7–19, http://digitalcommons.georgefox.edu/tcl/vol57/iss1/3.

Altbach, P. G. and de Wit, H. (2023) Global Patterns of Higher Education Development. In Bastedo, M. N., Altbach, P. G. and Gumport, P. J. (eds) *American Higher Education in the Twenty-first Century: Social, Political, and Economic Challenges*, 181–206, Johns Hopkins University Press.

Altbach, P. G. and Finkelstein, M. (2023) Harsh Realities: The Professoriate in the Twenty-first Century. In Bastedo, M. N., Altbach, P. G. and Gumport, P. J. (eds) *American Higher Education in the Twenty-first Century: Social, Political, and Economic Challenges*, 94–118, Johns Hopkins University Press.

American Library Association (2020) *The State of America's Libraries 2020: A Report from the American Library Association*, www.ala.org/news/sites/ala.org.news/files/content/State-of-Americas-Libraries-2020-web-2.pdf.

American Library Association (2024) *Core Values of Librarianship*, www.ala.org/advocacy/advocacy/intfreedom/corevalues.

Anderson, R. (2011) The Crisis in Research Librarianship, *Journal of Academic Librarianship*, **37** (4), 289–90, https://doi.org/10.1016/j.acalib.2011.04.001.

Anderson, R. (2016) *Libraries, Leadership, and Scholarly Communication: Essays by Rick Anderson*, American Library Association.

Andersson, B. (2018) A New Dawn? Academia Moving Eastwards. In Heijnen, A. and van der Vaart, R. (eds) *Places of Engagement: Reflections on Higher Education in 2040 – a Global Approach*, 101–7, Amsterdam University Press, https://doi.org/10.2307/j.ctvfjd0xs.

Anonymous (2023) Afghan Universities are Losing their Scholars and Students, *Times Higher Education*, 4 December, www.timeshighereducation.com/opinion/afghan-universities-are-losing-their-scholars-and-students.

Appleton, L. (2010) Living Through Super-convergence: Creating Library and Student Support at Liverpool John Moores University, *SCONUL Focus,* (49), 67–70.

Appleton, L. (2018) Positioning the Academic Library Within the Institution: Structures and Challenges, *New Review of Academic Librarianship,* **24** (33–4), 209–16, https://doi.org/10.1080/13614533.2019.1582078.

Appleton, L. (2020) Leading Liberation in the Library. In Weaver, M. and Appleton, L. (eds) *Bold Minds: Library Leadership in a Time of Disruption,* 47–61, Facet Publishing.

Appleton, L. (ed.) (2021) *Positioning the Academic Library Within the Institution: Structures and Challenges,* Routledge.

Appleton, L. (2022) Trendspotting – Looking to the Future in a Post-Pandemic Academic Library Environment, *New Review of Academic Librarianship,* **28** (1), 1–6, https://doi.org/10.1080/13614533.2022.2058174.

Appleton, L. (2024) AI and Academic Libraries: What's All the Fuss About? *New Review of Academic Librarianship,* **30** (1), 1–3, https://doi.org/10.1080/13614533.2024.2356474.

Appleton, L. and Woolley, N. (2023) The Role of Academic Libraries in Climate Action, *New Review of Academic Librarianship,* **29** (2), 117–22, https://doi.org/10.1080/13614533.2023.2230652.

Appleton, L., Stevenson, V. and Boden, D. (2011) Developing Learning Landscapes: Academic Libraries Driving Organisational Change, *Reference Services Review,* **39** (3), 343–61, https://doi.org/10.1108/00907321111161368.

Archer, V., Jones, O. A. H., Sands, D., Isaacson, R., Sword, H., Sanders, D. A., . . . Hendon, C. H. (2019) How Can Academics Keep Up with the Literature? *Times Higher Education,* 22 August, www.timeshighereducation.com/features/how-can-academics-keep-literature.

Association of College and Research Libraries (2016) *Value of Academic Libraries Statement,* www.acrl.ala.org/value/wp-content/uploads/2016/07/Value-of-Academic-Libraries-Statement-FINAL.pdf.

Association of College and Research Libraries (2018) *Standards for Libraries in Higher Education,* www.ala.org/acrl/standards/standardslibraries.

Association of Research Libraries (2010) *The ARL 2030 Scenarios: A User's Guide for Research Libraries,* www.arl.org/resources/the-arl-2030-scenarios-a-users-guide-for-research-libraries.

Association of Research Libraries (2013) *Library Expenditure as % of Total University Expenditure,* www.libqual.org/documents/admin/EG_2.pdf.

Atkins, S. E. (1991) *The Academic Library in the American University,* Parallel Press, http://digital.library.wisc.edu/1711.dl/History.AcadLib.

Atkinson, J. (2018) Reflections on Collaboration and Academic Libraries. In Atkinson, J. (ed.) *Collaboration and the Academic Library: Internal and External, Local and Regional, National and International,* 221–32, Chandos Publishing.

Atkinson, J. (2019) Collaboration by Academic Libraries: What are the Benefits, What are the Constraints, and What Do You Need to Do to be Successful? *New Review of Academic Librarianship,* **25** (1), 1–7, https://doi.org/10.1080/13614533.2019.1575016.

Baker, D. (2017) The End of Wisdom? The Future of Libraries in the Digital Age. In Baker, D. and Evans, W. (eds) *The End of Wisdom? The Future of Libraries in a Digital Age,* 1–37, Chandos Publishing.

Baker, D. and Allden, A. (2017) *Leading Libraries: The View from Above,* SCONUL, www.sconul.ac.uk/knowledge-hub/organisational-development/[illegible] links.

Baker, M. (2016) 1,500 Scientists Lift the Lid on Reproducibility, *Nature,* **533** (7604), 452–4, https://doi.org/10.1038/533452a.

Bakkalbasi, N. (2017) Assessment and Evaluation, Promotion, and Marketing of Academic Library Services. In Gilman, T. and Lynch, B. P. (eds) *Academic Librarianship Today,* 211–21, Rowman & Littlefield.

Barnett, R. (2022) *The Philosophy of Higher Education: A Critical Introduction,* Routledge.

Barney, J. B. (1991) Firm Resources and Sustained Competitive Advantage, *Journal of Management,* **17** (1), 99–120, https://doi.org/10.1177/014920639101700108.

Barney, J. B. (1995) Looking Inside for Competitive Advantage, *Academy of Management Executive,* **9** (4), 49–61, https://doi.org/10.5465/ame.1995.9512032192.

Basken, P. (2023a) Conservatives Aim at Harvard and MIT Heads After Magill Quits, *Times Higher Education,* 4 December, www.timeshighereducation.com/news/conservatives-aim-harvard-and-mit-heads-after-magill-quits.

Basken, P. (2023b) US Campus Protests on Israel-Hamas War Raise Divestment Pressure, *Times Higher Education,* 29 November, www.timeshighereducation.com/news/us-campus-protests-israel-hamas-war-raise-divestment-pressure.

Bastedo, M. N., Altbach, P. G. and Gumport, P. J. (eds) (2023) *American Higher Education in the Twenty-first Century: Social, Political, and Economic Challenges,* Johns Hopkins University Press.

Baughman, S., Brillat, A., Daines, G., Davis, G., McReynolds, S. J. H. and Roller, M. (2023) *Building a Community of Assessment: Final Report of the Research Library Impact Framework Pilot Initiative,* Association of Research Libraries, www.arl.org/wp-content/uploads/2023/03/2023.03.10-building-a-community-of-assessment-rlif-final-report.pdf.

Beilin, I. G. (2017) The Academic Research Library's White Past and Present. In Schlesselman-Tarango, G. (ed.) *Topographies of Whiteness: Mapping Whiteness in Library and Information Science,* 77–96, Library Juice Press, https://doi.org/10.7916/D82F94R2.

Bekhradnia, B. (2024) *Student Demand to 2035*, Higher Education Policy Institute, www.hepi.ac.uk/wp-content/uploads/2024/10/Student-Demand-to-2035.pdf.

Bell, S. (2015) Evolution in Higher Education Matters to Libraries. In Allen, N. (ed.) *New Roles for the Road Ahead: Essays Commissioned for ACRL's 75th Birthday*, 13–18, Association of College and Research Libraries, www.ala.org/acrl/sites/ala.org.acrl/files/content/publications/whitepapers/new_roles_75th.pdf.

Belluigi, D. Z. (2023) Why Decolonising 'Knowledge' Matters: Deliberations for Educators on That Made Fragile. In Czerniewicz, L. and Cronin, C. (eds) *Higher Education for Good: Teaching and Learning Futures*, 137–59, Open Book Publishers, https://doi.org/10.11647/obp.0363.05.

Bergenäs, E. and Dorthé, L. (2021) Why the Simple Act of Listening Will Help Us Design Strong and Sustainable Post Pandemic Library Services, *LIBER Quarterly*, **31** (1), 1–8, https://doi.org/10.18352/lq.10931.

Bergstrom, T. and Ruediger, D. (2024) *A Third Transformation? Generative AI and Scholarly Publishing*, Ithaka S+R, https://doi.org/10.18665/sr.321519.

Bergstrom, T., Rieger, O. Y. and Schonfeld, R. C. (2024) *The Second Digital Transformation of Scholarly Publishing: Strategic Context and Shared Infrastructure*, Ithaka S+R, https://doi.org/10.18665/sr.320210.

Biagioli, M. and Lippman, A. (eds) (2020) *Gaming the Metrics: Misconduct and Manipulation in Academic Research*, MIT Press, https://doi.org/10.7551/mitpress/11087.001.0001.

Bickley, R. and Corrall, S. (2011) Student Perceptions of Staff in the Information Commons: A Survey at the University of Sheffield, *Reference Services Review*, **39** (2), 223–43, https://doi.org/10.1108/00907321111135466.

Bieraugel, M. (2015) Managing Library Innovation Using the Lean Startup Method, *Library Management*, **36** (4/5), 351–61, https://doi.org/10.1108/LM-10-2014-0131.

Björk, B.-C. (2021) Why is Access to the Scholarly Journal Literature So Expensive? *portal: Libraries and the Academy*, **21** (2), 177–92, https://doi.org/10.1353/pla.2021.0010.

Bladek, M. (2021) Student Well-being Matters: Academic Library Support for the Whole Student, *Journal of Academic Librarianship*, **47** (3), 102349, https://doi.org/10.1016/j.acalib.2021.102349.

Blake, J. (2025) Higher Ed Alarmed by Trump's Plan to Freeze Federal Grants, *Inside Higher Ed*, 28 January, www.insidehighered.com/news/government/politics-elections/2025/01/28/trumps-federal-funding-freeze-concerns-colleges.

Blake, M. and Gallimore, V. (2018) Understanding Academics: A UX Ethnographic Research Project at the University of York, *New Review of Academic Librarianship*, **24** (33–4), 363–75, https://doi.org/10.1080/13614533.2018.1466716.

Blankstein, M. (2022) *Ithaka S+R US Faculty Survey 2021*, Ithaka S+R, https://doi.org/10.18665/sr.316896.

Bledsoe, K., Cooper, D. M., Schonfeld, R. C. and Rieger, O. Y. (2022) *Leading by Diversifying Collections: A Guide for Academic Library Leadership*, Ithaka S+R, https://doi.org/10.18665/sr.317833.

Blumenstyk, G. (2024) Fundamental Change is Coming Quickly to Higher Ed. Will the Sector Respond in Time? In *What Higher Ed Will Look Like in 10 Years: Fundamental Change is Coming Quickly*, 3–7, *Chronicle of Higher Education*, www.chronicle.com/report/free/what-higher-ed-will-look-like-in-10-years.

Blummer, B. and Kenton, J. M. (2017) Learning Commons in Academic Libraries: Discussing Themes in the Literature from 2001 to the Present, *New Review of Academic Librarianship*, **23** (4), 329–52, https://doi.org/10.1080/13614533.2017.1366925.

Bolman, L. G. and Deal, T. E. (2021) *Reframing Organizations: Artistry, Choice, and Leadership*, 7th edn, Jossey-Bass.

Bolton, P. (2025) *Higher Education Student Numbers*, House of Commons Library, https://researchbriefings.files.parliament.uk/documents/CBP-7857/CBP-7857.pdf.

Bothwell, E. (2023) World University Rankings 2024: Results Announced. *Times Higher Education*, 28 September, www.timeshighereducation.com/news/world-university-rankings-2024-results-announced.

Bowers Sharpe, K. (2024) Library Magic!, www.youtube.com/channel/UCrLS6BXkXHA3hd_pTVmGLUQ/videos.

Bracke, P. J. (2022a) Conclusion: Into the Social Future. In Schlak, T., Corrall, S. and Bracke, P. J. (eds) *The Social Future of Academic Libraries: New Perspectives on Communities, Networks, and Engagement*, 299–305, Facet Publishing.

Bracke, P. J. (2022b) Networks, Higher Education and the Social Future of Libraries. In Schlak, T., Corrall, S. and Bracke, P. J. (eds) *The Social Future of Academic Libraries: New Perspectives on Communities, Networks, and Engagement*, 35–58, Facet Publishing.

Brayman, K., Devenney, A., Dobson, H., Marques, M. and Vernon, A. (2024) *A Review of Transitional Agreements in the UK*, Jisc, https://doi.org/10.5281/zenodo.10787392.

Brembs, B., Huneman, P., Schönbrodt, F., Nilsonne, G., Susi, T., Siems, R., . . . Rodriguez-Cuadrado, S. (2023) Replacing Academic Journals, *Royal Society Open Science*, **10**, 230206, https://doi.org/10.1098/rsos.230206.

Brewerton, A. and Woolley, B. (2016) Study Happy: Library Wellbeing Initiatives from the University of Warwick, *SCONUL Focus*, (68), 15–25, www.sconul.ac.uk/news/sconul-focus-archive.

Brindley, L. (2006) Re-defining the Library, *Library Hi Tech*, **24** (4), 484–95, https://doi.org/10.1108/07378830610715356.

Brook, F., Ellenwood, D. and Lazzaro, A. E. (2015) In Pursuit of Antiracist Social Justice: Denaturalizing Whiteness in the Academic Library, *Library Trends*, **64** (2), 246–84, http://doi.org/10.1353/lib.2015.0048.

Brown, K. and Malenfant, K. J. (2017) *Academic Library Impact on Student Learning and Success: Findings from Assessment in Action Team Projects*, Association of College and Research Libraries, www.ala.org/acrl/sites/ala.org.acrl/files/content/issues/value/findings_y3.pdf.

Brown, S., Alvey, E., Danilova, E., Morgan, H. and Thomas, A. (2018) Evolution of Research Support Services at an Academic Library: Specialist Knowledge Linked by Core Infrastructure, *New Review of Academic Librarianship*, **24** (33–4), 337–48, https://doi.org/10.1080/13614533.2018.1473259.

Brunner, M. and Osorio, J. (2017) Recruitment, Retention, Diversity, and Professional Development. In Gilman, T. and Lynch, B. P. (eds) *Academic Librarianship Today*, 143–59, Rowman & Littlefield.

Bruxvoort, D. (2023) The Power of Place. In Baker, D., Ellis, L., Williams, C. and Wragg, C. (eds) *Benchmarking Library, Information and Education Services*, 111–16, Chandos Publishing.

Bryant, R., Dortmund, A. and Lavoie, B. (2020) *Social Interoperability in Research Support: Cross-campus Partnerships and the University Research Enterprise*, OCLC Research, https://doi.org/10.25333/wyrd-n586.

Bryant, R., Clements, A., Feltes, C., Groenewegen, D., Huggard, S., Mercer, H., . . . Wright, J. (2017) *Research Information Management: Defining RIM and the Library's Role*, OCLC Research, http://dx.doi.org/10.25333/C3NK88.

Buckland, M. (1992) *Redesigning Library Services: A Manifesto*, American Library Association, https://digitalassets.lib.berkeley.edu/sunsite/Redesigning%20Library%20Services_%20A%20Manifesto%20%28HTML%29.pdf.

Bucy, R. (2022) Native American Student Experiences of the Academic Library, *College & Research Libraries*, **83** (3), 416–33, https://doi.org/10.5860/crl.83.3.416.

Budd, J. M. (2018) *The Changing Academic Library: Operations, Culture, Environments*, 3rd edn, Association of College and Research Libraries.

Budd, J. M. (2022) Foreword. In McCallon, M. L. and Tucker, J. M. (eds) *The Academic Library in the United States: Historical Perspectives*, 1–2, McFarland.

Bulpitt, G. (ed.) (2012) *Leading the Student Experience: Super-convergence of Organisation, Structure and Business Processes*, Leadership Foundation for Higher Education, www.advance-he.ac.uk/knowledge-hub/leading-student-experience-super-convergence-organisation-structure-and-business.

Burress, T., Mann, E. Z., Montgomery, S. E. and Walton, R. (2021) Data Literacy in Undergraduate Education: Faculty Perspectives and Pedagogical Approaches. In Bauder, J. (ed.) *Data Literacy in Academic Libraries: Teaching Critical Thinking with Numbers*, 1–22, American Library Association.

Butterfield, B. (2015) Environmental Scanning and Futures Analysis. In Cox, J. B. and Radwan, S. S. (eds) *ASAE Handbook of Professional Practices in Association Management*, 3rd edn, 139–51, Jossey-Bass.

Caldwell, J. (2022a) 'People Don't Understand What Our Role Is, It Is Definitely Seen as an Inferior Job to an Academic': Perceptions on Relationships Between Professional Services and Academic Staff in the UK, *Journal of Higher Education Management*, **37** (1), 24–35, https://issuu.com/aaua10/docs/1.jhem_37_1_final_8-23_.

Caldwell, J. (2022b) Professional Identity and Professional Services Staff: Understanding and Impact, *Perspectives: Policy and Practice in Higher Education*, **26** (4), 140–7, https://doi.org/10.1080/13603108.2022.2073288.

Caldwell, J. (2024) Nomenclature in Higher Education: 'Non-academic' as a Construct, *Journal of Higher Education Policy and Management*, **46** (5), 507–22, https://doi.org/10.1080/1360080X.2024.2306569.

Callender, C., Locke, W. and Marginson, S. (eds) (2020) *Changing Higher Education for a Changing World*, Bloomsbury Academic, https://doi.org/10.5040/9781350108448.

Campbell, A. (2023) *But What Can I Do? Why Politics Has Gone Wrong and How You Can Help Fix It*, Hutchinson Heinemann.

Campbell-Meier, J. and Hussey, L. (2018) Exploring Becoming, Doing, and Relating Within the Information Professions, *Journal of Librarianship and Information Science*, **51** (4), 962–73, https://doi.org/10.1177/0961000618757298.

Chambers, C., Dumitrescu, I., Oliver, R., Seeliger, J., Zaretsky, R., Eichhorn, K. and Pietsch, T. (2020) Life in the Zoomiverse: What We Miss About the Physical Campus, *Times Higher Education*, 30 April, www.timeshighereducation.com/features/life-zoomiverse-what-we-miss-about-physical-campus.

Cheng, J. and Hoffman, S. (2020) Librarians and Administrators on Academic Library Impact Research: Characteristics and Perspectives, *College & Research Libraries*, **81** (3), 538–69, https://doi.org/10.5860/crl.81.3.538.

Christensen, C. M. and Overdorf, M. (2000) Meeting the Challenge of Disruptive Change, *Harvard Business Review*, **78** (2), 66–76, https://hbr.org/2000/03/meeting-the-challenge-of-disruptive-change.

Christensen, C. M., Anthony, S. D. and Roth, E. A. (2004) *Seeing What's Next: Using the Theories of Innovation to Predict Industry Change*, Harvard Business School Press.

Chronicle of Higher Education (2025a) DEI Legislation Tracker, www.chronicle.com/article/here-are-the-states-where-lawmakers-are-seeking-to-ban-colleges-dei-efforts.

Chronicle of Higher Education (2025b) Tracking Trump's Higher-ed Agenda, www.chronicle.com/article/tracking-trumps-higher-ed-agenda.

Clancy, P. (2021) The Governance of European Higher Education in Transition. In Eggins, H., Smolentseva, A. and de Wit, H. (eds) *Higher Education in the Next Decade: Global Challenges, Future Prospects*, 167–85, Brill.

Clarke, M. (2022) Liberating the Library: What It Means to Decolonise and Why It Is Necessary. In Crilly, J. and Everitt, R. (eds) *Narrative Expansions: Interpreting Decolonisation in Academic Libraries*, 127–38, Facet Publishing.

Colby, G. (2023) *Data Snapshot: Tenure and Contingency in US Higher Education*, American Association of University Professors, www.aaup.org/sites/default/files/AAUP%20Data%20Snapshot.pdf.

Connaway, L. S., Harvey, W., Kitzie, V. and Mikitish, S. (2017) *Academic Library Impact: Improving Practice and Essential Areas to Research*, Association of College and Research Libraries, www.ala.org/acrl/sites/ala.org.acrl/files/content/publications/whitepapers/academiclib.pdf.

Connell, R. (2019) *The Good University: What Universities Actually Do and Why It's Time for Radical Change*, Zed Books.

Conner, M. (2014) *The New University Library: Four Case Studies*, ALA Editions.

Cooper, D. M., Hill, C. B. and Schonfeld, R. C. (2022) *Aligning the Research Library to Organizational Strategy*, Ithaka S+R, https://doi.org/10.18665/sr.316656.

Copper, C. M. (2023) *The Experimental Library: A Guide to Taking Risks, Failing Forward, and Creating Change*, ALA Editions.

Cornish, E. (2005) *Futuring: the Exploration of the Future*, World Future Society.

Corrado, E. M. (2024) Environmental Sustainability and Libraries, *Technical Services Quarterly*, **41** (3), 265–74, https://doi.org/10.1080/07317131.2024.2357015.

Corrall, S. (2000) *Strategic Management of Information Services: A Planning Handbook*, Aslib/IMI.

Corrall, S. (2022a) Renewing and Revitalising the Social Mission of Higher Education. In Schlak, T., Corrall, S. and Bracke, P. J. (eds) *The Social Future of Academic Libraries: New Perspectives on Communities, Networks, and Engagement*, 59–90, Facet Publishing.

Corrall, S. (2022b) The Social Mission of Academic Libraries in Higher Education. In Schlak, T., Corrall, S. and Bracke, P. J. (eds) *The Social Future of Academic Libraries: New Perspectives on Communities, Networks, and Engagement*, 109–47, Facet Publishing.

Corrall, S. (2022c) The Social Turn in Communities, Professions and the Economy. In Schlak, T., Corrall, S. and Bracke, P. J. (eds) *The Social Future of Academic Libraries: New Perspectives on Communities, Networks, and Engagement*, 3–33, Facet Publishing.

Corrall, S. (2023a) Alignment, Collaboration and the Social Turn: Our Agenda for the Relational Library, *New Review of Academic Librarianship*, **29** (1), 1–10, https://doi.org/10.1080/13614533.2023.2196277.

Corrall, S. (2023b) Seven Strategies to Turn Academic Libraries Into Social Organisations, *Times Higher Education*, 10 March, www.timeshighereducation.com/campus/seven-strategies-turn-academic-libraries-social-organisations.

Corrall, S. (2024) Foreword – the Network is the Message. In Pavey, S., *The Networked Librarian: The School Librarian's Role in Fostering Connections, Collaboration and Co-Creation Across the Community*, xi-xvii, Facet Publishing.

Cox, A. M. (2021) *The Impact of AI, Machine Learning, Automation and Robotics on the Information Professions*, CILIP, www.cilip.org.uk/page/researchreport.

Cox, A. M. (2023) Factors Shaping Future Use and Design of Academic Library Space, *New Review of Academic Librarianship*, **29** (1), 33–50, https://doi.org/10.1080/13614533.2022.2039244.

Cox, A. M. (2025) *AI and the UK Library Profession: Survey Results*, CILIP, https://www.cilip.org.uk/page/AISurveyReport2025.

Cox, A. M. and Benson-Marshall, M. (2021) *Drivers for the Usage of SCONUL Member Libraries*, SCONUL, www.sconul.ac.uk/knowledge-hub/space-and-design/resources-and-links.

Cox, A. M. and Brewster, L. (2019) Services for Student Well-being in Academic Libraries: Three Challenges, *New Review of Academic Librarianship*, **27** (2), 149–64, https://doi.org/10.1080/13614533.2019.1678493.

Cox, A. M. and Mazumdar, S. (2024) Defining Artificial Intelligence for Librarians, *Journal of Librarianship and Information Science*, **56** (2), 330–40, https://doi.org/10.1177/09610006221142029.

Cox, A. M., Pinfield, S. and Rutter, S. (2019a) Academic Libraries' Stance Toward the Future, *portal: Libraries and the Academy*, **19** (3), 485–509, https://doi.org/10.1353/pla.2019.0028.

Cox, A. M., Pinfield, S. and Rutter, S. (2019b) Extending McKinsey's 7S Model to Understand Strategic Alignment in Academic Libraries, *Library Management*, **40** (5), 313–26, https://doi.org/10.1108/LM-06-2018-0052.

Cox, A. M., Pinfield, S. and Rutter, S. (2019c) The Intelligent Library: Thought Leaders' Views on the Likely Impact of Artificial Intelligence on Academic Libraries, *Library Hi Tech*, **37** (3), 418–35, https://doi.org/10.1108/LHT-08-2018-0105.

Cox, A. M., Kennan, M. A., Lyon, L. and Pinfield, S. (2017) Developments in Research Data Management in Academic Libraries: Towards an Understanding of Research Data Service Maturity, *Journal of the Association for Information Science and Technology*, **68** (9), 2182–200, http://dx.doi.org/10.1002/asi.23781.

Cox, C. (2020) Changed, Changed Utterly, *Inside Higher Ed*, 5 June, www.insidehighered.com/views/2020/06/05/academic-libraries-will-change-significant-ways-result-pandemic-opinion.

Cox, J. (2016a) Communicating New Library Roles to Enable Digital Scholarship: A Review Article, *New Review of Academic Librarianship*, **22** (22–3), 132–47, http://dx.doi.org/10.1080/13614533.2016.1181665.

Cox, J. (2016b) Ten Years of a Future Leaders Programme Reflective Journal, *SCONUL Focus*, (66), 26–9, www.sconul.ac.uk/news/sconul-focus-archive.

Cox, J. (2018) Positioning the Academic Library Within the Institution: A Literature Review, *New Review of Academic Librarianship*, **24** (3–4), 217–41, https://doi.org/10.1080/13614533.2018.1466342.

Cox, J. (2019) *Technology and the Positioning of the Library on Campus: Challenges and Opportunities*. Paper presented at the IATUL 2019 conference, Perth, Western Australia, https://docs.lib.purdue.edu/iatul/2019/strategic/1.

Cox, J. (2021) The Higher Education Environment Driving Academic Library Strategy: A Political, Economic, Social and Technological (PEST) Analysis, *Journal of Academic Librarianship*, **47** (1), 102219, https://doi.org/10.1016/j.acalib.2020.102219.

Cox, J. (2023a) The Position and Prospects of Academic Libraries: Strengths and Opportunities, *New Review of Academic Librarianship*, **29** (4), 367–93, https://doi.org/10.1080/13614533.2023.2238692.

Cox, J. (2023b) The Position and Prospects of Academic Libraries: Weaknesses, Threats and Proposed Strategic Directions, *New Review of Academic Librarianship*, **29** (3), 263–87, https://doi.org/10.1080/13614533.2023.2238691.

Cox, J. (2024) Politics, Persuasion and Persistence: The Learning Commons Project at the University of Galway. In Everitt, R. and Everitt, N. (eds) *Privileged Spaces: Academic Libraries in University Estates Strategy*, 117–37, Facet Publishing.

Crawford, K. (2021) *Atlas of AI: Power, Politics, and the Planetary Costs of Artificial Intelligence*, Yale University Press.

Crilly, J. (2024) Diversifying, Decentering and Decolonising Academic Libraries: A Literature Review, *New Review of Academic Librarianship*, **30** (22–3), 112–52, https://doi.org/10.1080/13614533.2023.2287450.

Crow, M., Anderson, D. and Whitman, K. (2018) Academic Enterprise as a New Institutional Logic for Public Higher Education. In Heijnen, A. and van der Vaart, R. (eds) *Places of Engagement: Reflections on Higher Education in 2040 – A Global Approach*, 121–30, Amsterdam University Press, https://doi.org/10.2307/j.ctvfjd0xs.

Curtin Open Knowledge Initiative (2025) Open Access, https://open.coki.ac/open.

Curtis, P. (2005) Bangor Librarians Face Internet Threat, *The Guardian*, 16 February, www.theguardian.com/technology/2005/feb/16/highereducation.careers.

Davies, R. (2020) Top Down and Bottom Up – the Librarian as a Senior Leader and Preparing for Senior Leadership by 'Managing Up'. In Weaver, M. and Appleton, L. (eds) *Bold Minds: Library Leadership in a Time of Disruption*, 227–38, Facet Publishing.

De Paor, S. and Heravi, B. (2020) Information Literacy and Fake News: How the Field of Librarianship Can Help Combat the Epidemic of Fake News, *Journal of Academic Librarianship*, **46** (5), 102218, https://doi.org/10.1016/j.acalib.2020.102218.

De Rosa, C. and Johnson, J. (2008) *From Awareness to Funding: A Study of Library Support in America*, OCLC, www.oclc.org/content/dam/oclc/reports/funding/fullreport.pdf.

De Rosa, C., Cantrell, J., Gallagher, P., Hawk, J., Hoffman, I. and Page, R. (2014) *At a Tipping Point: Education, Learning and Libraries*, OCLC, www.oclc.org/research/publications/2014/tipping-point.html.

de Wit, H. and Altbach, P. G. (2021) Internationalization in Higher Education: Global Trends and Recommendations for Its Future. In Eggins, H., Smolentseva, A. and de Wit, H. (eds) *Higher Education in the Next Decade: Global Challenges, Future Prospects*, 303–25, Brill.

Deards, K. and Puente, M. A. (2020) Improving Diversity, Equity, and Inclusion in Libraries: Programs and Methodologies to Consider, *Research Library Issues*, (301), 43–70, https://doi.org/10.29242/rli.301.4.

Dekker, H., Ferria, A. G. and Mandal, I. (2022) URI Libraries' AI Lab – Evolving to Meet the Needs of Students and Research Communities. In Hervieux, S. and Wheatley, A. (eds) *The Rise of AI: Implications and Applications of Artificial Intelligence in Academic Libraries*, 15–34, Association of College and Research Libraries.

Dempsey, L. (2012) Libraries and the Informational Future: Some Notes, *Information Services & Use*, **32** (3–4), 203–14, http://doi.org/10.3233/ISU-2012-0670.

Dempsey, L. (2015) Intra-institutional Boundaries: New Contexts of Collaboration on Campus. In Allen, N. (ed.) *New Roles for the Road Ahead: Essays Commissioned for ACRL's 75th Birthday*, 80–2, Association of College and Research Libraries, www.ala.org/acrl/sites/ala.org.acrl/files/content/publications/whitepapers/new_roles_75th.pdf.

Dempsey, L. (2016) Library Collections in the Life of the User: Two Directions, *LIBER Quarterly*, **26** (4), 338–59, http://doi.org/10.18352/lq.10170.

Dempsey, L. (2018a) *The Powers of Library Consortia 1: How Consortia Scale Capacity, Learning, Innovation and Influence*, www.lorcandempsey.net/the-powers-of-library-consortia-1-how-consortia-scale-capacity-learning-innovation-and-influence.

Dempsey, L. (2018b) *The Powers of Library Consortia 4: Scoping, Sourcing and Scaling*, www.lorcandempsey.net/the-powers-of-library-consortia-4-scoping-sourcing-and-scaling.

Dempsey, L. and Malpas, C. (2018) Academic Library Futures in a Diversified University System. In Gleason, N. W. (ed.) *Higher Education in the Era of the Fourth Industrial Revolution*, 65–89, Palgrave Macmillan, https://doi.org/10.1007/978-981-13-0194-0_4.

DeRosa, R. (2023) Writing from the wreckage: austerity and the public university. In Czerniewicz, L. and Cronin, C. (eds) *Higher Education for Good: Teaching and Learning Futures*, 53–80, Open Book Publishers, https://doi.org/10.11647/obp.0363.01.

Dewey, B. I. (2014) Leading the Library by Leading the Campus: A Dean's Perspective, *Library Leadership & Management*, **29** (1), 1–10, https://doi.org/10.5860/llm.v29i1.7099.

Dewey, B. I. (2017) College and University Governance: The Role of the Academic Library. In Gilman, T. and Lynch, B. P. (eds) *Academic Librarianship Today*, 17–28, Rowman & Littlefield.

Dillon, A. (2022) Design as an Accelerator of Social Capital in Academic Libraries. In Schlak, T., Corrall, S. and Bracke, P. J. (eds) *The Social Future of Academic Libraries: New Perspectives on Communities, Networks, and Engagement*, 287–98, Facet Publishing.

Dixon, E. (2024) Compensation Call After Students with 'non-Dutch' Names Targeted, *Times Higher Education*, 10 April, www.timeshighereducation.com/news/compensation-call-after-students-non-dutch-names-targeted.

Drabinski, E. (2019) What is Critical About Critical Librarianship? *Art Libraries Journal*, **44** (2), 49–57, https://doi.org/10.1017/alj.2019.3.

Drucker, P. F. (1997) The Future That Has Already Happened, *Harvard Business Review*, **75** (5), 20–4, https://hbr.org/1997/09/looking-ahead-implications-of-the-present.

Drucker, P. F. (2017) Planned Abandonment: Out with the Old, in with the New, https://drucker.institute/wp-content/uploads/2018/08/Reading_Drucker-on-Planned-Abandonment-1.pdf.

Dunford, A. (2019) *Obviously Awesome: How to Nail Product Positioning So Customers Get It, Buy It, Love It*, Ambient Press.

Dunne, K. (n.d.) *SWOT Analysis: Understanding Your Business, Informing Your Strategy*, www.mindtools.com/amtbj63/swot-analysis.

Dyer, A. (2024) Guest Editorial. Re-managing the Library, *College & Research Libraries*, **85** (3), 312–15, https://doi.org/10.5860/crl.85.3.312.

Eggins, H., Smolentseva, A. and de Wit, H. (2021a) Challenges and Prospects for Higher Education. In Eggins, H., Smolentseva, A. and de Wit, H. (eds) *Higher Education in the Next Decade: Global Challenges, Future Prospects*, 9–18, Brill.

Eggins, H., Smolentseva, A. and de Wit, H. (eds) (2021b) *Higher Education in the Next Decade: Global Challenges, Future Prospects*, Brill.

Eldridge, J., Fraser, K., Simmonds, T. and Smyth, N. (2016) Strategic Engagement: New Models of Relationship Management for Academic Librarians, *New Review of Academic Librarianship*, **22** (2–3), 160–75, http://dx.doi.org/10.1080/13614533.2016.1193033.

Ellingrud, K., Sanghvi, S., Dandona, G. S., Madgavkar, A., Chui, M., White, O. and Hasebe, P. (2023) *Generative AI and the Future of Work in America*, McKinsey Global Institute, www.mckinsey.com/mgi/our-research/generative-ai-and-the-future-of-work-in-america.

Emanuel, R. (2020) Let's Make Sure This Crisis Doesn't Go to Waste, *Washington Post*, 25 March, www.washingtonpost.com/opinions/2020/03/25/lets-make-sure-this-crisis-doesnt-go-waste.

Ettarh, F. (2018) Vocational Awe and Librarianship: The Lies We Tell Ourselves, *In the Library with the Lead Pipe*, 10 January, http://www.inthelibrarywiththeleadpipe.org/2018/vocational-awe.

Evangeliste, M. and Furlong, K. (eds) (2014) *Letting Go of Legacy Services: Library Case Studies*, ALA Editions.

Everitt, R. (2022) Intelligent Leaders, Intelligent Spaces. In Crilly, J. and Everitt, R. (eds) *Narrative Expansions: Interpreting Decolonisation in Academic Libraries*, 13–24, Facet Publishing.

Everitt, R. (2024) 'Selling' the University: The Role of the Academic Library. In Everitt, R. and Everitt, N. (eds) *Privileged Spaces: Academic Libraries in University Estates Strategy*, 73–86, Facet Publishing.

Fagan, J. C., Ostermiller, H., Price, E. and Sapp, L. (2021) Librarian, Faculty, and Student Perceptions of Academic Librarians: Study Introduction and Literature Review, *New Review of Academic Librarianship*, **27** (1), 38–75, https://doi.org/10.1080/13614533.2019.1691026.

Fagan, J. C., Ostermiller, H., Price, E. and Sapp, L. (2022a) Faculty Perceptions of Academic Librarians: Experts, Connectors, and Resource Stewards, *New Review of Academic Librarianship*, **28** (1), 79–116, https://doi.org/10.1080/13614533.2020.1819354.

Fagan, J. C., Ostermiller, H., Price, E. and Sapp, L. (2022b) Student Perceptions of Academic Librarians and the Librarian-Faculty-Student Dynamic: Minding Our Gaps, *New Review of Academic Librarianship*, **28** (2), 125–71, https://doi.org/10.1080/13614533.2021.1906717.

Faires, D. (2017) Serving Campus and Remote Students and Faculty: Online Learning, Distance Education, and MOOCs. In Gilman, T. and Lynch, B. P. (eds) *Academic Librarianship Today*, 177–96, Rowman & Littlefield.

Farley, A., Langham-Putrow, A., Shook, E., Sterman, L. B. and Wacha, M. (2021) Transformative Agreements: Six Myths, Busted: Lessons Learned, *College & Research Libraries News*, **82** (7), 298–301, https://doi.org/10.5860/crln.82.7.298.

Feather, J. (2013) Space in the University Library: An Historical Perspective. In Matthews, G. and Walton, G. (eds) *University Libraries and Space in the Digital World*, 19–34, Ashgate.

Fisher, T. (2024) The 'Phygital' Future: What Campuses Will Look Like. In *What Higher Ed Will Look Like in 10 Years: Fundamental Change Is Coming Quickly*, 10–12, Chronicle of Higher Education, www.chronicle.com/report/free/what-higher-ed-will-look-like-in-10-years.

Fister, B. (2015a) Libraries as Catalysts for on-campus Collaboration. In Allen, N. (ed.) *New Roles for the Road Ahead: Essays Commissioned for ACRL's 75th Birthday*, 56–7, Association of College and Research Libraries, www.ala.org/acrl/sites/ala.org.acrl/files/content/publications/whitepapers/new_roles_75th.pdf.

Fister, B. (2015b) The Value of Our Values. In Allen, N. (ed.) *New Roles for the Road Ahead: Essays Commissioned for ACRL's 75th Birthday*, 77–9, Association of College and Research Libraries, www.ala.org/acrl/sites/ala.org.acrl/files/content/publications/whitepapers/new_roles_75th.pdf.

Fister, B. (2015c) Valuing Libraries. In Allen, N. (ed.) *New Roles for the Road Ahead: Essays Commissioned for ACRL's 75th Birthday*, 100–2, Association of College and Research Libraries, www.ala.org/acrl/sites/ala.org.acrl/files/content/publications/whitepapers/new_roles_75th.pdf.

Fitzpatrick, K. (2019) *Generous Thinking: A Radical Approach to Saving the University*, Johns Hopkins University Press.

Foundation for Individual Rights and Expression (2025) Free Speech Makes Free People, www.thefire.org.

Fraser, N., Brierley, L., Day, G., Polka, J. K., Pálfy, M., Nanni, F. and Coates, J. A. (2021) The Evolving Role of Preprints in the Dissemination of Covid-19 Research and Their Impact on the Science Communication Landscape, *PLOS Biology*, **19** (4), e3000959, https://doi.org/10.1371/journal.pbio.3000959.

Frederick, J. K. and Wolff-Eisenberg, C. (2020a) *Academic Library Strategy and Budgeting During the COVID-19 Pandemic: Results from the Ithaka S+R US Library Survey 2020*, Ithaka S+R, https://doi.org/10.18665/sr.314507.

Frederick, J. K. and Wolff-Eisenberg, C. (2020b) *Ithaka S+R US Library Survey 2019*, Ithaka S+R, https://doi.org/10.18665/sr.312977.

Frederick, J. K. and Wolff-Eisenberg, C. (2020c) Leading the Library by Looking Beyond the Library, Ithaka S+R, https://sr.ithaka.org/blog/leading-the-library-by-looking-beyond-the-library.

Frederick, J. K. and Wolff-Eisenberg, C. (2020d) Measuring What Matters: Equity, Diversity, Inclusion, and Accessibility in Academic Library Strategic Plans, Ithaka S+R, https://sr.ithaka.org/blog/measuring-what-matters.

Freedman, S. (2014) Faculty Status, Tenure, and Professional Identity: A Pilot Study of Academic Librarians in New England, *portal: Libraries and the Academy*, **14** (4), 533–65, https://doi.org/10.1353/pla.2014.0023.

Fukuyama, F. (2018) Against Identity Politics: The New Tribalism and the Crisis of Democracy, *Foreign Affairs*, **97** (5), 90–114, www.jstor.org/stable/44823914.

Fukuyama, F. (2020) 30 Years of World Politics: What Has Changed? *Journal of Democracy*, **31** (1), 111–21, https://doi.org/10.1353/jod.2020.0001.

Gasparini, A. and Kautonen, H. (2022) Understanding Artificial Intelligence in Research Libraries – Extensive Literature Review, *LIBER Quarterly*, **32** (1), 1–36, https://doi.org/10.53377/lq.10934.

Geiger, R. L. (2019) *American Higher Education Since World War II*, Princeton University Press.

Gibson, A., Hughes-Hassell, S. and Threats, M. (2018) Critical Race Theory in the LIS Curriculum. In Percell, J., Sarin, L. C., Jaeger, P. T. and Bertot, J. C. (eds) *Re-envisioning the MLS: Perspectives on the Future of Library and Information Science Education*, 49–70, Emerald Publishing, https://doi.org/10.1108/S0065-28302018000044B005.

Giesecke, J., Cawthorne, J. and Pearson, D. (2015) *Navigating the Future with Scenario Planning: A Guidebook for Librarians*, Association of College and Research Libraries.

Givens, M., Macklin, L. A. and Mangiafico, P. (2017) Faculty Profile Systems: New Services and Roles for Libraries, *portal: Libraries and the Academy*, **17** (2), 235–55, https://doi.org/10.1353/pla.2017.0014.

Gorman, M. (1992) Foreword. In Buckland, M., *Redesigning Library Services: A Manifesto*, American Library Association, https://digitalassets.lib.berkeley.edu/sunsite/Redesigning%20Library%20Services_%20A%20Manifesto%20%28HTML%29.pdf.

Gorman, M. (2015) *Our Enduring Values Revisited: Librarianship in an Ever-Changing World*, ALA Editions.

Gormley, D. M. (1974) A Bibliographic Essay of Western Library Architecture to the Mid-twentieth Century, *The Journal of Library History*, **9** (1), 4–24, www.jstor.org/stable/25540547.

Greenhall, M. (2020) *Covid-19 and the Digital Shift in Action: RLUK Report*, Research Libraries UK, www.rluk.ac.uk/covid-19-and-the-digital-shift-in-action.

Griffey, J. (ed.) (2019) Artificial Intelligence and Machine Learning in Libraries, *Library Technology Reports*, **55** (1), 5–29, https://doi.org/10.5860/ltr.55n1.

Grimes, D. J. (1998) *Academic Library Centrality: User Success Through Service, Access, and Tradition*, Association of College and Research Libraries.

Grove, J. (2025a) Trump's 'Unprecedented' Executive Orders Wreak Havoc on Science, *Times Higher Education*, 1 February, www.timeshighereducation.com/news/trumps-unprecedented-executive-orders-wreak-havoc-science.

Grove, J. (2025b) Trump's DEI Crackdown 'Could Block US–UK Research Collaborations', *Times Higher Education* 14 February, www.timeshighereducation.com/news/trumps-dei-crackdown-could-block-us-uk-research-collaborations.

Guillén, M. F. (2021) *2030: How Today's Biggest Trends Will Collide and Reshape the Future of Everything*, FLINT.

Guri-Rosenblit, S. (2021) Diverse Higher Education Systems Reflecting Local and Regional Academic Cultures. In Eggins, H., Smolentseva, A. and de Wit, H. (eds) *Higher Education in the Next Decade: Global Challenges, Future Prospects*, 205–24, Brill.

Guthro, C. (2019) The 21st Century Academic Library: Six Metaphors for a New Age, *Library Leadership & Management*, **33** (2), 11–12, https://llm.corejournals.org/llm/article/view/7334.

Gwyer, R. (2015) Identifying and Exploring Future Trends Impacting on Academic Libraries: A Mixed Methodology Using Journal Content Analysis, Focus Groups, and Trend Reports, *New Review of Academic Librarianship*, **21** (3), 269–85, https://doi.org/10.1080/13614533.2015.1026452.

Gwyer, R. (2018) 'This is an Opportunity for Librarians to Reinvent Themselves, but it is About Moving Out of Their Areas': New Roles for Library Leaders? *New Review of Academic Librarianship*, **24** (3–4), 428–41, https://doi.org/10.1080/13614533.2018.1473258.

Hamad, F., Elfadel, M., Fakhouri, H. and Abu-Qaadan, A. (2024) Advancing Climate Change Literacy: Are Academic Libraries Part of the Solution? *New Review of Academic Librarianship*, **30** (4), 345–67, https://doi.org/10.1080/13614533.2024.2369503.

Hanson, M. (2025a) College Enrollment & Student Demographic Statistics, Education Data Initiative, https://educationdata.org/college-enrollment-statistics.

Hanson, M. (2025b) Student Loan Debt Statistics, Education Data Initiative, https://educationdata.org/student-loan-debt-statistics.

Hanson, T. (ed.) (2005) *Managing Academic Support Services in Universities: The Convergence Experience*, Facet Publishing.

Hardesty, L. (1991) The Bottomless Pit Revisited, *College & Research Libraries*, **52** (3), 219–30, https://doi.org/10.5860/crl_52_03_219.

Harland, F., Stewart, G. and Bruce, C. (2017) Ensuring the Academic Library's Relevance to Stakeholders: The Role of the Library Director, *Journal of Academic Librarianship*, **43** (5), 397–408, https://doi.org/10.1016/j.acalib.2017.06.009.

Harland, F., Stewart, G. and Bruce, C. (2018) Aligning Library and University Strategic Directions: A Constructivist Grounded Theory Study of Academic Library Leadership in Australia and the U.S.A. *New Review of Academic Librarianship*, **24** (33–4), 263–85, https://doi.org/10.1080/13614533.2018.1498797.

Harrison, R. (2018) Reshaping Academic Librarianship in the Context of Twenty-first Century Scholarly Communications and Information Fluency: A Case Study of the Scholarly Communications Management Team at Imperial College London Library Services, *New Review of Academic Librarianship*, **24** (33–4), 349–62, https://doi.org/10.1080/13614533.2018.1519490.

Harvey, R. (2015) Australasia. In Richards, P. S., Wiegand, W. A. and Dalbello, M. (eds) *A History of Modern Librarianship: Constructing the Heritage of Western Cultures*, 179–204, Libraries Unlimited.

Hauke, P. (2018) *From Information Literacy to Green Literacy: Training Librarians As Trainers for Sustainability Literacy*. Paper presented at the IFLA World Library and Information Conference (WLIC), 24–30 August 2018, Kuala Lumpur, Malaysia, https://library.ifla.org/id/eprint/2147/1/116-hauke-en.pdf.

Held, D. and McGrew, A. (2001) Globalization. In Krieger, J. (ed.) *The Oxford Companion to Politics of the World*, 2nd edn, 324–7, Oxford University Press.

Helms, M. M. and Nixon, J. (2010) Exploring SWOT Analysis – Where Are We Now? A Review of Academic Research from the Last Decade, *Journal of Strategy and Management*, **3** (3), 215–51, https://doi.org/10.1108/17554251011064837.

Henkel, M. (2010) Introduction: Change and Continuity in Academic and Professional Identities. In Gordon, G. and Whitchurch, C. (eds) *Academic and Professional Identities in Higher Education: The Challenges of a Diversifying Workforce*, 3–12, Routledge.

Henriques, M. (2024) Climate Change: the 1.5C Threshold Explained, www.bbc.com/future/article/20231130-climate-crisis-the-15c-global-warming-threshold-explained.

Herman, E., Nicholas, D., Clark, D., Boukacem-Zeghmouri, C., Rodríguez-Bravo, B., Abrizah, A., . . . Allard, S. (2023) Outside the Library: Early Career Researchers and Use of Alternative Information Sources in Pandemic Times, *Learned Publishing*, **36** (2), 141–55, https://doi.org/10.1002/leap.1522.

Heseltine, R. (2020) Painting Books on the Walls: Why Libraries Have Lost Their Way and How They Can Rediscover Their Real Purpose in a Fragmented World. In Weaver, M. and Appleton, L. (eds) *Bold Minds: Library Leadership in a Time of Disruption*, 3–23, Facet Publishing.

Hickerson, H. T., Lippincott, J. K. and Crema, L. (2022) Looking Ahead. In Hickerson, H. T., Lippincott, J. K. and Crema, L. (eds) *Designing Libraries for the 21st Century*, 411–14, American Library Association, www.ala.org/sites/default/files/acrl/content/publications/booksanddigitalresources/digital/9780838936726_OA.pdf.

Higham, N. (1980) *The Library in the University: Observations on a Service*, Andre Deutsch.

Hilton, J. (2019) Dr. James Hilton, Vice Provost for Academic Innovation, University Librarian and Dean of Libraries, University Library, University of Michigan. In Lo, P., Chiu, D. K. W., Cho, A. and Allard, B. (eds) *Conversations with Leading Academic and Research Library Directors: International Perspectives on Library Management*, 85–98, Chandos Publishing.

Hinchcliffe, E. (2023) Women CEOs Run 10.4% of Fortune 500 Companies. A Quarter of the 52 Leaders Became CEO in the Last Year, https://fortune.com/2023/06/05/fortune-500-companies-2023-women-10-percent.

Hoare, P. (2006) Introduction: Higher Education and Libraries. In Black, A. and Hoare, P. (eds) *The Cambridge History of Libraries in Britain and Ireland: Volume III: 1850–2000*, 317–20, Cambridge University Press, https://doi.org/10.1017/CHOL9780521780971.028.

Hoare, P. (2015) Europe. In Richards, P. S., Wiegand, W. A. and Dalbello, M. (eds) *A History of Modern Librarianship: Constructing the Heritage of Western Cultures*, 1–67, Libraries Unlimited.

Holley, E. G. (1972) Organization and Administration of Urban University Libraries, *College & Research Libraries*, **33** (3), 175–89, https://doi.org/10.5860/crl_33_03_175.

Hoodless, C. and Pinfield, S. (2018) Subject vs. Functional: Should Subject Librarians Be Replaced by Functional Specialists in Academic Libraries? *Journal of Librarianship and Information Science*, **50** (4), 345–60, http://dx.doi.org/10.1177/0961000616653647.

Hooley, G., Nicoulaud, B., Rudd, J. M. and Lee, N. (2020) *Marketing Strategy and Competitive Positioning*, 7th edn, Pearson.

Hosoi, M., Reiter, L. and Zabel, D. (2021) Reshaping Perspectives on Flexible Work: The Impact of Covid-19 on Academic Library Management, *portal: Libraries and the Academy*, **21** (4), 695–713, https://doi.org/10.1353/pla.2021.0038.

Huang, Y., Cox, A. M. and Cox, J. (2023) Artificial Intelligence in Academic Library Strategy in the United Kingdom and the Mainland of China, *Journal of Academic Librarianship*, **49** (6), 102772, https://doi.org/10.1016/j.acalib.2023.102772.

Hulbert, I. G. (2023) *US Library Survey 2022: Navigating the New Normal*, Ithaka S+R, https://doi.org/10.18665/sr.318642.

Institute of International Education (2025) *Project Atlas*, www.iie.org/research-initiatives/project-atlas.

Ishaq, M. and Hussain, A. M. (2022) Do Black Employees' Rights Matter? The Lived Experience of BAME Staff in UK Academic Libraries. In Crilly, J. and Everitt, R. (eds) *Narrative Expansions: Interpreting Decolonisation in Academic Libraries*, 39–55, Facet Publishing.

Jaeger-McEnroe, E. (2024) Conflicts of Neutrality: Exploring Definitions, Values, and Practices Among Canadian Academic Librarians, *Journal of Academic Librarianship*, **50** (6), 1–11, https://doi.org/10.1016/j.acalib.2024.102958.

Jaguszewski, J. M. and Williams, K. (2013) *New Roles for New Times: Transforming Liaison Roles in Research Libraries*, Association of Research Libraries, www.arl.org/wp-content/uploads/2015/12/nrnt-liaison-roles-revised.pdf.

Jantz, R. C. (2017a) Creating the Innovative Library Culture: Escaping the Iron Cage Through Management Innovation, *New Review of Academic Librarianship*, **23** (4), 323–8, https://doi.org/10.1080/13614533.2017.1388055.

Jantz, R. C. (2017b) A Vision for the Future: New Roles for Academic Librarians. In Gilman, T. and Lynch, B. P. (eds) *Academic Librarianship Today*, 223–35, Rowman & Littlefield.

Jesse, D. (2023) After Protests and a Resignation, a New University Withdraws a Plan for a Digital-First Library, *Chronicle of Higher Education*, 25 April, www.chronicle.com/article/after-protests-and-a-resignation-a-new-university-withdraws-a-plan-for-a-digital-first-library.

Johnson, J. and Crenna-Jennings, W. (2018) *Prevalence of Mental Health Issues Within the Student-aged Population*, Education Policy Institute, https://epi.org.uk/publications-and-research/prevalence-of-mental-health-issues-within-the-student-aged-population.

Kaplan, L. (1988) On the Road to Participative Management: The American Academic Library, 1934–1970, *Libri*, **38**, 314–20.

Kasten, K. (2018) Library as Forum: Building Relationships and Identity Through Faculty Speaker Events, *New Review of Academic Librarianship*, **24** (3–4), 404–15, https://doi.org/10.1080/13614533.2018.1498796.

Keene, J. and Downes, J. (2020) Do Library Partnerships Work and How Can They Help Build a Strong Future for the Library? In Weaver, M. and Appleton, L. (eds) *Bold Minds: Library Leadership in a Time of Disruption*, 65–79, Facet Publishing

Kelderman, E., Elias, J. and O'Leary, B. (2023) What the Public Really Thinks About Higher Education, *Chronicle of Higher Education*, 5 September, www.chronicle.com/article/what-the-public-really-thinks-about-higher-education.

Kendrick, C. L. and Hulbert, I. G. (2023) *By Any Measure: The Racial Demographics of Librarians*, Ithaka S+R, https://doi.org/10.18665/sr.318716.

Kendrick, T. (2021) *Engaging Your Community Through Active Strategic Marketing: A Practical Guide for Librarians and Information Professionals*, Facet Publishing.

Kent, A., Jacob, C., Montgomery, K. L., Williams, J. G., Bulick, S., Flynn, R. R., . . . Manfield, U. (1979) *Use of Library Materials: The University of Pittsburgh Study*, Marcel Dekker.

Khalid, A., Malik, G. F. and Mahmood, K. (2021). Sustainable Development Challenges in Libraries: A Systematic Literature Review (2000–2020), *Journal of Academic Librarianship*, **47** (3), 102347, https://doi.org/10.1016/j.acalib.2021.102347.

Kim, B. (2019) AI and Creating the First Multidisciplinary AI Lab, *Library Technology Reports*, **55** (1), 16–20, https://doi.org/10.5860/ltr.55n1.

Knott, K. (2025) 5 Ways the Education Department Affects Higher Ed, *Inside Higher Ed*, 7 February, www.insidehighered.com/news/government/student-aid-policy/2025/02/07/five-ways-education-department-impacts-higher-ed.

Knox, S. (2004) Positioning and Branding Your Organisation, *Journal of Product & Brand Management*, **13** (2), 105–15, https://doi.org/10.1108/10610420410529735.

Koehler, W. (2015) *Ethics and Values in Librarianship: A History*, Rowman & Littlefield.

Kotler, P. (1997) *Marketing Management: Analysis, Planning, Implementation and Control*, 9th edn, Prentice Hall.

Kramer, B. and Bosman, J. (2015) *101 Innovations in Scholarly Communication – the Changing Research Workflow*, https://doi.org/10.6084/m9.figshare.1286826.v1.

Lancaster, F. W. (1978a) *Toward Paperless Information Systems*, Academic Press.

Lancaster, F. W. (1978b) Whither Libraries? or, Wither Libraries? *College & Research Libraries*, **39** (5), 345–57, https://doi.org/10.5860/crl_39_05_345.

Latimer, K. (2011) Collections to Connections: Changing Spaces and New Challenges in Academic Library Buildings, *Library Trends*, **60** (1), 112–33, https://doi.org/10.1353/lib.2011.0035.

Law, D. (2010) The Changing Roles and Identities of Library and Information Services Staff. In Gordon, G. and Whitchurch, C. (eds) *Academic and Professional*

Identities in Higher Education: The Challenges of a Diversifying Workforce, 185–198, Routledge.

Levitt, T. (1980) Marketing Success Through Differentiation – of Anything, *Harvard Business Review*, **58** (1), 83–91, https://hbr.org/1980/01/marketing-success-through-differentiation-of-anything.

Lewis, D. W. (2007) A Strategy for Academic Libraries in the First Quarter of the 21st Century, *College & Research Libraries*, **68** (5), 418–34, https://doi.org/10.5860/crl.68.5.418.

Lewis, D. W. (2016) *Reimagining the Academic Library*, Rowman & Littlefield.

Lewis, D. W. (2017) Library as Place. In Gilman, T. and Lynch, B. P. (eds) *Academic Librarianship Today*, 161–76, Rowman & Littlefield.

Lewis, D. W. (2019) Innovation and Growth: Applying Clayton M. Christensen's Theories to Academic Libraries, *Library Leadership & Management*, **34** (1), 1–13, https://llm.corejournals.org/llm/article/view/7377.

Lewis, D. W., Baich, T., Palmer, K. and Miller, W. M. (2022) The Efficient Provision of Information Resources in Academic Libraries: Theory and Practice, *Library Trends*, **70** (3), 323–54, http://doi.org/10.1353/lib.2022.0007.

Lewis, D. W., Goetsch, L., Graves, D. and Roy, M. (2018) Funding Community Controlled Open Infrastructure for Scholarly Communication: The 2.5% Commitment Initiative, *College & Research Libraries News*, **79** (3), 133–6, https://doi.org/10.5860/crln.79.3.133.

Lippincott, J. K. (2022) 21st-century Libraries for Students: Learning and Belonging. In Hickerson, H. T., Lippincott, J. K. and Crema, L. (eds) *Designing Libraries for the 21st Century*, 41–52, American Library Association, www.ala.org/sites/default/files/acrl/content/publications/booksanddigitalresources/digital/9780838936726_OA.pdf.

Liu, L. and Liu, W. (2023) The Engagement of Academic Libraries in Open Science: A Systematic Review, *Journal of Academic Librarianship*, **49** (3), 102711, https://doi.org/10.1016/j.acalib.2023.102711.

Lo, L. S. (2023) An Initial Interpretation of the U.S. Department of Education's AI Report: Implications and Recommendations for Academic Libraries, *Journal of Academic Librarianship*, **49** (5), 102761, https://doi.org/10.1016/j.acalib.2023.102761.

Lo, L. S. and Hudson-Vitale, C. (2025) *Tracking the AI Evolution in Research Libraries: Findings from ARL's Third AI Quick Poll*, Association of Research Libraries, www.arl.org/blog/tracking-the-ai-evolution-in-research-libraries-findings-from-arls-third-ai-quick-poll.

Locke, W. (2020) Visions of Higher Education Futures: The Shape of Things to Come? In Callender, C., Locke, W. and Marginson, S. (eds) *Changing Higher Education for a Changing World*, 18–32, Bloomsbury Academic, www.bloomsburycollections.com/encyclopedia-chapter?docid=b-9781350108448&tocid=b-9781350108448-chapter2.

Lombard, E. (2022) *The Internationalization of the Academic Library*, Routledge, https://doi.org/10.4324/9781003128878-1.

Long, D. and Magerko, B. (2020) *What is AI Literacy? Competencies and Design Considerations*. Paper presented at the 2020 CHI Conference on Human Factors in Computing Systems, https://doi.org/10.1145/3313831.3376727.

Lu, A. (2024) 'A Luxury That We Can't Afford': Why One University Axed its Entire Library Faculty, *Chronicle of Higher Education*, 10 December, www.chronicle.com/article/a-luxury-that-we-cant-afford.

Lutz, K. D. and Schonfeld, R. C. (2020) *Leading a Library Today. How Library Directors Are Approaching the Challenges of the Current Moment*, Ithaka S+R, https://sr.ithaka.org/blog/leading-a-library-today.

Lynch, B. P. (1997) The Development of the Academic Library in American Higher Education and the Role of the Academic Librarian. In McCallon, M. L. and Tucker, J. M. (eds) *The Academic Library in the United States: Historical Perspectives*, 45–59, McFarland.

Lynch, B. P., Murray-Rust, C., Parker, S. E., Turner, D., Parr Walker, D., Wilkinson, F. C. and Zimmerman, J. (2007) Attitudes of Presidents and Provosts on the University Library, *College & Research Libraries*, **68** (3), 213–27, https://doi.org/10.5860/crl.68.3.213.

Ma, L. (2022) Metrics and Epistemic Injustice, *Journal of Documentation*, **78** (7), 392–404, https://doi.org/10.1108/JD-12-2021-0240.

Ma, L. (2023a) The Platformisation of Scholarly Information and How to Fight It, *LIBER Quarterly*, **33** (1), 1–20, https://doi.org/10.53377/lq.13561.

Ma, L. (2023b) *The Scholarly Communication Handbook: From Research Dissemination to Societal Impact*, Facet Publishing.

Macfarlane, B. (2011) The Morphing of Academic Practice: Unbundling and the Rise of the Para-Academic, *Higher Education Quarterly*, **65** (1), 59–73, https://doi.org/10.1111/j.1468-2273.2010.00467.x.

Machovec, G. (2017) Trends in Higher Education and Library Consortia, *Journal of Library Administration*, **57** (5), 577–84, https://doi.org/10.1080/01930826.2017.1326266.

Makoe, M. (2023) Visioning Futures of Higher Education for the Common Good. In Czerniewicz, L. and Cronin, C. (eds) *Higher Education for Good: Teaching and Learning Futures*, 303–16, Open Book Publishers, https://doi.org/10.11647/obp.0363.12.

Makos, J. (2024) PEST Analysis: Examples and Meaning in Business, https://pestleanalysis.com/pest-analysis.

Malpas, C., Schonfeld, R. C., Stein, R., Dempsey, L. and Marcum, D. (2018) *University Futures, Library Futures: Aligning Library Strategies with Institutional Directions*, OCLC Research, https://doi.org/10.25333/WS5K-DD86.

Marcum, D. B. (2016) *Library Leadership for the Digital Age*, Ithaka S+R, https://doi.org/10.18665/sr.277583.

Marcum, D. B. (2017) Historical Context and Contemporary Challenges. In Gilman, T. and Lynch, B. P. (eds) *Academic Librarianship Today*, 7–16, Rowman & Littlefield.

Marginson, S. (2020a) Public and Common Goods: Key Concepts in Mapping the Contributions of Higher Education. In Callender, C., Locke, W. and Marginson, S. (eds) *Changing Higher Education for a Changing World*, 249–63, Bloomsbury Academic, www.bloomsburycollections.com/encyclopedia-chapter?docid=b-9781350108448&tocid=b-9781350108448-chapter17.

Marginson, S. (2020b) The World Research System: Expansion, Diversification, Network and Hierarchy. In Callender, C., Locke, W. and Marginson, S. (eds) *Changing Higher Education for a Changing World*, 35–51, Bloomsbury Academic, www.bloomsburycollections.com/encyclopedia-chapter?docid=b-9781350108448&tocid=b-9781350108448-chapter3.

Marginson, S., Callender, C. and Locke, W. (2020) Higher Education in Fast Moving Times: Larger, Steeper, More Global and More Contested. In Callender, C., Locke, W. and Marginson, S. (eds) *Changing Higher Education for a Changing World*, 3–17, Bloomsbury Academic, www.bloomsburycollections.com/encyclopedia-chapter?docid=b-9781350108448&tocid=b-9781350108448-chapter1.

Martin, E. A. and Sheehan, L. A. (2018) The New 'Jack of All': The Evolution of the Functionality and Focus of the Academic Librarian in New Spaces and New Roles. In Fowler, G. J. and Hines, S. S. (eds) *Challenging the 'Jacks of All Trades But Masters of None' Librarian Syndrome*, 67–90, Emerald Publishing, https://doi.org/10.1108/S0732-067120180000039006.

Martinez, M. and Wolverton, M. (2009) *Innovative Strategy Making in Higher Education*, Information Age Publishing.

Mathews, B. (2014a) Flip the Model: Strategies for Creating and Delivering Value, *Journal of Academic Librarianship*, **40** (1), 16–24, https://doi.org/10.1016/j.acalib.2013.09.004.

Mathews, B. (2014b) Librarian as Futurist: Changing the Way Libraries Think About the Future, *portal: Libraries and the Academy*, **14** (3), 453–62, https://dx.doi.org/10.1353/pla.2014.0019.

Mathews, B., Metko, S. and Tomlin, P. (2018) Empowerment, Experimentation, Engagement: Embracing Partnership Models in Libraries, *EDUCAUSE Review*, **53** (3), 52–3, https://er.educause.edu/articles/2018/5/empowerment-experimentation-engagement-embracing-partnership-models-in-libraries.

Mathiasson, M. H. and Jochumsen, H. (2022) Libraries, Sustainability and Sustainable Development: A Review of the Research Literature, *Journal of Documentation*, **78** (6), 1278–304, https://doi.org/10.1108/JD-11-2021-0226.

Matthews, G. and Walton, G. (2014) Strategic Development of University Library Space: Widening the Influence, *New Library World*, **115** (5/6), 237–49, https://doi.org/10.1108/NLW-05-2014-0062.

McAnally, A. M. and Downs, R. B. (1973) The Changing Role of Directors of University Libraries, *College & Research Libraries*, **34** (2), 103–25, https://doi.org/10.5860/crl_34_02_103.

McCaffrey, C. (2021) Planning and Implementing an Automated Storage and Retrieval System at the University of Limerick. In Atkinson, J. (ed.) *Technology Change and the Academic Library: Case Studies, Trends and Reflections*, 143–50, Chandos Publishing, https://doi.org/10.1016/B978-0-12-822807-4.00014-2.

McCallon, M. L. and Tucker, J. M. (2022) From the Bequest of John Harvard to the Dream of Alexandria: Historiography of the Academic Library in the United States, 1638–2015. In McCallon, M. L. and Tucker, J. M. (eds) *The Academic Library in the United States: Historical Perspectives*, 3–41, McFarland.

McKenna, R. O. (1980) University Library Organization. In Thompson, J. (ed.) *University Library History: An International Review*, 92–108, K. G. Saur/Clive Bingley.

McRae, H. (2023) *The World in 2050: How to Think About the Future*, Bloomsbury.

Melling, M. (2013) Collaborative Service Provision Through Super-convergence. In Melling M. and Weaver, M. (eds) *Collaboration in Libraries and Learning Environments*, 149–66, Facet Publishing.

Metzger, R. L. (2022) Beyond Individual Relationships: Programmatic Approaches to Outreach and Engagement at UC Santa Barbara Library. In Schlak, T., Corrall, S. and Bracke, P. J. (eds) *The Social Future of Academic Libraries: New Perspectives on Communities, Networks, and Engagement*, 243–56, Facet Publishing.

Mintz, S. (2023) Higher Ed's Top 10 Developments of 2023, *Inside Higher Ed*, 18 December, www.insidehighered.com/opinion/blogs/higher-ed-gamma/2023/12/18/higher-eds-top-10-developments-2023.

Mintz, S. (2024) The Evolving University Library: What's Gained, What's Lost, *Inside Higher Ed*, 28 October, www.insidehighered.com/opinion/blogs/higher-ed-gamma/2024/10/28/whats-gained-whats-lost-evolving-university-library.

Mizrachi, D., Salaz, A. M., Kurbanoglu, S. and Boustany, J. (2018) Academic Reading Format Preferences and Behaviors Among University Students Worldwide: A Comparative Survey Analysis, *PLoS ONE*, **13** (5), 1–32, https://doi.org/10.1371/journal.pone.0197444.

Moran, J. (2020) I Can't Wait for Universities to Reopen Their Beating, Bookish Hearts, *Times Higher Education*, 24 December, www.timeshighereducation.com/opinion/i-cant-wait-universities-reopen-their-beating-bookishhearts.

Morgan, J. (2023) Conservative Attacks on Universities 'Not a Vote Winner', *Times Higher Education*, 10 October, www.timeshighereducation.com/news/conservative-attacks-universities-not-vote-winner.

Mowat, I. (2006) Academic Libraries and the Expansion of Higher Education Since the 1960s. In Black, A. and Hoare, P. (eds) *The Cambridge History of Libraries in Britain and Ireland: Volume III: 1850–2000*, 377–401, Cambridge University Press, https://doi.org/10.1017/CHOL9780521780971.032.

Munn, R. F. (1968) The Bottomless Pit, Or the Academic Library as Viewed from the Administration Building, *College & Research Libraries*, **29** (1), 51–4, https://doi.org/10.5860/crl_29_01_51.

Murray, A. and Ireland, A. (2018) Provosts' Perceptions of Academic Library Value and Preferences for Communication: A National Study, *College & Research Libraries*, **79** (3), 336–65, https://doi.org/10.5860/crl.79.3.336.

National Science Foundation. National Science Board (2021) *Publications Output: U.S. and International Comparisons*, https://ncses.nsf.gov/pubs/nsb20214.

Neal, J. G. (2015) Still 'Choosing Our Futures': How Many Apples in the Seed? *College & Research Libraries*, **76** (3), 310–15, https://doi.org/10.5860/crl.76.3.310.

Nguyen, B. (2023) World Population Grew by Over 75 Million People in 2023 – but Population Growth Rate is Slowing, www.forbes.com/sites/britneynguyen/2023/12/28/world-population-grew-by-over-75-million-people-in-2023-but-population-growth-rate-is-slowing.

Nicholas, D., Boukacem-Zeghmouri, C., Rodríguez-Bravo, B., Xu, J., Watkinson, A., Abrizah, A., . . . Świgoń, M. (2017) Where and How Early Career Researchers Find Scholarly Information, *Learned Publishing*, **30** (1), 19–29, https://doi.org/10.1002/leap.1087.

Nicholas, D., Jamali, H. R., Herman, E., Watkinson, A., Abrizah, A., Rodríguez-Bravo, B., . . . Polezhaeva, T. (2020) A Global Questionnaire Survey of the Scholarly Communication Attitudes and Behaviours of Early Career Researchers, *Learned Publishing*, **33** (3), 198–211, https://doi.org/10.1002/leap.1286.

Nicholas, D., Rodríguez-Bravo, B., Abrizah, A., Revez, J., Herman, E., Clark, D., . . . Watkinson, A. (2025) Where Will AI Take Scholarly Communication? Voices from the Research Frontline. *Learned Publishing*, **38** (2), e2008, https://doi.org/10.1002/leap.2008.

Nicholson, K. P. (2015) The McDonaldization of Academic Libraries and the Values of Transformational Change, *College & Research Libraries*, **76** (3), 328–38, https://doi.org/10.5860/crl.76.3.328.

Noorda, S. (2018) Autonomy: A Practice Serving a Purpose. In Heijnen, A. and van der Vaart, R. (eds) *Places of Engagement: Reflections on Higher Education in 2040 – a Global Approach*, 23–9, Amsterdam University Press, https://doi.org/10.2307/j.ctvfjd0xs.

North Carolina State University Libraries (2022) The NC State University Libraries: Our Strategic Plan – 2022–2027, www.lib.ncsu.edu/strategic-priorities.

Oakleaf, M. (2010) *The Value of Academic Libraries: A Comprehensive Research Review and Report for the Association of College and Research Libraries*, www.ala.org/sites/default/files/2024-06/val_report.pdf.

O'Bryan, C. (2018) The Influence of Political Capital on Academic Library Leadership, *Library Leadership & Management*, **32** (4), 1–18, https://llm.corejournals.org/llm/article/view/7292.

ODonnell, P. and Anderson, L. (2022) The University Library: Places for Possibility, *New Review of Academic Librarianship*, **28** (3), 232–55, https://doi.org/10.1080/13614533.2021.1906718.

Office for Students (2018) *Value for Money: The Student Perspective*, Trendence Research UK, www.officeforstudents.org.uk/media/3105/value-for-money-the-student-perspective-final-final-final.pdf.

Oliphant, T. and Brundin, M. R. (2019) Conflicting Values: An Exploration of the Tensions Between Learning Analytics and Academic Librarianship, *Library Trends*, **68** (1), 5–23, https://doi.org/10.1353/lib.2019.0028.

Orne, J. (1980) The Evolution of Academic Library Staff in the United States. In Thompson, J. (ed.) *University Library History: An International Review*, 77–91, K. G. Saur/Clive Bingley.

Orzech, M. J. (2020) Openness, Scholarly Communication and Evolving Expectations for Academic Libraries. In Diamond, T. (ed.) *The Academic Librarian in the Digital Age: Essays on Changing Roles and Responsibilities*, 7–21, McFarland.

Ovenden, R. (2020) *Burning the Books: A History of Knowledge Under Attack*, John Murray.

Oxford University Press (2022) *Oxford English Dictionary*, www.oed.com.

Palmer, K. (2024) Library Faculty Eliminated Amid 'Fiscal Insanity' at Western Illinois, *Inside Higher Ed*, 20 August, www.insidehighered.com/news/business/cost-cutting/2024/08/20/library-faculty-eliminated-western-illinois-university.

Palmowski, J. (2008) Climate Change. In Palmowski, J. (ed.) *A Dictionary of Contemporary World History: from 1900 to the Present Day*, 3rd edn, 140–1, Oxford University Press.

Panagiotou, G. (2003) Bringing SWOT into Focus, *Business Strategy Review*, **14** (2), 8–10, https://doi.org/10.1111/1467-8616.00253.

Parsons, S., Azevedo, F., Elsherif, M. M., Guay, S., Shahim, O. N., Govaart, G. H., . . . Aczel, B. (2022) A Community-sourced Glossary of Open Scholarship Terms, *Nature Human Behaviour*, **6** (3), 312–18, https://doi.org/10.1038/s41562-021-01269-4.

Pearson, A. (2018) Consuming Education. In Geelan, T., González Hernando, M. and Walsh, P. W. (eds) *From Financial Crisis to Social Change: Towards Alternative Horizons*, 67–86, Palgrave Macmillan.

Pechenkina, E. (2023) Artificial Intelligence for Good? Challenges and Possibilities of AI in Higher Education from a Data Justice Perspective. In Czerniewicz, L. and

Cronin, C. (eds) *Higher Education for Good: Teaching and Learning Futures*, 239–66, Open Book Publishers, https://doi.org/10.11647/obp.0363.09.

Pelletier, K., McCormack, M., Muscanell, N., Reeves, J., Robert, J. and Arbino, N. (2024) *2024 EDUCAUSE Horizon Report, Teaching and Learning Edition*, https://library.educause.edu/resources/2024/5/2024-educause-horizon-report-teaching-and-learning-edition.

Pelletier, K., Robert, J., Arbino, N., Muscanell, N., McCormack, M., Reeves, J., . . . Grajek, S. (2023a) *2023 EDUCAUSE Horizon Report: Holistic Student Experience Edition*, https://library.educause.edu/-/media/files/library/2023/9/2023hrholisticstudentexperience.pdf.

Pelletier, K., Robert, J., Muscanell, N., McCormack, M., Reeves, J., Arbino, N. and Grajek, S. (2023b) *2023 EDUCAUSE Horizon Report, Teaching and Learning Edition*, https://library.educause.edu/resources/2023/5/2023-educause-horizon-report-teaching-and-learning-edition.

Penniman, W. D. (1997) Strategic Positioning of Information Services in a Competitive Environment, *Bulletin of the American Society for Information Science*, **23** (4), 11–14, https://doi.org/10.1002/bult.55.

Pennock, J. R. (2001) Equality and Inequality. In Krieger, J. (ed.) *The Oxford Companion to Politics of the World*, 2nd edn, 257–60, Oxford University Press.

Penprase, B. E. (2018) The Fourth Industrial Revolution and Higher Education. In Gleason, N. W. (ed.) *Higher Education in the Era of the Fourth Industrial Revolution*, 207–29, Palgrave Macmillan, https://doi.org/10.1007/978-981-13-0194-0_9.

Penprase, B. E. (2024) 5 Forces Reshaping Higher Education, www.forbes.com/sites/bryanpenprase/2024/12/23/the-five-forces-reshaping-higher-education.

Perna, L. W., Ruiz, R. and Brickfield, J. (2023) Technology: The Solution to Higher Education's Pressing Problems? In Bastedo, M. N., Altbach, P. G. and Gumport, P. J. (eds) *American Higher Education in the Twenty-first Century: Social, Political, and Economic Challenges*, 396–423, Johns Hopkins University Press.

Peston, R. and Koria, K. (2023) *Bust? Saving the Economy, Democracy and Our Sanity*, Hodder & Stoughton.

Pinfield, S., Cox, A. M. and Rutter, S. (2017) *Mapping the Future of Academic Libraries: A Report for SCONUL*, https://sconul.ac.uk/knowledge-hub/library-structures-and-strategies/resources-and-links.

Pinfield, S., Cox, A. M. and Smith, J. (2014) Research Data Management and Libraries: Relationships, Activities, Drivers and Influences, *PLoS ONE*, **9** (12), e114734, https://doi.org/10.1371/journal.pone.0114734.

Pokornowski, E. and Schonfeld, R. C. (2024) *Censorship and Academic Freedom in the Public University Library*, Ithaka S+R, https://doi.org/10.18665/sr.320506.

Porter, M. E. (1979) How Competitive Forces Shape Strategy, *Harvard Business Review*, **57** (2), 137–45, https://hbr.org/1979/03/how-competitive-forces-shape-strategy.

Porter, M. E. (1996) What is Strategy? *Harvard Business Review*, **74** (6), 61–78, https://hbr.org/1996/11/what-is-strategy.

Porter, M. E. (2008) The Five Competitive Forces That Shape Strategy, *Harvard Business Review*, **78** (1), 78–93, https://hbr.org/2008/01/the-five-competitive-forces-that-shape-strategy.

Posner, M. (2013) No Half Measures: Overcoming Common Challenges to Doing Digital Humanities in the Library, *Journal of Library Administration*, **53** (1), 43–52, http://dx.doi.org/10.1080/01930826.2013.756694.

Quan, J. (2022) Toward Reproducibility: Academic Libraries and Open Science. In Herndon, J. (ed.) *Data Science in the Library: Tools and Strategies for Supporting Data-driven Research and Instruction*, 49–68, Facet Publishing.

Ramsey, E. and Aagard, M. C. (2018) Academic Libraries As Active Contributors to Student Wellness, *College & Undergraduate Libraries*, **25** (4), 328–34, https://doi.org/10.1080/10691316.2018.1517433.

Raschke, G. K. (2022) Library As Platform: The Transformed Library's Impact on Teaching, Learning, and Research. In Hickerson, H. T., Lippincott, J. K. and Crema, L. (eds) *Designing Libraries for the 21st Century*, 17–26, American Library Association, www.ala.org/sites/default/files/acrl/content/publications/booksanddigitalresources/digital/9780838936726_OA.pdf.

Ratcliffe, F. W. (1980) The Growth of University Library Collections in the United Kingdom. In Thompson, J. (ed.) *University Library History: An International Review*, 5–32, K. G. Saur/Clive Bingley.

Ratcliffe, F. W. (2006) The Civic Universities and Their Libraries. In Black, A. and Hoare, P. (eds) *The Cambridge History of Libraries in Britain and Ireland: Volume III: 1850–2000*, 357–76, Cambridge University Press, https://doi.org/10.1017/CHOL9780521780971.031.

Rauf, T. (2017) Funding and Budgeting. In Gilman, T. and Lynch, B. P. (eds) *Academic Librarianship Today*, 47–68, Rowman & Littlefield.

Reddington, M. (2023) *A Study of the UK's Information Workforce 2023: Mapping the Library, Archives, Records, Information Management and Knowledge Management and Related Professions in the United Kingdom & Ireland*, UK Information Workforce Data Consortium, www.cilip.org.uk/page/workforcemapping.

Rider, F. (1944) *The Scholar and the Future of the Research Library: A Problem and Its Solution*, Hadham Press.

Ries, A. and Trout, J. (2001) *Positioning: The Battle for Your Mind – How to Be Seen and Heard in the Overcrowded Marketplace*, McGraw-Hill.

Robert, J., Muscanell, N., McCormack, M., Pelletier, K., Arnold, K. , . . . Reeves, J. (2025) *2025 EDUCAUSE Horizon Report, Teaching and Learning Edition*, https://library.educause.edu/resources/2025/5/2025-educause-horizon-report-teaching-and-learning-edition.

Roberts, N. (1980) Financing of University Libraries in the United Kingdom. In Thompson, J. (ed.) *University Library History: An International Review*, 109–27, K. G. Saur/Clive Bingley.

Robertson, M. (2015) Perceptions of Canadian Provosts on the Institutional Role of Academic Libraries, *College & Research Libraries*, **76** (4), 490–511, https://doi.org/10.5860/crl.76.4.490.

Ross, J. (2024) New Zealand Universities' Financial Woes 'Unprecedented', *Times Higher Education*, 9 February, www.timeshighereducation.com/news/new-zealand-universities-financial-woes-unprecedented.

Ross, L. and Sennyey, P. (2008) The Library Is Dead, Long Live the Library! The Practice of Academic Librarianship and the Digital Revolution, *Journal of Academic Librarianship*, **34** (2), 145–52, https://doi.org/10.1016/j.acalib.2007.12.006.

Roubini, N. (2023) *Megathreats: Ten Threats to Our Future and How to Survive Them*, John Murray.

Rouse, W. B. (2016) *Universities as Complex Enterprises: How Academia Works, Why It Works These Ways, and Where the University Enterprise Is Headed*, Wiley.

Rubin, R. E. and Rubin, R. G. (2020) *Foundations of Library and Information Science*, 5th edn, ALA Neal-Schuman.

Salisbury, F. and Peseta, T. (2018) The 'Idea of the University': Positioning Academic Librarians in the Future University, *New Review of Academic Librarianship*, **24** (3–4), 242–62, https://doi.org/10.1080/13614533.2018.1472113.

Salisbury, F. and Peseta, T. (2023) The Heart of the University: Revisiting an Enduring Metaphor, *portal: Libraries and the Academy*, **23** (2), 269–92, https://doi.org/10.1353/pla.2023.0020.

Salisbury, F., Dollinger, M. and Vanderlelie, J. (2020) Students as Partners in the Academic Library: Co-designing for Transformation, *New Review of Academic Librarianship*, **26** (2–4), 304–21, https://doi.org/10.1080/13614533.2020.1780275.

Santayana, G. (2017) *The Life of Reason*, Open Road Integrated Media.

Sapp, G. and Gilmour, R. (2002) A Brief History of the Future of Academic Libraries: Predictions and Speculations from the Literature of the Profession, 1975 to 2000 – Part One, 1975 to 1989, *portal: Libraries and the Academy*, **2** (4), 553–76, https://doi.org/10.1353/pla.2002.0086.

Sapp, G. and Gilmour, R. (2003) A Brief History of the Future of Academic Libraries: Predictions and Speculations from the Literature of the Profession, 1975 to 2000 – Part Two, 1990 to 2000, *portal: Libraries and the Academy*, **3** (1), 13–34, https://doi.org/10.1353/pla.2003.0008.

Saqib, N. (2021) Positioning – a Literature Review, *PSU Research Review*, **5** (2), 141–69, https://doi.org/10.1108/PRR-06-2019-0016.

Sarsby, A. (2016) *SWOT Analysis: A Guide to SWOT for Business Studies Students*, Spectaris.

Saunders, L. (2016) Room for Improvement: Priorities in Academic Libraries' Strategic Plans, *Journal of Library Administration*, **56** (1), 1–16, https://doi.org/10.1080/01930826.2015.1105029.

Saunders, L. (2020) Core Knowledge and Specialized Skills in Academic Libraries, *College & Research Libraries*, **81** (2), 288–311, https://doi.org/10.5860/crl.81.2.288.

Sayre, F. and Riegelman, A. (2018) The Reproducibility Crisis and Academic Libraries, *College & Research Libraries*, **79** (1), 2–9, https://doi.org/10.5860/crl.79.1.2.

Sayre, F. and Riegelman, A. (2019) Replicable Services for Reproducible Research: A Model for Academic Libraries, *College & Research Libraries*, **80** (2), 260–72, https://doi.org/10.5860/crl.80.2.260.

Schlak, T. (2022a) Forecasting a Future for Academic Libraries: Engagement, Community Building and Organisational Development. In Schlak, T., Corrall, S. and Bracke, P. J. (eds) *The Social Future of Academic Libraries: New Perspectives on Communities, Networks, and Engagement*, 149–69, Facet Publishing.

Schlak, T. (2022b) Introduction: Charting a Course to the Social Future of Academic Libraries. In Schlak, T., Corrall, S. and Bracke, P. J. (eds) *The Social Future of Academic Libraries: New Perspectives on Communities, Networks, and Engagement*, xxix–xxxix, Facet Publishing.

Schlak, T. (2022c) Social Capital and Academic Libraries: The Basics. In Schlak, T., Corrall, S. and Bracke, P. J. (eds) *The Social Future of Academic Libraries: New Perspectives on Communities, Networks, and Engagement*, 91–108, Facet Publishing.

Schlak, T. and Macklin, A. (2022) Open Access Overtaking Academic Library Leadership: Staying Ahead of the Organisational Dynamics an Increasingly Open Future May Bring, *New Review of Academic Librarianship*, **28** (2), 117–24, https://doi.org/10.1080/13614533.2022.2079539.

Schlak, T., Corrall, S. and Bracke, P. J. (eds) (2022) *The Social Future of Academic Libraries: New Perspectives on Communities, Networks, and Engagement*, Facet Publishing.

Schmidt, B., Chiarelli, A., Loffreda, L. and Sondervan, J. (2024) Emerging Roles and Responsibilities of Libraries in Support of Reproducible Research, *LIBER Quarterly*, **33** (1), 1–21, https://doi.org/10.53377/lq.14947.

Schonfeld, R. C. (2014) *Does Discovery Still Happen in the Library? Roles and Strategies for a Shifting Reality*, Ithaka S+R, https://doi.org/10.18665/sr.24914.

Schonfeld, R. C. (2016) *Organizing the Work of the Research Library*, Ithaka S+R, https://doi.org/10.18665/sr.283717.

Schonfeld, R. C. and Sweeney, L. (2017) *Inclusion, Diversity, and Equity: Members of the Association of Research Libraries: Employee Demographics and Director Perspectives*, Ithaka S+R, https://doi.org/10.18665/sr.304524.

Schonfeld, R. C. and Wolff-Eisenberg, C. (2020) Academic Libraries at a Pivotal Moment, *The Scholarly Kitchen*, 6 April, https://scholarlykitchen.sspnet.org/2020/04/06/academic-libraries-pivotal-moment.

SCONUL (2012) The Value of Academic Libraries, https://web.archive.org/web/20160314005320/www.sconul.ac.uk/page/the-value-of-academic-libraries.

SCONUL (2023) *Annual Library Statistics 2021–2022*.

Scott, R. E., Harrington, C. and Dubnjakovic, A. (2021) Exploring Open Access Practices, Attitudes, and Policies in Academic Libraries, *portal: Libraries and the Academy*, **21** (2), 365–88, https://doi.org/10.1353/pla.2021.0020.

Seemiller, C. and Grace, M. (2016) *Generation Z Goes to College*, Jossey-Bass.

Senge, P. M. (2006) *The Fifth Discipline: The Art and Practice of the Learning Organization*, Currency/Doubleday.

Shiflett, O. L. (1994) Academic Libraries. In Wiegand, W. A. and Davis, D. G. (eds) *Encyclopedia of Library History*, 5–14, Garland.

Simons, M. (2017) *Academic Library Metamorphosis and Regeneration*, Rowman & Littlefield.

Smethurst, J. M. (1980) University Library Staffing in the United Kingdom. In Thompson, J. (ed.) *University Library History: An International Review*, 56–76, K. G. Saur/Clive Bingley.

Smith, M. D. (2023) The Public Is Giving Up on Higher Ed, *Chronicle of Higher Education*, 5 October, www.chronicle.com/article/the-public-is-giving-up-on-higher-ed.

Sotirakopoulos, N. (2021) *Identity Politics and Tribalism: The New Culture Wars*, Imprint Academic.

Stanford University Libraries (n.d.) About the Libraries, https://library.stanford.edu/about-stanford-libraries/about-libraries.

Steel, V. (2019) Virginia Steel, Norman and Armena Powell University Librarian, University of California, Los Angeles (UCLA). In Lo, P., Chiu, D. K. W., Cho, A. and Allard, B. (eds) *Conversations with Leading Academic and Research Library Directors: International Perspectives on Library Management*, 43–74, Chandos Publishing.

Stoffle, C. J. and Cuillier, C. (2010) From Surviving to Thriving, *Journal of Library Administration*, **51** (1), 130–55, https://doi.org/10.1080/01930826.2011.531645.

Stoffle, C. J., Renaud, R. and Veldof, J. R. (1996) Choosing Our Futures, *College & Research Libraries*, **57** (3), 213–25, https://doi.org/10.5860/crl_57_03_213.

Stoffle, C. J., Allen, B., Morden, D. and Maloney, K. (2003) Continuing to Build the Future: Academic Libraries and Their Challenges, *portal: Libraries and the Academy*, **3** (3), 363–80, https://doi.org/10.1353/pla.2003.0068.

Stromquist, N. P. (2021) A Faculty in Crisis: External and Internal Challenges to the Academic Profession. In Eggins, H., Smolentseva, A. and de Wit, H. (eds) *Higher Education in the Next Decade: Global Challenges, Future Prospects*, 21–40, Brill.

Stueart, R. D. (1984) Preparing Libraries for Change, *Library Journal*, **109** (15), 1724–6.

Sullivan, M. C. (2018) Why Librarians Can't Fight Fake News, *Journal of Librarianship and Information Science*, **51** (4), 1146–56, https://doi.org/10.1177/0961000618764258.

Sun, J. C. (2023) Academic Freedom: Its Historical Development, Current State, and Future Challenges. In Bastedo, M. N., Altbach, P. G. and Gumport, P. J. (eds) *American Higher Education in the Twenty-first Century: Social, Political, and Economic Challenges*, 36–67, Johns Hopkins University Press.

Susskind, D. (2021) *A World Without Work: Technology, Automation and How We Should Respond*, Penguin.

Szekeres, J. (2004) The Invisible Workers, *Journal of Higher Education Policy and Management*, **26** (1), 7–22, https://doi.org/10.1080/1360080042000182500.

Szekeres, J. (2011) Professional Staff Carve Out a New Space, *Journal of Higher Education Policy and Management*, **33** (6), 679–91, https://doi.org/10.1080/1360080X.2011.621193.

Technopolis Group (2020) *Read & Publish Contracts in the Context of a Dynamic Scholarly Publishing System: A Study on Future Scenarios for the Scholarly Publishing System*, https://eua.eu/downloads/publications/read%20and%20publish%20contracts%20in%20the%20context%20of%20a%20dynamic%20scholarly%20publishing%20system.pdf.

Teixeira, P. (2021) Global Funding Trends in Higher Education: The Challenges of Competition, Selectivity, and Differentiation. In Eggins, H., Smolentseva, A. and de Wit, H. (eds) *Higher Education in the Next Decade: Global Challenges, Future Prospects*, 245–70, Brill.

Tennant, R. (2002) Factoring in the Only Constant, *Library Journal*, **127** (3), 28.

Tenopir, C., Talja, S., Horstmann, W., Late, E., Hughes, D., Pollock, D., . . . Allard, S. (2017) Research Data Services in European Academic Research Libraries, *LIBER Quarterly*, **27** (1), 23–44, http://doi.org/10.18352/lq.10180.

Teplitzky, S. (2023) Generation Open. In Bonn, M., Bolick, J. and Cross, W. (eds) *Scholarly Communication Librarianship and Open Knowledge*, 363–71, Association of College and Research Libraries, www.ala.org/sites/default/files/acrl/content/publications/booksanddigitalresources/digital/9780838936566_OA.pdf.

Terrile, V. C. (2024) Community College Library Services: Meeting Students Where They Are, *Teachers College Record*, **126** (6–7), 46–63, https://doi.org/10.1177/01614681241285739.

Thompson, H. (2022) *Disorder: Hard Times in the 21st Century*, Oxford University Press.

Thompson, J. (1980) Introduction. In Thompson, J. (ed.) *University Library History: An International Review*, 1–4, K. G. Saur/Clive Bingley.

Thompson, J. (1982) *The End of Libraries*, Clive Bingley.

Tribelhorn, S. K. (2023) Preliminary Investigation of Sustainability Awareness and Activities Among Academic Libraries in the United States, *Journal of Academic Librarianship*, **49** (3), 102661, https://doi.org/10.1016/j.acalib.2022.102661.

UN Global Pulse (2022) *Horizon Scan User Manual: A Step-by-step Guide*, www.unglobalpulse.org/wp-content/uploads/2023/12/HorisonScanManual_ENG-1.pdf.

UNESCO (2023) *Open Science Outlook 1: Status and Trends Around the World*, https://doi.org/10.54677/GIIC6829.

UNESCO Institute for Statistics (2022) Higher Education Figures at a Glance, www.uis.unesco.org/sites/default/files/medias/fichiers/2025/03/f_unesco1015_brochure_web_en.pdf.

United Nations (2015) *Sustainable Development Goals*, https://sdgs.un.org/goals.

United States Office of Science and Technology Policy (2022) *Memorandum: Ensuring Free, Immediate, and Equitable Access to Federally Funded Research*, https://bidenwhitehouse.archives.gov/wp-content/uploads/2022/08/08-2022-OSTP-Public-Access-Memo.pdf.

Universities UK (2022) *Closing Ethnicity Degree Awarding Gaps: Three Years On*, www.universitiesuk.ac.uk/sites/default/files/uploads/Reports/closing-the-gap-three-years-on.pdf.

University Grants Committee (1921) *Report of the University Grants Committee, 3rd February 1921, [Cmd. 1163]*, H.M.S.O.

University Grants Committee (1967) *Report of the Committee on Libraries*, H.M.S.O.

University of Leeds Libraries (2022) Knowledge for All: University of Leeds Libraries Vision for 2030, https://spotlight.leeds.ac.uk/libraries-vision.

University of Toronto Scarborough Library (n.d.) UTSC Library Values, https://utsc.library.utoronto.ca/library-values.

University of Western Australia (2024) Library Strategic Plan 2024–26, www.uwa.edu.au/library/-/media/uwa-library/documents/about-the-library/uwa-library-strategic-plan-2024-26.pdf.

Usher, W. and Curran, C. (2017) Predicting Australia's University Students' Mental Health Status, *Health Promotion International*, **34** (2), 312–22, https://doi.org/10.1093/heapro/dax091.

van der Zwaan, B. (2017) *Higher Education in 2040: A Global Approach*, Amsterdam University Press, https://doi.org/10.26530/oapen_625978.

Vandegrift, M. (2023) Defining Open Science. In Bonn, M., Bolick, J. and Cross, W. (eds) *Scholarly Communication Librarianship and Open Knowledge*, 349–61, Association of College and Research Libraries, www.ala.org/sites/default/files/acrl/content/publications/booksanddigitalresources/digital/9780838936566_OA.pdf.

Vandegrift, M. and Varner, S. (2013) Evolving in Common: Creating Mutually Supportive Relationships Between Libraries and the Digital Humanities, *Journal of Library Administration*, **53** (1), 67–78, http://dx.doi.org/10.1080/01930826.2013.756699.

Veaner, A. B. (1985) 1985 to 1995: The Next Decade in Academic Librarianship, Part I, *College & Research Libraries*, **46** (3), 209–29, https://doi.org/10.5860/crl_46_03_209.

Veles, N., Graham, C. and Ovaska, C. (2023) University Professional Staff Roles, Identities, and Spaces of Interaction: Systematic Review of Literature Published in 2000–2020, *Policy Reviews in Higher Education*, **7** (2), 127–68, https://doi.org/10.1080/23322969.2023.2193826.

Verbaan, E. and Cox, A. M. (2014) Occupational Sub-Cultures, Jurisdictional Struggle and Third Space: Theorising Professional Service Responses to Research Data Management, *Journal of Academic Librarianship*, **40** (3), 211–19, https://doi.org/10.1016/j.acalib.2014.02.008.

Vosoughi, S., Roy, D. and Aral, S. (2018) The Spread of True and False News Online, *Science*, **359** (6380), 1146–51, https://doi.org/10.1126/science.aap9559.

Wade, W. (2012) *Scenario Planning: A Field Guide to the Future*, Wiley.

Wales, T. (2018) The View from Within: A Personal Reflection on Library Strategy Development in Three Academic Libraries, *New Review of Academic Librarianship*, **24** (33–4), 442–56, https://doi.org/10.1080/13614533.2018.1460728.

Walters, S. and Jackson, K. (2013) *Breakthrough Branding: Positioning Your Library to Survive and Thrive*, American Library Association.

Walters, W. H. (2016) Faculty Status of Librarians at U.S. Research Universities, *Journal of Academic Librarianship*, **42** (2), 161–71, https://doi.org/10.1016/j.acalib.2015.11.002.

Walton, G. (2018) Supporting Student Wellbeing in the University Library: A Core Service Or a Distraction? *New Review of Academic Librarianship*, **24** (2), 121–3, https://doi.org/10.1080/13614533.2017.1418240.

Wang, F., Tucker, A. and Seo, J. D. (2022) Incubating AI: The Collaboratory at Ryerson University Library. In Hervieux, S. and Wheatley, A. (eds) *The Rise of AI: Implications and Applications of Artificial Intelligence in Academic Libraries*, 47–60, Association of College and Research Libraries.

Weaver, M. (2020) Students Lead the Future: Academic Library Space and Place. In Weaver, M. and Appleton, L. (eds) *Bold Minds: Library Leadership in a Time of Disruption*, 125–48, Facet Publishing.

Weaver, M. and Appleton, L. (2020) Introduction. In Weaver, M. and Appleton, L. (eds) *Bold Minds: Library Leadership in a Time of Disruption*, xxi–xxxii, Facet Publishing.

Weiner, S. G. (2005) The History of Academic Libraries in the United States: A Review of the Literature, *Library Philosophy and Practice*, **7** (2), 1–12, https://digitalcommons.unl.edu/libphilprac/58.

Westermann, M. (2023) After a Year of ChatGPT, Is Academia Getting to Grips with Generative AI? *Times Higher Education*, 23 November, www.timeshighereducation.com/depth/after-year-chatgpt-academia-getting-grips-generative-ai.

Whitchurch, C. (2008) Shifting Identities and Blurring Boundaries: The Emergence of Third Space Professionals in UK Higher Education, *Higher Education Quarterly*, **62** (4), 377–96, https://doi.org/10.1111/j.1468-2273.2008.00387.x.

Whitchurch, C. (2010) Convergence and Divergence in Professional Identities. In Gordon, G. and Whitchurch, C. (eds) *Academic and Professional Identities in Higher Education: The Challenges of a Diversifying Workforce*, 167–83, Routledge.

Whitchurch, C. (2013) *Reconstructing Identities in Higher Education: The Rise of 'Third Space' Professionals*, Routledge.

Whyte, S. and McLaren, L. (2023) *SCONUL Equality, Diversity and Inclusion Statistics Report: Ethnicity of Our Workforce 2021–22*, www.sconul.ac.uk/knowledge-hub/equality-diversity-and-inclusion.

Willenborg, A. and Detmering, R. (2024) Student Success As a Value Proposition in ARL Libraries' Strategic Plans, *Journal of Library Administration*, **64** (8), 957–72, https://doi.org/10.1080/01930826.2024.2403751.

Williams, C. (2021) Labour Gains. The Future of Work: Special Report, *The Economist*, 10 April, www.economist.com/special-report/2021-04-10.

Williams, C. A. (2025) Academic Libraries: Overview. In Baker, D. and Ellis, L. (eds) *Encyclopedia of Libraries, Librarianship, and Information Science*, Volume 1, 114–28, Academic Press, https://doi.org/10.1016/B978-0-323-95689-5.00241-8.

Wilson, K. (2022) Decolonising Library Collections: Contemporary Issues, Practical Steps and Examples from London School of Economics. In Crilly, J. and Everitt, R. (eds) *Narrative Expansions: Interpreting Decolonisation in Academic Libraries*, 225–50, Facet Publishing.

Woodsworth, A., Allen, N., Hoadley, I., Lester, J., Molholt, P., Nitecki, D. and Wetherbee, L. (1989) The Model Research Library: Planning for the Future, *Journal of Academic Librarianship*, **15** (3), 132–8.

World Economic Forum (2023) *Global Gender Gap Report 2023*, www.weforum.org/publications/global-gender-gap-report-2023/in-full/benchmarking-gender-gaps-2023.

Worsley, P. (2001) Populism. In Krieger, J. (ed.) *The Oxford Companion to Politics of the World*, 2nd edn, 678–9, Oxford University Press.

Writer, P. (2021) What is Positioning Strategy: How Does It Work? https://paulwriter.com/what-is-positioning-strategy.

Wynne, B., Dixon, S., Donohue, N. and Rowlands, I. (2016) Changing the Library Brand: A Case Study, *New Review of Academic Librarianship*, **22** (2–3), 337–49, https://doi.org/10.1080/13614533.2016.1156000.

Zahneis, M. (2018) UVa Library's Plan to Cut Stacks by Half Sparks Faculty Concerns, *Chronicle of Higher Education*, 7 June, www.chronicle.com/article/uva-librarys-plan-to-cut-stacks-by-half-sparks-faculty-concerns.

Zelinsky, W. (2009) Human Dimensions of Global Change. In Cuff, D. J. and Goudie, A. S. (eds) *The Oxford Companion to Global Change*, 325–9, Oxford University Press.

Zhao, X., Cox, A. and Cai, L. (2024) ChatGPT and the Digitisation of Writing, *Humanities and Social Sciences Communications*, **11** (1), Article 482, https://doi.org/10.1057/s41599-024-02904-x.

Index